SPEAK
OUT IN
THUNDER TONES

SPEAK
OUT IN
THUNDER TONES

Letters and other writings
by Black Northerners, 1787–1865

edited by

DOROTHY STERLING

Doubleday & Company, Inc.
GARDEN CITY, NEW YORK

All pictures not otherwise credited are from Dorothy Sterling's files.
ISBN: 0-385-02474-6 Trade
       0-385-01909-2 Prebound
Library of Congress Catalog Card Number 72–92245
Printed in the United States of America
FIRST EDITION

CONTENTS

FOREWORD

Fifteen years ago while I was sitting on a beach reading *The Life and Writings of Frederick Douglass,*[*] a scholarly-looking stranger peered over my shoulder and asked, "How could he have written enough to fill a *whole book?*" I replied that this was only one of four volumes of Douglass' writings. The man shook his head in disbelief and walked on toward the water.

The stranger's disbelief was rooted in the century-old insistence of historians that black people had not had any role in United States history or that their role was limited to a few unique individuals. Between Denmark Vesey, Harriet Tubman, Frederick Douglass, Booker T. Washington and Martin Luther King, Jr., it seemed that there were only great blank spaces in which nothing worth recording had

[*] Edited by Philip Foner (New York, 1950).

happened and no one worth knowing about had lived.

Blacks, however, have been recording their history in the United States ever since 1841 when the Reverend James W. C. Pennington, once a slave, published a small book titled, *A Textbook of the Origin and History of the Colored People*. In later decades of the nineteenth century, more ambitious works were produced by William C. Nell, Martin R. Delany, William Wells Brown and George Washington Williams. These writings were known only to a small black readership and few white scholars paid attention to them.

In the twentieth century, there were new and more powerful challenges by such fine black scholars as Carter Woodson, W. E. B. Du Bois, Rayford Logan, Benjamin Quarles, John Hope Franklin, and by white historians like Herbert Aptheker, C. Vann Woodward and others. Though their researches and writings made significant inroads, they could not entirely reverse white Academia's long denial of the black role in United States history. They did much, however, to shape the self-image of a new black generation, which since the 1960s has achieved a fresh understanding of and a positive pride in its identity.

The Black Consciousness explosion of the 1960s set off a publishing explosion not only of new works on black history but also of long-forgotten out-of-print books. The dust settled at the end of the decade, leaving behind a feeling that at last we know it all, and if we don't, we never will because by now, certainly, we have exhausted all the sources.

Not so. While I was working on a biography of Martin R. Delany in 1968–70, my hunt for facts and meanings moved repeatedly toward black sources. And I was repeatedly astonished that so much should remain to be discovered, written about, interpreted.

Later, my Delany files tantalized me. I knew they held only surface scrapings from the large body of materials I had encountered. And if the surface was that rich, who could resist digging deeper?

I began to plan a three-volume collection of letters, diaries and other writings to present the viewpoints of succeeding black generations—the records of blacks who, as individuals, had helped to make history or had commented on history in the making. Most of them lived their lives without distinction except in their own communities; many were as famous as black people could become in their time.

This is volume one, which takes the story through the Civil War. My first source was the black newspapers. Almost three dozen weekly papers edited by black men and women appeared between 1827 and 1865. Many lasted only a few months but five—*Freedom's Journal, The Colored American, The North Star* (later *Frederick Douglass' Paper* and *Douglass' Monthly*), *The Weekly Anglo-African* and *The Pacific Appeal*—continued for years and are now available on microfilm. These papers have long been known to researchers but have been little used. Their editorials, news stories and, particularly, their letters to the editors provided rich and exciting insights into the black communities of the North. Here were people talking about themselves, their struggles and dreams, frustrations and achievements. The antislavery papers edited by whites, particularly *The Liberator*, supplemented the black papers. They, too, contained letters from blacks and reports of their meetings.

The newspapers were only the beginning. Following up on hints in black history books and some hunches of my own, I visited or corresponded with university and public libraries, historical societies and the National Archives. Some had only a letter or two. In others a wealth of material turned up. Alongside reports from community leaders were letters from young men about their girls, accounts of whaling voyages, correspondence from soldiers at the front and, over and over again, tales of prejudice and discrimination.

There were some surprises too. Perhaps the most exciting find was a dusty leatherbound notebook on loan to the Newport (Rhode Island) Historical Society. Here was the record of an extensive back-to-Africa movement in the eighteenth century. Only twenty-five miles from Newport, in the Free Public Library of New Bedford, Massachusetts, Paul Cuffe's correspondence with blacks in Northern cities carried the movement into the first decades of the nineteenth century. The identification of American blacks with Africa at this time and their widespread interest in resettlement there has never been reported before.

Even material known to historians sometimes took on a new meaning. When, from ten different sources, I put together the writings of black men and women who had known John Brown, a fresh picture of Brown emerged. It does not diminish his greatness to discover that he was not a great white savior who singlehandedly struck a blow for freedom. Rather, it adds a new dimension to find that scores of blacks knew Brown's plans and backed him all along the way.

Early in this effort, it became clear that I would have to choose between presenting relatively few documents in full or offering many more in abridged form. I chose the latter because I found that the material was arranging itself into a narrative—more or less chronological—of black life in the United States. Further choices were necessary when I called a halt to my research and discovered that my bulging files contained enough for four volumes the size of this one. Reluctantly I was forced to drop the tales of slavery as seen by slaves, accounts from free blacks in the slave South and the rich literature of the black-run Underground Railroad. I have also refrained from quoting extensively from Frederick Douglass, David Walker and one or two others whose writings are available elsewhere.

In this book, then, free blacks who lived in the North between 1787 and 1865 tell their story. The text, except for my introductions, was written by them. Almost all of it will be new to modern readers.

Sources are given after each selection, except in the opening sections where, as indicated, the bulk of the material comes from manuscript collections in Newport and New Bedford. The first time a writer's name is mentioned, he is briefly identified. For further information there are thumb-nail sketches of the most important men and women of the period at the end of the book.

To make the selections more readable, spelling and punc-tuation have been modernized. Although extensive cuts have been made, the original meaning of the writer has not been altered. Where an occasional word has been inserted to make this meaning clear, my additions are in brackets.

In only one way have I tampered with the material. When white writers interviewed blacks or took down their speeches, the blacks' language, as reported, was often heavy with "dem," "dat," "dose," "gwine" for "going," "lobe" for "love," and so forth. I have removed all of this dialect with a clear conscience. There *were* regional and class differences in speech, of course, but the reporters, sympathetic though they were, glossed over these real differences in favor of a stereotype. Harriet Tubman, for instance, grew up in Mary-land, while Sojourner Truth was born in New York and spoke only Dutch in her childhood. Yet those who wrote for them reduced the speech of both women to an identical dialect. Equally telling is a reporter's interview with Robert Smalls on the day he turned a Confederate gunboat over to the Union. Smalls is quoted as saying, "I tells you what it is, sar. I was born under the old flag and I'se getting old and jist feel as though I'd like to die under it." Well and good, except that Robert Smalls was twenty-three years old at the time!

As I have read and re-read these writings I have been struck by how much light they shed on the present as well as on the past. Many studies have been made to determine why black children fail in schools. Wouldn't it be useful to examine New York's African Free Schools where black chil-dren in 1820–60 were signally successful? Records show that they surpassed their white contemporaries in both school-work and attendance.

Sociologists are currently debating the strengths and weaknesses of the black family. In a government report published in 1965, Daniel Moynihan wrote, "It was by destroying the Negro family under slavery that white America broke the will of the Negro people." He concluded that the major problems that blacks face today stem from their weakened family structure. But *was* the black family destroyed by slavery? The *actual* testimony of black families, as given here, might lead to different conclusions.

Many of the issues of the modern black revolution were under discussion before the Civil War. Should blacks be called Negro, colored or Afro-American? They were talking about that in the 1830s. The fight against segregated accommodations? That began in 1840, not in 1955. Separatism versus integration? The United States versus Africa? Those were the big debates in black circles in the 1850s and earlier. Job discrimination? That goes back one hundred and fifty years.

The history of the United States is usually described as a history of progress. The continent was tamed; the frontier moved westward. And each succeeding generation of immigrants climbed another rung up the ladder of success.

But the history of black people—and of Indians and Mexican-Americans—does not show this steady progression. Blacks tamed the continent as slaves and were denied equality on the frontier. Their history tells of a constant struggle against oppression in which they have taken a step forward, only to be pushed back again. Time after time victories were won, then snatched away a decade or so later.

One hundred and thirty years ago, Boston's black community asked the School Committee to close the inferior segregated school which their children were forced to attend. They drew up petitions, held meetings, organized boycotts, sued in court. After more than ten years of agitation, they won. Boston's schools were integrated and parents and community leaders held a great victory celebration.

What is the school situation in Boston at present? In 1973 a Federal judge ruled that the Boston School Committee was operating two school systems—one for blacks and one for whites. Progress? Hardly.

Today, when black people demand equal opportunities for jobs, housing and schools, a common response from the children and grandchildren of European immigrants is: "Our parents made it without any help. Why can't they?"

Here are some of the answers to that question.

Dorothy Sterling

ACKNOWLEDGMENTS

I am greatly indebted to the staffs of the libraries, historical societies and government archives whose manuscript collections were consulted, and particularly to Dr. Dorothy Porter, curator of the Moorland-Spingarn Collection at Howard University, and to Mrs. Jean Hutson, curator of the Schomburg Collection. Not only are Moorland-Spingarn and Schomburg the most important collections of black history materials in the country, but Dr. Porter and Mrs. Hutson are immensely knowledgeable as well as generous with their time.

My thanks are also due to many historians and writers in the black-history field. Benjamin Quarles, whose *Black Abolitionists* supplied indispensable background information for this book, answered innumerable inquiries promptly and patiently. James McPherson, author of *The Negro's Civil War,* loaned me his microfilm of *The Pacific Appeal,* a valuable source of information on blacks in the West. Joseph Boromé, a biographer of Robert

Purvis, made the records of the Philadelphia Vigilant Committee available to me. Carleton Mabee, author of *Black Freedom*, told me where the full story of the Boston school fight of the 1840–50s could be found, and Elizabeth Bark made repeated trips to the Boston Public Library to dig out the documents. Sarah Jackson of the National Historical Publications Commission sent me correspondence from black soldiers, and Richard O. Boyer—whose *The Legend of John Brown* has recently been published—gave me letters from some of John Brown's men. Herbert Gutman, author of a forthcoming study of the black family, pointed out the letter in which Henry Highland Garnet described his return to his birthplace (Part VI) and Paul Silbert found the account of the Kentucky slave who traveled to Canada on the Underground Railroad (Part III). Victor and Louise Ullman sent me the reminiscences of Dr. Anderson Abbott (Part VI) from their files of *Look To the North Star*. And everyone exploring the black past owes special thanks to Herbert Aptheker for his groundbreaking *Documentary History of the Negro People in the United States*.

My greatest debt is to my husband, Philip Sterling, who spent innumerable hours developing a narrative structure for the book and gave me the courage to select and cut from the large number of documents I had gathered.

We are proscribed and pressed down by prejudices more wicked and fatal than even slavery itself. These evils pervade the length and breadth of the land. Colored men must do something. They must establish and maintain the PRESS, and through it, speak out in THUNDER TONES, until the nation repent and render to every man that which is just and equal.

The Colored American, March 4, 1837

SPEAK OUT IN THUNDER TONES

I · BELOVED AFRICANS (1787–1830)

The abolition of the African Slave Trade [in 1808] was celebrated throughout the country by the colored people in meetings, prayers, thanksgivings. The terms by which orators addressed their hearers on that day was universally "Beloved Africans!" The people in those days rejoiced in their nationality and hesitated not to call each other "Africans" or "descendants of Africa." In after years the term "African" fell into disuse and finally discredit.

—Dr. James McCune Smith

1. We Have No City! No Country!

In the last half of the eighteenth century, almost a quarter of the population of the American colonies was black. It was natural for people who had been born in Africa or whose parents or friends had been born there to think of themselves as Africans. Advertisements for runaway slaves showed that large numbers could speak only the language of their native continent:

Virginia Gazette, January 30, 1752:
Stolen, or ran away, a likely young Eboe Negro Man Slave who was imported last summer. Went by the name of Cuffee and can speak but few words in English.

New York-Mercury, November 6, 1752:
Run-away. A Negro Man lately imported from Africa. He cannot speak a word of English or Dutch, or any other language but that of his own country.

Georgia Gazette, March 7, 1765:
Run away. A young new Negro wench named Sidney. Has her country marks on her breast and arms. Talks no English.

Georgia Gazette, December 3, 1766:
Brought to the Work-house, a Well-set able Negro fellow about 24 years old. He speaks very little English, cannot tell his master's name so as to be understood.

Even American-born blacks thought of themselves as Africans. They belonged to America, but America did not, in any way, belong to them. Listening to the Sons of Liberty cry out against British oppression, slaves in New England towns petitioned for their own freedom. "We have no Property! We have no Wives! No Children! We have no City! No Country!" one petition reminded the American patriots. Another, in 1773—the year of the Boston Tea Party—asked for the right of slaves to work for themselves one day a week, to buy their freedom. This petition, "In behalf of our fellow slaves," concluded, "We are willing to submit to regulations and laws until we leave the province, which we determine to do as soon as we can procure money to transport ourselves to the coast of Africa where we propose a settlement."

For five thousand black men who served in the Revolutionary army and navy, freedom became real and immediate. It was the reward promised to them for fighting against the British. Thousands more were freed after the Revolution when Northern states provided for gradual emancipation of their slaves. By 1790 when the first U. S. Census was taken there were 697,897 slaves in the country and almost 60,000 free black people.

Powerless as individuals, these free Africans keenly felt the need of organization. In cities of the North, and in Maryland and Virginia, they formed societies to help each other. The Free African Society of Philadelphia was organized in 1787 "to support one another in sickness and for the benefit of widows and fatherless children." The African Society of Boston (1796) and the New York African Society for Mutual Relief (1809) had similar goals.

The African Union Society of Newport, Rhode Island, was probably the earliest organization of black people in the United States. Formed some time before 1787, its members pooled their money to care for the sick and bury the dead. Their main goal, however, was to return to their homeland.

Africa seemed especially close to anyone who lived in Newport, the leading slave port of New England. Before the Revolution, hundreds of vessels left its wharves each year for the coast of Guinea. There, hogsheads of Newport rum were traded for men, women, children (one man for 100 gallons; a woman for 85). The slaves were sold in the West Indies, except for a select few. These, branded with the letter "P" for "Privilege," were brought back to Newport, along with cargoes of sugar cane to make more rum for the African trade. Even after 1787, when further importation of slaves was forbidden in Rhode Island, Newport's ships continued to carry Africans to the South. Many of Newport's "privileged" slaves had been taught to read and write. They worked as clerks on the wharves or in their masters' countinghouses. And as Christians, worshipping in their masters' churches, they heard a good deal about the need to civilize Africa.

In 1774 the Reverend Samuel Hopkins and a fellow clergyman, Ezra Stiles, had sent two Newport blacks to the College of New Jersey (now Princeton) to train as missionaries. The war interrupted this plan, but afterwards the African Union Society went to work in earnest on the idea of a black Christian settlement in Africa. Salmar Nubia, the Society's first secretary, was African born. Brought to Newport as a boy, he won his freedom before the Revolution. As secretary, Nubia was paid "twelve shillings lawful money per annum and also five shillings for purchasing paper, ink, quills and materials for writing copies, &c."

There was no allowance for carbon paper. It didn't exist. Instead, Nubia copied the dozens of letters sent and received by the society, and the reports of its meetings, into a large leather-bound ledger. This volume and later records have remained in the possession of Newport's black community for almost two hundred years. When the Union Congregational Church, which was known as "the Church of Color," united with the United Congregational Church in 1963, the papers were loaned to the Newport Historical Society.

The first letter in the ledger was addressed to William Thornton, a white man who had recently visited Newport. Thornton wanted to start a colony of American blacks in Africa, with himself as leader. The correspondence that follows shows that the blacks were willing to accept financial support from whites, but not their leadership.

Newport, January 24, 1787

Mr. Thornton
Sir:

Our earnest desire of returning to Africa and settling there has induced us further to trouble you in order to

Newport's Union Congregational Church, "the Church of Color"
(*Newport Historical Society*)

convey a more particular idea of our proposal:

That a number of men from among ourselves shall be sent to Africa to see if they can obtain, by gift or purchase, lands sufficient to settle upon. And if such land can be obtained, then some of these men shall return and bring information. The company then shall go without their wives and children, to make preparation for their families.

This plan is agreeable to us. But as we are unable to prosecute it for want of money, this is the only reason of our troubling our superiors for assistance.

We want to know by what right we shall possess said lands when we settle upon them, for we think it unwise to settle in Africa unless the right and fee of the land is first made over to us and to our heirs.

Anthony Taylor, in the name of Union Society

When Thornton left Newport he carried a letter from the Union Society to the African Company of Boston. Eighty black Bostonians had just petitioned their state officials, asking for financial help in returning to Africa. Replying to Newport some months later, they still had hope that their petition would be granted:

Boston, June 1, 1787

Dear Brethren:

We received your letter by the hand of Mr. Thornton. We have conversed with the gentleman and find him, we think, a friend to the blacks. We heartily agree with you in sending circular letters to free blacks to all the states, as it will strengthen our number.

We have presented our petition to the General Court [of Massachusetts] and [it] is accepted. They will grant us all we require if we find a place to settle in.

We do not approve of Mr. Thornton's going [to] settle a place for us. We think it would be better if we could charter a vessel and send some of our own blacks.

Samuel Stevens for the African Company

Newport, October 4, 1787

To Mr. Samuel Stevens to African Company at Boston
Dear Brethren:

We have much the same opinion of Mr. Thornton which you express. We think he ought to be treated with respect and encouraged in his honest zeal to promote the welfare of the Africans, while we behave with caution and are on our guard against being imposed upon. We hope his exertions may be some way serviceable to our proposed plan.

We are waiting and longing to hear what has been the success of the attempt made in England to make a settlement of blacks in Africa, hoping this will open the way for us. We rejoice to hear of the encouragement given by the General Court in Boston to assist in making a settlement.

We like your plan of chartering a vessel and are desirous to join with you in it, but our poverty renders us unable to do much. We hope God will raise up friends and benefactors.

Anthony Taylor in ye name of Union Society

Newport's African Union Society followed up on its plan to send circular letters to other cities. A lengthy manifesto-letter "To all the Africans in Providence" resulted in the formation of a society there. One of several letters from Providence described the structure of their organization:

Providence, September 22, 1789

To Anthony Taylor, Esq.
Dear Brethren:

We assembled our brethren together and laid your Rules and Regulations before them. We have established ourselves in the name of the Union Society to be subordinate [to] your part of the Society in Newport. The officers are as following: a Vice-President, Moderator, six Representatives, Treasurer, Secretary and a Sheriff to convene the members at every quarterly and annual meeting.

The Treasurer shall give a sufficient bond of security in land for his faithful performance of his trust. There shall be [no] members admitted into this Society without paying two shillings lawful money into the Treasury and at every quarterly meeting one shilling sixpence. And anyone that should make application for admission shall give notice of his intention three months before his admittance and shall be examined and by approbation of two-thirds of the committee, the candidate shall be admitted.

By your Brethren in Affliction,
James McKenzie, Secretary

The Newport society approved the rules set up by its new branch in Providence, but had a request to make, in a letter dated October 15, 1789:

Whenever you shall favor us with a letter, we should take it kind that the scrivener be careful that those letters may easily be read and understood. We were much perplexed to find out the meaning of the [letter] of 22d September last. It appears to us that the gentleman who wrote the first page is a good writer but somewhat careless in forming his letters. We beg leave to be excused in being so plain with you.

The Newport people also tried to interest the Free African Society of Philadelphia in the back-to-Africa movement. Philadelphia's answer was cool:

The Union Society, Newport   [undated]
Respected Friends:
    Your epistle dated the first of September 1789 claimed our serious attention. With regard to emigration to Africa, we have at present but little to communicate, [believing] every pious man is a good citizen to the whole world. However, if any apprehend a divine injunction is laid upon them to undertake such a long and perilous journey, we hope such may meet encouragement and that the arm of divine protection may hover over them.

                Joseph Clark, Clerk of the Free African Society

In the 1790s, black Rhode Islanders turned their attention to Sierra Leone, a new colony on Africa's west coast. It was started by British antislavery men as a place to resettle freed slaves. Some of the Sierra Leoneans came from the West Indies; others were American slaves who had run away to fight for the British during the Revolution. A letter from Providence proposed that trusted men be sent to check out the situation in Sierra Leone:

                    Providence, January 15, 1794
Brethren of the Union Society in Newport:
    We have voted to send a petition to the General Assembly of this state to grant us permission to go to Sierra

Leone. To inform ourselves of what we would wish to know [we propose] sending a man of our own complexion, a person in Providence sufficiently qualified to the undertaking.

But us would wish to have three black men go on this important business, on account of accidents—one from Boston, one from Providence and one from Philadelphia. We have wrote to Boston and Philadelphia acquainting them with our resolution.

We have some hopes of receiving assistance from the white people. Now is the time for us to try to distinguish ourselves, as the more remote we are situated from the white people the more we shall be respected.

By order of the African Society in Providence,
Bonner Brown, President
James McKenzie, Secretary

Newport, not ready to let Providence call the shots, replied with some suggestions of its own:

Newport, February 13, 1794

Brethren of the African Society in Providence:

Concerning the petition to the General Assembly, we thought best to acquaint all our brethren, the free people of color, in every town in this state of our proceedings. And if they agreed with us, to establish [a] Union Assembly consisting of one or two members from every society in the state to meet and draft this petition.

Also the [Union] Assembly shall determine how many men to send to Africa to procure a place for us to settle. And the candidates shall be named so that every member in every society may vote for the same.

It seemed to us that you have already agreed with the brethren in Boston and Philadelphia to fix upon three candidates to go to Africa. We thank you for the invitation to partake with you, but we wish to know whether the Providence candidates are to act for the society in Newport as well.

Dear brethren, we approved of our emigration to Africa. We also approved of petitioning the General Assembly for their assistance. But this business is so weighty, we think best for as many of us as approved of this plan to meet and agree upon certain mode which we shall all follow with united hearts.

By order of the African Union Society

Charles Chaloner, President
Newport Gardner, Secretary

A reply from Providence, meeting Newport's objections half way, was brought to Newport by William Olney and London Spear:

February 25, 1794

Brethren of the African Union Society in Newport:

Your letter of February 13 was agreeably received. We have drawn up a petition to present to the inhabitants of this state. Enclosed we send you a copy for your inspection, together with our Emigration Bill [to be presented to the Rhode Island General Assembly].

We wish you to procure a list of your inhabitants who are disposed to emigrate, including your young women. You will be pleased to lay our petition, together with our Emigration Bill, before the [white] Abolition Society in Newport, as their influence with the inhabitants of this town and state is very great.

The bearer, Mr. William Olney, [is] the person we have made choice of to accompany Mr. James McKenzie to Sierra Leone. His extensive knowledge in land affairs was a sufficient inducement to nominate Mr. Olney. You will, my worthy friends, be pleased to make a choice of a person in your society to represent your members and others who may be disposed to emigrate. [He should] be ready to embark at a moment's warning.

My brethren, it is impossible for you to form any idea of the encouragement we meet. Every white person in town seems to be forward in promoting the matter.

In behalf of the African Society in Providence
                                    Bonner Brown, President
                                    James McKenzie, Secretary

The logical man to represent Newport's blacks in Africa was Newport Gardner, then secretary of the Union Society. Born Ocramar Marycoo, he was brought to America in 1760 when he was fourteen. Owned by Captain Caleb Gardner, a slave trader, he was not able to buy freedom for himself and his family until 1791—and then because he held a share in a winning lottery ticket. While still a slave he taught himself music. He composed songs and hymns and started a singing school which was patronized by Newport's leading families. Although widely respected by both blacks and whites, he never gave up hope of returning to Africa. "Newport Gardner used to say that he was very careful to cultivate his recollection of his African tongue so that in case Providence should open a way, he might return to Africa and find a people with whom he might converse intelligently," a white fellow townsman recalled.

Newport, February 26, 1794

Brethren of the African Society in Providence:

We received your letter and called a special meeting. To represent the business of our society we have chosen Mr. Newport Gardner, a worthy member, in whom we can confide. Him we think sufficient to accompany Mr. McKenzie and Mr. Olney.

And as to your petition and emigration bill, we approve of them and have concluded to lay them before our Abolition Society here.

As to the names of the inhabitants who will be disposed to emigrate, we cannot at present inform you, but in our next we will write more particular. We have sent you a list of members belonging to the society and in our next shall include the number of their families.

In behalf of the African Union Society

. Charles Chaloner, President

Newport Gardner, Secretary

This letter is the last in the Union Society's record of correspondence about returning to Africa. Later communications, if any, were not copied into the ledger and thus were lost.

James McKenzie did go to Sierra Leone in 1795, representing the Rhode Island black community, but he met with little encouragement there. The colony had just been bombarded by French naval forces and its governor agreed to admit no more than twelve families—and these only if the Reverend Samuel Hopkins or the president of Newport's Abolition Society would testify that they were pious Christians who had not been infected with "the poison of The Age of Reason."

The big stumbling block, however, was lack of money. "A vessel must be obtained, and a cargo procured of such things as will sell there," the Reverend Hopkins wrote. "A captain must be found who can be relied on and a sufficient number of blacks for sailors."

The dream did not die. Fifteen years after James McKenzie's trip, a black sea captain commanding a black crew sailed to Sierra Leone, to investigate the possibility of an American black settlement there.

2. The Dust of Africa Lodged on Our Rigging

Paul Cuffe, born in 1759, was the son of a slave who had been captured in Africa and who later bought his freedom. Cuffe's mother was an Indian of the Wampanoag tribe. From the time he was fourteen, Paul Cuffe farmed, fished, hunted whales and saved his money. Self-taught, he built a school for his own and his neighbors' children on his farm in West-port, Massachusetts. He became a prominent member of the Society of Friends (Quakers). At fifty he was a prosperous shipowner, doing business with leading merchants along the Atlantic coast and sending his vessels overseas to Spain, Sweden, Russia. At last he felt able to devote his time and talents to fellow Africans.

In a letter to two Quaker merchants in Philadelphia, Cuffe explained his interest in Africa. His correspondence, ship's logs and account books are now in the Free Public Library of New Bedford, Massachusetts.

Westport, June 10, 1809

John James & Alexander Wilson
Esteemed friends:

I have for some years had it on my mind to make a voyage to Sierra Leone, feeling a real desire that the inhabitants of Africa might become an enlightened people, in the true light of Christianity. As I am of the African race I feel myself interested for them. If I am favored with a talent, I am willing that they should be benefited thereby.

The Sierra Leone Company wrote that if Paul Cuffe should make a voyage there he should have every privilege that its government could afford. If you think it expedient [would you] write to England that I have some concern in navigation which if I concluded to settle [in Africa] I would wish to take with me so that the inhabitants might be benefited both with agriculture and commerce. And in case I engage in whale fishery [would you ask] whether I could have some encouragement such as a bounty, or to carry the products of the country duty-free to England?

If times should be settled between this & next fall for such a voyage, it looks pretty clear to be put into execution. I think there are several families of good credit that may like to go.

Paul Cuffe

Cuffe set sail for Sierra Leone in the fall of 1810, aboard his favorite ship, the Traveller. *He carried a cargo of goods to trade with the Africans, as well as Bibles and Quaker religious writings. Unlike the slave traders who still visited the African coast, Cuffe, a strict teetotaler, brought no rum. The following are selections from his log:*

On Board the Brig *Traveller* of Westport, Thomas Wainer, Master. Her crew consisting of nine in number, all people of color, except 1 apprentice boy. We left Westport for Philadelphia, November 25, 1810.

February 21, 1811. Days out 50. Fresh trades and a large sea wind. The weather clear but very smoky. The dust of Africa lodged on our rigging. We judged the land to be about 25 leagues off.

February 24. Days out 53. Small wind and a hot sun. At 10 A.M. sounded and got bottom for the first ground that we got on the coast of Africa. 65 fathoms. Caught 1 dolphin and many sucker fish so we had excellent fish dinner for the first time since we sailed from America.

March 1. Out 59 days. At half-past 8 o'clock we came to in Sierra Leone Road.

March 2. At 7 this morning the governor arrived. His excellency permitted all of our cargo to be landed but the 6 bales of India goods.

March 4. Invitation was given me this day to dine with the

Paul Cuffe and his brig, *Traveller*
(*Whaling Museum, New Bedford*)

governor at whose table an extensive observation took place
on the slave trade and the colony of Sierra Leone.

March 8. We passeth this day with landing flour and ships
cargo. Bartered for 316 Elephants Teeth which weighed
2,352 lbs. and am to give 2 yards of cloth for 1 lb. of ivory.

March 13. King Thomas came on board to see me. He was
an old man, gray-headed, appeared to be sober and grave. I
treated him with civility and made him a present of a Bible,
a history of Elizabeth Webb [a Quaker] and an essay on
War; together with a letter of advice from myself, such as
appeared to be good to hand to the King for the use of the
nations of Africa. He and retinue was thirteen in number. I
served him with victuals. It appeared that there was rum
wanting, but none was given.

March 14. King George from Bullom Shore sent his mes-
senger on board with present of three chickens and invited
me over to see him.

March 18. This day I went to visit King George, King of
Bullom, who received us very cordially. We went in a long
canoe. I presented the king with a Bible, a testament, a

treatise of Benjamin Holmes and two of Elizabeth Webb, and an epistle from the Yearly Meeting.

March 26. This morning was some rainy. I breakfasted with the governor. After breakfast had conference with him on the subject of the country and settling in it, to good satisfaction.

March 31. Attended the church. The Mandingo men have the Scripture in their tongue, the Old Testament, but deny the New Testament. They own Mahomet a prophet.

From Africa Cuffe sailed to England to work out a three-cornered trade betweeen England, Sierra Leone and the United States which would benefit both the Africans and American blacks who decided to join them. During a two-month stay there he conferred with members of the African Institution, an organization working to strengthen Britain's influence in Africa. One of its directors was the Duke of Gloucester, a member of the British royal family. From Cuffe's log:

August 27. This day met with the Committee of the African Institution who expressed great satisfaction on the information I gave them, and felt that I was endeavoring to assist them in the good cause. I made the Duke a present of an African robe, a letter box and a dagger, to show that the Africans were capable of mental endowments &c.

Cuffe returned to Sierra Leone, took on a cargo of African goods and sailed for home. By the time he reached American coastal waters in April 1812, the United States was on the brink of war with England. Trade with Great Britain, France and their colonies had been forbidden. When Cuffe attempted to land, customs officials confiscated the Traveller *and its cargo.*

Armed with letters from governors, judges and prominent citizens of New England, Cuffe went to Washington to argue for the return of his ship. He was received warmly by President James Madison and Secretary of the Treasury Albert Gallatin. Many public officials of that period believed that the solution of "the Negro problem" was to ship all free blacks to Africa. They were glad to co-operate with Paul Cuffe who seemed to be offering to do the job for them. Gallatin was also concerned with something else—brandy that he could no longer obtain from France. Cuffe was as firm with him as he had been with King Thomas.

Selections from Paul Cuffe's diary:

May 2, 1812. At 11 o'clock waited on the President, accompanied with my friend Samuel Hutchinson. From the President, waited on the Secretary and then on those that I had letters unto. Obtained favorable countenance and assurance of an answer. I likewise went to Congress. The construction was magnificent.

The Secretary observed to me that French brandy could not be imported from a British port but observed whether it would be inconvenient to me to have it entered for exportation [from Africa]. I told him my funds were small, and it would lock up my funds.

May 4. Little after 12 waited on the Secretary. The President had sent for him. We waited until one o'clock, then was sent for into the Secretary's office. He told me that all of my property was to be restored to me without reserve. I thanked him for his services. He then observed to me anything that the government could do to promote the good cause I was pursuing, they would certainly be always ready to render me their help.

My much-esteemed friend Samuel Hutchinson attended with me at all the Departments and was eye and ear witness to what is afore-written.

From Washington, Cuffe went to Baltimore, Philadelphia and New York to confer with white antislavery men and influential free "people of color." As a result of his meetings, blacks formed African Institutions in each of the three cities. Entries in his diary sum up the results of the trip:

May 14. New York. It rested thus that there should be a Society united with that of Philadelphia, Baltimore &c. for the further promotion of Africa, of which Sierra Leone at present seems to be the principally established colony.

May 22. Arrived at Newport. I called on the Collector [of Customs]. He told me that he had orders to return vessel and cargo without taxing costs.

May 23. Left Newport last evening. Arrived home at 8 o'clock. Found all well for which I desire ever to be thankful, world without end.

The War of 1812 had already started when Cuffe began an exchange of correspondence with Prince Saunders, teacher of Boston's African School, to suggest that black Bostonians also form an African Institution. Saunders replied:

Portrait of a black Philadelphian, thought to be James Forten
(*Historical Society of Pennsylvania*)

Boston, August 3, 1812

Capt. Paul Cuffe

Dear Sir:

There are several men in this place who calculate to go to Africa with you, whenever there is an opening. An attempt was made to call a general meeting of the people of color [to] consult upon the best method of organizing a society for making arrangements for going to Africa. But there was a diversity of opinions on political ground. The Democratic Party are opposed to the plan on account of its being under British government and say that those who go are going for the purpose of speculation & trading in slaves.

From such insinuations, it was thought best that the society should consist of those persons who wish to go. They have accordingly chosen a committee. We should be glad to see you here as soon as you can make it convenient.

> Prince Saunders, Secretary, Boston African Institution
> Thomas Jarvis, Chairman
> Perry Locke, President

Cuffe had decided to make an annual trip to Sierra Leone to carry emigrants and to bring back African produce. But he was stymied until a peace treaty was signed on February 14, 1815. A day later, James Forten, secretary of Philadelphia's African Institution, wrote to him. War veteran, inventor and sailmaker with contracts to outfit U. S. Navy vessels, Forten was one of the wealthiest black men in America.

Philadelphia, February 15, 1815

Dear Friend:

I approve very highly of your proposition of building a ship for the African trade by the men of color and shall lay it before the Society when next we meet. We have had a very severe winter. The Delaware is all frozened over and has been so for some time. The news from Washington is that the Treaty of Peace has been unanimously ratified by the Senate. Charlotte and the family join me in love to you and your family.

James Forten

Soon letters from would-be emigrants began to reach Westport. A typical one:

Providence, February 23, 1815

To Paul Cuffe, Esq.
Sir:

I congratulate you on the happy event of peace. You have now an opportunity of putting your benevolent plans into execution.

There is several of us here who are anxious to visit our brethren in Sierra Leone and settle among them. Although we have not learning nor property to bestow on them, yet we are willing to place ourselves in a situation to be useful to them. Some of us have families.

We beg you to write whether we can have passage with you and how long it will be before you sail and what the terms will be.

William Brown

With Peter Williams, Jr., secretary of the African Institution in New York, Cuffe discussed the possibilities of trade with Sierra Leone on a regular basis. Williams, the son of a prosperous tobacco manufacturer, became pastor of St. Philip's Episcopal Church in 1820.

Westport, August 30, 1815

To Peter Williams, Jr.
Esteemed friend:

In consequence of what thee mentioned, that we, the people of color, might establish a mercantile business from the United States to Africa, &c., should this still be in your mind

Peter Williams, Jr.

and you propose to carry it into effect this fall, we have no time to lose.

After consulting thyself and friends, please to inform me your resolutions. And also the price of prime tobacco, soap and candles. And also what size vessel would be most advantageous.

Thy assured friend, Paul Cuffe

In the fall of 1815, Cuffe completed arrangements for his second voyage to Africa. Two weeks before Christmas the Traveller *set sail, with thirty-eight passengers—eighteen men and women and twenty children. Eight paid their own way; the expenses of the others were borne by Cuffe. In addition to trading goods, the* Traveller *carried a wagon, a plow and iron to build a sawmill. Writing from Sierra Leone to an English Friend, Cuffe described some of the emigrants:*

April 1, 1816

Dear friend William Allen:

The people I took over were all common laborers. They are inclined to cultivate the land, to make trial with tobacco for the present year. Five of them has about 10 acres of ground cut away. One has undertaken to work the governor's plantation, the seventh to farm for one of the citizens, the eighth to farm with the Congo people, as he is one of the nation, a little out of Sierra Leone. He intends to go to Congo. The ninth is a native of Senegal and thinks of getting to Senegal.

This Congo man is about 40 years old. Has a wife but no children. He paid his passage and is not inclined to receive any assistance. He has some property in Philadelphia. He was sold among the French at St. Domingo. At the time of their revolution, he got over to America and thereby obtained his freedom. Since has acquired some education so far as to write a good hand, read well, and pretty well-versed in arithmetic. Also has made himself acquainted with the rules of navigation. However, he will not make a mariner on account of his seasickness.

Samuel Wilson is about 36 years of age. Has a wife but not children. He was from Philadelphia and paid his passage but had no property left but a little furniture. He is an industrious man and proposes to be acquainted with raising of tobacco.

William Guin, the man that works the governor's farm, is about 60 years of age. Has a wife and one daughter, from Boston. Paid nothing. He is a member of the Methodist order.

Perry Locke, 30 years old, has a wife and four children. The oldest boy, 11, the youngest girl, 5. He is member of the Methodist Society and is licensed to preach. I believe him to be an honest character, but has rather a hard voice for a preacher.

As to my opinion in rendering the chiefs friendly toward civilization, I recommend opening roads from tribe to tribe, with their consent and establish[ing] factories. Making presents to the chiefs only helps to whet their appetite for more. If these factories were in different places with such

articles as they needed, it would help to make them more industrious.

Paul Cuffe

The Traveller's successful voyage to Sierra Leone stirred
the imagination of influential white Americans who favored
a mass transfer of free black people from the United States
to Africa. Not all of them were attracted to the idea for the
same reason. Most of them were slaveowners who felt that
free blacks, some of them educated and successful, were a
threat to the slave system. Their presence gave the lie to the
argument that blacks were naturally inferior, one of the
standard justifications for slavery.

The others were antislavery church people who saw a
double humanitarian benefit in colonization. Slaveholders
would be more willing to free their slaves if they could be
shipped out of the country. And black colonists from Amer-
ica could be trained as missionaries to Christianize Africa.

In December 1816 an all-white group of politicians,
planters and clergymen met in the Hall of the House of
Representatives in Washington to establish the American
Society for Colonizing the Free People of Color, later known
as the American Colonization Society. Among those present
were Henry Clay, Speaker of the House; General Andrew
Jackson, Congressman John Randolph and Supreme Court
Justice Bushrod Washington. William Thornton, by then
Commissioner of the U. S. Patent Office, was elected to the
Board of Managers. Other active members included Samuel
J. Mills and the Reverend Robert Finley. Mills and Finley
immediately asked for Paul Cuffe's advice. He replied:

Westport, January 6, 1817

Respected friend Samuel J. Mills:

[Sierra Leone] may do for small settlements but were
there a willingness for a pretty general removal and the
south part of Africa, viz, the Cape of Good Hope, could be

obtained, I think it most favorable. There is [also] the great river Congo which layeth near the equator. Its powerful population and the fertility of the land, I hope will not always be neglected.

I much approve of a vessel being sent, as thou has mentioned. I take the liberty of naming Peter Williams, Jr., secretary to the African Institution in New York, to be a suitable man to make one of the number for such a plan. There is a similar institution established in Philadelphia. James Forten is the corresponding secretary. I wish these institutions to be brought as much into action as would be best. By that means, the colored population of these large cities would be more awakened than from a stranger and be prevailed on for their own good.

I observe what I have experienced. 1815, I carried out to Africa 9 families. In 1816 I have had so many applications for taking more that I believe I could have had the greater part out of Boston.

As to the length of the voyage, it would depend on the extent of the discoveries. I think from 12 to 18 months, especially if voyage were to extend as far as the Cape. I have not calculated on going out myself, but all my voyages, I hope, may be in behalf of forwarding the great cause in contemplation.

Paul Cuffe

Two days later Cuffe wrote to James Forten:

Westport, January 8, 1817

Esteemed friend James Forten:

I have lately received a letter from a gentleman in the city of Washington announcing to me the concern that rests at the seat of government for the welfare of the people of color. They mention whether I will join them in going to Africa to seek a place where the people of color might be colonized. I have answered informing [him] of the African Institutions in Philadelphia and New York.

Give my love to the members of the African Institution and tell them I wish them a joyful New Year, hoping they have all their energies engaged to celebrate the year in behalf of the African Race and to the honor and glory of God.

Give my love to Charlotte and the children. Dear James, thou art often the companion of my mind.

Paul Cuffe

Forten too had heard from the Colonization Society. One of its spokesman, Robert Finley, paid a visit to Philadelphia to meet with him and Richard Allen, bishop of the African Methodist Episcopal Church. If there was to be a large-scale emigration, the Colonization Society realized that the co-operation of these men was needed. According to Finley, Forten was enthusiastic about colonization:

He said their people would become a great nation. He remarked on the oppressive situation of his people in our land, observing that neither riches nor education could put them on a level with the whites, and that the more wealthy and the better informed any became, the more wretched they were made; for they felt their degradation more acutely. He gave it as his decided opinion that Africa was the proper place for a colony.

[Richard Allen also] spoke warmly in favor of colonization in Africa, declaring that were he young he would go himself. He considered the present plan of colonization as holding out great advantages for the blacks who are now young.

Isaac Van Arsdale Brown, *Memoirs of the Rev. Robert Finley*
(New Brunswick, 1819)

The majority of blacks in Philadelphia, however, disagreed strongly with their leaders. To them, the program of the Colonization Society meant a forced deportation of free blacks, in order to strengthen slavery. Soon after Finley's

visit, three thousand men—almost the whole male black pop-
ulation of Philadelphia—crowded into Richard Allen's
church to say, "WE WON'T GO!" Forten, who had been
elected chairman of the meeting described it to Paul Cuffe:

Philadelphia, January 25, 1817

Esteemed friend:

The African Institution met at the Rev. R. Allen's, the
very night your letter came to hand. I read that part to them
that wished them a happy New Year, for which they desired
me to return you many thanks.

I must mention to you that the whole continent seems to
be agitated concerning colonizing the people of color. Indeed, the people here was very much frightened at first.
They were afraid that all the free people would be compelled to go, particularly in the Southern states. We had a
large meeting of males at the Rev. R. Allen's church, the
other evening. Three thousand at least attended and there
was not one soul that was in favor of going to Africa. They
think that the slaveholders want to get rid of them so as to
make their property more secure.

We, however, have agreed to remain silent as the people
here, both white and color, are decided against the measure. My opinion is that they will never become a people until they come out from amongst the white people. But as the
majority is decidedly against me, I am determined to remain
silent, except as to my opinion which I freely give when
asked.

Charlotte has been very ill with the sore throat, but
thanks to God she has quite recovered. She thought during
her indisposition could she but have seen you, it would have
made her well. All the family join me in love to you all.

James Forten

Cuffe, his reply delayed by illness, was not disturbed by

the report of the Philadelphia meeting:

Westport, March 1, 1817

Dear friend James Forten:

I was glad to be informed that the African Institution were assembling, although they seemed to be alarmed at the movement of being colonized. Don't be uneasy, but trust in God who hath done all things well.

I have been asked again and again concerning colonizing the free people of color. I have pointed out the Cape of Good Hope. It certainly would be best to obtain a peaceful and quiet possession in whatever part of the globe we might pitch.

I have suggested settling two colonies, one in the United States and the other in Africa. If the free people of color would exert themselves more in industry and honesty, it would be a great help toward liberating those who remain in bondage.

Paul Cuffe

After a sickness of several months, Paul Cuffe died on September 9, 1817. The dream of a black-led emigration movement ended with him. James Forten had already done an about-face. A month before Cuffe's death, he had been co-author of an address which said, "The plan of colonizing is not asked for by us. We renounce and disclaim any connection with it."

Despite black disapproval, the American Colonization Society continued with its plans. With semiofficial backing from the United States government, the Society bought land on the coast of Africa, south of Sierra Leone, and named its colony Liberia. In the 1820s, a small number of free blacks, most of them from the South, emigrated there.

In 1826 a group of thirty-two black emigrants from Rhode Island went to Boston to embark on the brig Vine, *desti-*

nation: Liberia. Among them were two white-haired old men. One of them, a man of eighty, said:

I go to set an example to the youth of my race. I go to encourage the young. They can never be elevated here. I have tried it sixty years—in vain. Could I by my example lead them to set sail, and I die the next day, I should be satisfied.

E. A. Park, *Memoir of the Life and Character of Samuel Hopkins* (Boston, 1854)

He was Newport Gardner, going home at last. His companion was Salmar Nubia. Both men died in Liberia, a few months later.

3.   The Impassable Barrier

In a letter written in 1817, a founder of the Coloniza-
tion Society described "the impassable barrier" between
blacks and whites in the United States:

Be their industry ever so great, and their conduct ever so
correct, we never could consent, and they never could hope,
to see the two races placed on a footing of perfect equality
with each other. There is no State in the Union where a
Negro can ever hope to be member of Congress, a judge, a
militia officer, or even a justice of the peace, to sit down at
the same table with respectable whites, or to mix freely in
their society. I may safely assert that Paul Cuffe, respectable,
intelligent and wealthy as he is, has no expectation of ever
being invited to dine with any gentleman in Boston; of
marrying his daughter, whatever may be her fortune or education, to one of their sons; or of seeing his son obtain a
wife among their daughters.

First Annual Report of the American Society for
Colonizing the Free People of Color (Washington, 1818)

This barrier forced blacks to establish churches and schools
of their own and to live in separate neighborhoods. Richard
Allen described the incident, in 1787, that led to the forma-
tion of the first African churches:

A number of us usually attended St. George's church in
Fourth Street. When the colored people began to get numerous in attending the church, they moved us from the seats
we usually sat on, and placed us around the wall. On Sabbath morning we went to the church, and the sexton stood
at the door and told us to go in the gallery. We expected to

Richard Allen
(*Free Library of Philadelphia*)

take the seats over the ones we formerly occupied, not knowing any better.

Meeting had begun. They were nearly done singing, and just as we got to the seats, the elder said, "Let us pray." We had not been long upon our knees before I heard considerable scuffling and low talking.

I raised my head up and saw one of the trustees, H.M., having hold of Absalom Jones, pulling him up off of his knees and saying, "You must get up—you must not kneel here."

Mr. Jones replied, "Wait until prayer is over."

Mr. H.M. said, "Now! You must get up now, or I will call for aid and force you away."

Mr. Jones said, "Wait until prayer is over, and I will get up and trouble you no more."

By this time prayer was over and we all went out of the church in a body, and they were no more plagued with us.

> Richard Allen, *The Life, Experiences and Gospel Labors of the Right Reverend Richard Allen* (Philadelphia, 1888)

By 1794, Allen and his associates had converted an old

blacksmith shop into a church of their own—the Bethel Af-
rican Methodist Episcopal Church. In a statement to the
public they explained that they still considered themselves
members of the Methodist Episcopal Church, and were to
be governed by it in all church matters. However, their
regulations provided for a measure of community control:

All elections for officers shall be held by ballot of all the male members.

We admit none to be enrolled as members but descendants of the African race.

We retain a right within ourselves by a majority of qualified voters to call any brother that appears to us adequate to the task to preach, without the interference of any other person whatsoever.

All temporal concerns of our Church be conducted by our Trustees, and whatever matter may be in suspense shall be decided by a majority of legal voters.

B. T. Tanner, *An Outline of Our History and Government*
(Philadelphia, 1884)

Bethel African Methodist Episcopal Church, Philadelphia
(*Free Library of Philadelphia*)

But the hope for a church-within-a-church faded from year to year. The white Methodists insisted on complete control. They ignored the demand for black ministers. Instead, they supplied Bethel with white men whose preachings were sometimes distasteful and who demanded high pay for their services. After twenty-two years of patient negotiation, the Bethel congregation decided to take care of business its own way. What it did was reported in a letter written by Richard Allen to Daniel Coker, a minister who faced the same situation in Baltimore:

February 18, 1816

To the Rev. Daniel Coker
Dear Brother:

On the 26th of December, the Rev. Mr. Burch, one of the white Methodist Elders, sent me a notification that he should preach on the 31st inst. in Bethel Church, and requested me to give notice to the congregation that he would preach at 3 o'clock in the afternoon. However, for fear that notice would not be given, he came down himself on Thursday evening, and gave out the appointment for himself. But I contradicted it, and told the congregation that I did not believe he would preach.

When the day arrived, we began meeting a little after 2 o'clock. The house was crowded, and the aisles all filled with people and benches, so that he could not get half way up the aisle. He came about a quarter before 3 o'clock.

He said, "Jacob Tapiscoe (who is one of our colored ministers), did you not know it was my appointment?"

Brother Tapiscoe demanded silence, and said he was preaching in the name of the Lord, and by the authority of the laws of his country.

The Elder presently withdrew. On Monday the 1st of January, 1816, he applied to the Supreme Court for a writ to restore him to the pulpit of Bethel Church. On the 11th of January, it was brought before the Supreme Court.

Mr. Binney pleaded that the Rev. Mr. Burch, nor any other Elder, had right to the pulpit of Bethel, contrary to the wish of the Society. This was the decided opinion of the judges. The judge further asked, what profit he expected by forcing himself upon them contrary to their wishes; and that they held too high a hand over the colored people.

I shall get the decision of the Supreme Court and forward it to you. No more at present, but remain your loving brother in the bonds of a pure gospel.

Rev. R. Allen, with his other colleagues

Read this letter in your Church as often as you think proper. It will be observed that the property of Bethel Society in Philadelphia is worth between twenty and thirty thousand dollars.

B. T. Tanner, *An Outline of Our History and Government*
(Philadelphia, 1884)

Allen told the rest of the story in his autobiography:

Many of the colored people in other places were in a situation nearly like those of Philadelphia and Baltimore, which induced us, in April 1816, to call a general meeting. Delegates from Baltimore and other places met those of Philadelphia. Taking into consideration their grievances, and in order to promote union and harmony among themselves, it was resolved "That the people of Philadelphia, Baltimore, etc. should become one body under the name of the African Methodist Episcopal Church."

Richard Allen, *The Life, Experiences and Gospel Labors of
the Right Reverend Richard Allen* (Philadelphia, 1888)

*Richard Allen was elected bishop of the new all-black de-
nomination, which soon had branches in cities all over the
North. In New York a similar series of incidents led, in 1821,
to the formation of a second separate denomination, the African Methodist Episcopal Zion Church.*

There were no segregated seats in schools. Black children attended separate schools or none at all. Quakers and white abolitionists established African schools in New York and Philadelphia before 1800. In other towns schools were organized by the black community. Boston's African Meetinghouse, built in 1806, had a lower floor fitted out as a schoolroom. Black teachers, including Prince Saunders, taught there for a dozen years, until the school was taken over by the Boston School Committee.

In Newport, Rhode Island, blacks organized an African Benevolent Society in 1808 for "the establishment of a free school for any person of color of this town." It continued until 1842 when the first public school for black children was opened. The members of the African Benevolent Society welcomed white financial support, but their constitution was carefully worded to prevent a white takeover:

The Directors shall consist of seven colored persons and four white. They shall have the complete direction of the school and shall render a full statement of their proceedings to the Society at every annual meeting. No vote shall be carried by the Directors without the concurrence of a majority of the colored and at least two of the white Directors.

With Newport Gardner as instructor—at a salary of $10 a quarter—the school was in existence for three years before there were signs of friction. Then, in their annual report to the Society, written by a white minister, the Directors said:

We have all fully believed in the fidelity and very respectable qualifications of the present instructor. He has been successful beyond our expectation. We, however, are unanimous in the opinion that your school would be more generally attended by persons of color, and especially young men, if a white man should hereafter be the instructor. We hope that in your address to the next Directors you will express the same opinion.

The minutes of the next meetings of the Benevolent Society gave the answer of the membership:

January 2, 1811. The Directors' report being read, that clause respecting a white instructor caused some debate, but was referred to a committee of three to endeavor to know the minds of all the members.

February 7. At a meeting of the African Benevolent Society to hear the answer to the Directors, Mr. Charles Sherman, one of the Committee, made a report in writing which was considered and approved of by all present. The sum of it was that we disapprove of a white instructor at present.

> Records of the African Benevolent Society, on loan to the Newport Historical Society.

An account of some of these early schools for black children was written by William J. Brown (1814–85). An obscure shoemaker in Providence, Rhode Island, he wrote an autobiography late in life. The Moses Brown whom he refers to was one of the Brown brothers, Rhode Island's wealthiest merchants. Moses Brown had originally owned slaves—including William Brown's grandfather—but had freed them and was an active antislavery man.

Some ladies opened a free school for colored youth. I was large enough to go into the lowest class. A semicircle was painted in front of the teacher's desk. When the class was called each scholar had to toe the circle. It extended across the room and would accommodate some twelve children, who stood front of the teacher to read and spell. My class read from a large alphabet card. Then there was a long desk with seats. On top was a place one foot wide and one inch deep, filled with sand. A piece of board was used to stroke the sand smooth. A copy of A B C was made for the scholars to learn to write, using wooden pens flattened out like a spoon handle. Each scholar had his own space to write on.

When the space was filled each one had to sit up straight and the teacher would call a monitor to level the sand and set another copy. This school continued six months.

The colored people called a meeting in 1819 to take measures to build a meetinghouse, with a basement for a schoolroom. The lot was selected and Mr. [Moses] Brown purchased it and then conveyed the lot to the colored people of Providence. The house was finished in 1821. The committee lost some time in trying to find a teacher. After searching, they procured a white gentleman by the name of Mr. Ormsbee. The school was not a free school, the price of tuition being $1.50 per quarter. The colored people sent their children and they soon had 125 scholars.

I attended the school at the opening. The scholars behaved pretty well. On the east side of the vestry there was a part which had never been dug out. It was partitioned off, leaving a dark hole 20 feet long having a door that opened in the vestry. Whenever any of the scholars misbehaved they were put in this hole. The children were very much afraid to be shut up in this place, for when they were digging the cellar they dug up a coffin and a man in it. They supposed it must have been some Indian that was buried there.

Mr. Ormsbee was a very severe teacher. He used the cowhide very freely. After keeping the school for one year, his labors came to a close. For a year and a half the school was suspended, not being able to procure a teacher. Colored teachers were very rarely to be found, and it was difficult to procure a white teacher as it was considered disgraceful employment to be a teacher of colored children.

After waiting a long time the Lord sent us a teacher and a preacher, Mr. Asa C. Goldberry. He was an octoroon, and many people took him to be white. He filled the pulpit on the Sabbath and on week days taught the school. He was here some two years, when he got married and went to Haiti. After his departure we succeeded in getting a white teacher, and he remained six months and left. The next teacher was the Rev. Jacob Perry, a colored man. He preached in the meetinghouse and taught the school, having the same salary that the former teacher had.

It was the custom for children on seeing their teacher to raise their hats and speak and the girls to make a courtsy. If we neglected these marks of politeness, we would be put in mind of our duty by an elderly person who might be passing. They would say to us, "Go home and tell your parents to teach you some manners."

But it was considered such a disgrace for white men to teach colored schools that they would be greatly offended if the colored children bowed or spoke to them on the street. Mr. Anthony who was at one time teaching the colored school became very angry because Zebedee Howland met him on the street, raised his hat and bowed. The next morning [he] took poor Zebedee and the whole school to task, saying, "When you meet me on the street, don't look towards me, or speak to me. If you do, I will flog you the first chance I get."

The Life of William J. Brown of Providence,
R.I., with Personal Recollections of Incidents
in Rhode Island (Providence, 1883)

4.   A Life of One's Own

Life was not always serious. The few personal writings of blacks in the Northern states that have survived from the eighteenth and early nineteenth century illustrate a wide range of moods and personalities.

Caesar Lyndon was a slave belonging to Josiah Lyndon, a governor of Rhode Island. He worked as his master's business agent. At the same time he traded on his own with the sea captains of Newport and Providence and loaned money to fellow slaves. Some selections from his diary, in which he recorded both business transactions and correspondence, follow. Most of his dealings were in pounds, shillings and pence; a pistareen was a West Indian coin.

1765. May 18. Sir: If you have sold those 2 kegs Pickled Lobsters I sent you sometime ago I should be glad you would please to send me ye amount in money & Cotton Caps, one half in cash. Please to keep what you think will satisfy you for the trouble. Pray don't fail to write. I am, Sir, Your most humble servant,

Caesar Lyndon.

1766. July 2. This day Capt. Knowles has had 6 bunches Turnips at £2.8.0

August 9. Lent Mrs. Sarah Robinson, an Indian or Mulatto, 1 pistareen.

August 12th. This day the following persons took a pleasant ride out to Portsmouth:

> Boston Vose
> Lingo Stephens and Phylis Lyndon
> Nepton Sipson and Wife
> Prince Thurston
> Caesar Lyndon and Sarah Searing

Necessaries [bought] for ye Support of Nature are as follows:

To a pig to roast	£8.10.0
To so much paid for house room	7. 4.0
To Wine	3.12.0
To Bread	1. 8.0
To Rum	2.10.0
To Green Corn 70 Limes for Punch 20	4.10.0
To Sugar	2. 4.0
To Butter	1. 0.0
To Tea 40 Coffee 15	2.15.0
To 1 pint Rum for killing Pig	.10.0
	£33.13.0

October 11. Bought 1 pr. Silver knee buckles at £10. Sold my old pair at ye same time. Also gave £3.15 for Yellow pair knee bands put on my Leather Breeches.

1768. August 9. Friend Boston Vose arrived from Surinam & brought home for me 6 China Cups and 6 saucers, also one Looking Glass, yellow round the Frame. Glass £12. Cups &c £9.16.

1769. March 15. Bought one Razor and a pair Pinchbeck knee buckles for 1 pistareen & 4 Coppers of a man who said he came from Boston. The knee buckles Caesar gave to his friend Bristol.

1770. June 15. Bought a sow pig, very extraordinary sort. Came from a sow formerly owned by Mr. Anthony. Gave £8 in hard money.

Rhode Island Historical Society

As might be expected of anyone wearing leather breeches and silver knee buckles, Lyndon was a ladies' man. As a result of one love affair, a fellow black threatened to kill him. Lyndon appealed to Moses Brown, who still maintained an interest in his ex-slaves:

Newport, September 3, 1781

Moses Brown, Esqr.

Honored Sir:

This day your humble servant received a Letter from one of his Complexion, a person heretofore under your good government, which Letter runs thus:

Providence, August 27, 1781

Sir: I am induced to inform you of my present circumstances. Caesar Lyndon has acted a shameful part. He has visited me, and under the mask of friendship persuaded my wife to leave me and keep with him. He had better not marry her. His life will be in danger.

Prime Brown

I should be glad if Esqr. Brown would be pleased to give Mr. Prime such advice as may be necessary in such cases, where any Person threatens another's Life. My Countryman, Mr. Prime does not consider that he has broken the Peace by thus threatening, but I hope he will consider the consequences that attends those found Guilty of Murder.

I humbly pray Esqr. Brown would do that which may appear perfectly right & just. I should be exceeding sorry if there should be any murder done.

As far as I can learn, the woman is no wife to Mr. Prime. They only kept each other's company for so long a time as they could agree; which time seems now to be at an end. Hoping happiness will always attend Esqr. Brown's family, I crave leave to subscribe myself

Your Obedient Humble Servant

Caesar Lyndon, now in the service and under the government of Mrs. Mary Lyndon, Widow to the late Honorable Josiah Lyndon, Esquire, deceased

Rhode Island Historical Society

Perhaps Moses Brown did convince Prime to accept his

loss peacefully. At any rate, Lyndon survived to win his freedom and become an officer of the African Union Society.

In contrast to the worldly Caesar Lyndon, Phillis Wheatley was sedate and pious to a fault. Brought from Africa as a slave at the age of seven, she was treated considerately by her mistress, Susannah Wheatley, and was educated well beyond the level of most American women in her time. She began to live a life of her own only after her abilities as a poet became public, to the astonishment and disbelief of New England literary circles. At twenty she went to Eng-land where her first book, Poems on Various Subjects, Reli-gious and Moral *was published. The following letter to a black friend in Newport tells what she felt about her owner/family:*

Boston, March 21, 1774

To Miss Obour Tanner
Dear Obour:

I received your obliging letter. I have lately met with a great trial in the death of my mistress. Let us imagine the loss of a parent, sister or brother—the tenderness of all these were united in her. I was a poor little outcast & a stranger when she took me in, not only in her house, but I presently became a sharer in her most tender affections. I was treated more like her child than her servant. No opportunity was left unimproved of giving me the best of advice, in terms how tender! how engaging!

I am very sorry to hear that you are indisposed, but hope this will find you in better health. I have been unwell the greater part of the winter, but am much better as spring approaches. I shall send the 5 books you wrote for. If you want more, they shall be ready for you.

Phillis Wheatley

Letters of Phillis Wheatley, The Negro Slave-Poet of Boston
(Boston, 1864)

Phillis Wheatley   (*New York Public Library Picture Collection*)

Miss Wheatley's feelings about her homeland were expressed in "On Being Brought from Africa to America":

> 'Twas mercy brought me from my Pagan land,
> Taught my benighted soul to understand
> That there's a God, and there's a Savior too.

Her interest in Christianizing Africa led to correspondence with the Reverend Samuel Hopkins of Newport. The Philip Quaque she discusses was a British-educated African who went to Guinea as a missionary. Miss Wheatley may have met him during her stay in England.

Boston, May 6, 1774

The Reverend S. Hopkins
Reverend Sir:

I received your kind letter last evening. I have also received the money for the five books I sent Obour and 2s 6d more for another.

I am very sorry to hear that Philip Quaque has very little or no *apparent* success in his mission. Let us not be discouraged, but still hope that God will bring about his great work, though Philip may *not* be the instrument to perform this work of wonder, turning the Africans *"from darkness to light."* Possibly if Philip would introduce himself properly to them he might be more successful. I observe your reference to the maps of Guinea and Salmon's Gazetteer and shall consult them.

I have received, in some of the last ships from London, three hundred more copies of my poems, and wish to dispose of them as soon as possible. If you know of any being wanted, you will be pleased to let me know.

Phillis Wheatley

E. A. Park, *Memoir of the Life and Character of Samuel Hopkins* (Boston, 1854)

Benjamin Banneker, America's first black man of science, was an astronomer, surveyor and mathematician. Selections from his diary show him to have been a serious naturalist, as well. His systematic observation of three generations of seventeen-year locusts over a period of fifty-one years produced accurate information about the life cycle of these insects long before entomology became an important branch of science.

December 2, 1790. About 3 o'clock, A.M. I heard the sound and felt the shock like unto heavy thunder. I went out but could not observe any cloud above the horizon. I therefore conclude it must be a great earthquake in some part of the globe.

August 27, 1797. Standing at my door I heard the discharge of a gun and in four or five seconds of time, after the discharge, the small shot came rattling about me, one or two of which struck the house; which plainly demonstrates that the velocity of sound is greater than that of a cannon bullet.

April 1800. The first great locust year that I can remember was 1749. I was then about seventeen years of age when thousands of them came and were creeping up the trees and bushes. I then imagined they came to eat and destroy the fruit of the earth and would occasion a famine in the land. I therefore began to kill and destroy them, but soon saw that my labor was in vain.

Again, in the year 1766, which is seventeen years after their first appearance, they made a second, and appeared to me to be full as numerous as the first. I then, being about thirty-four years of age, had more sense than to endeavor to destroy them, knowing they were not so pernicious to the fruit of the earth as I imagined they would be.

Again, in the year 1783, which was seventeen years since their second appearance to me, they made their third; and they may be expected again in the year 1800. The female has a sting in her tail as sharp and hard as a thorn, with which she perforates the branches of the trees and in the holes lays eggs. The branch soon dies and falls. Then the egg, by some occult cause, immerges a great depth into the earth and there continues for the space of seventeen years as aforesaid.

I like to forgot to inform, that if their lives are short they are merry. They begin to sing or make a noise from first they come out of the earth till they die.

February 2, 1803. In the morning part of the day, there arose a very dark cloud, followed by snow and hail, a flash of lightning and loud thunder crack; and then the storm abated until afternoon, when another cloud arose at the same point with a beautiful shower of snow. But what beautified the snow was the brightness of the sun. I looked for the rainbow, or rather snowbow, but I think the snow was of too dense a nature to exhibit the representation of the bow in the cloud.

"Memoir of Benjamin Banneker" by John H. B. Latrobe
in *African Repository* (November 1845)

Banneker often gave his friend and fellow-scientist George Ellicott mathematical problems in rhyme:

A Cooper and Vintner sat down for a talk,
Both being so groggy, that neither could walk,
Says Cooper to Vintner, "I'm the first of my trade,
There's no kind of vessel, but what I have made,
And of any shape, Sir,—just what you will,—
And of any size, Sir,—from a ton to a gill!"
"Then," says the Vintner, "you're the man for me,—
Make me a vessel, if we can agree.
The top and the bottom diameter define,
To bear that proportion as fifteen to nine;
Thirty-five inches are just what I crave,
No more and no less, in the depth, will I have;
Just thirty-nine gallons this vessel must hold,—
Then I will reward you with silver or gold,—
Give me your promise, my honest old friend?"
"I'll make it tomorrow, that you may depend!"
So the next day the Cooper his work to discharge,
Soon made the new vessel, but made it too large;—
He took out some staves, which made it too small,
And then cursed the vessel, the Vintner and all.
He beat on his breast, "By the Powers!" —he swore,
He never would work at his trade any more.
Now my worthy friend, find out, if you can,
The vessel's dimensions and comfort the man!

Benjamin Banneker

"A Sketch of the Life of Benjamin Banneker,"
read before the Maryland Historical Society,
October 5, 1854 (*Maryland Historical Society Pre-Fund Publications*, Vol. 2. No. 18)

The answer: the greater diameter of Banneker's tub was 24.746 inches; the lesser diameter 14.8476 inches.

Despite trips that kept him away from home for a year at

Title page from almanac compiled by Benjamin Banneker
(*Maryland Historical Society*)

a time, Paul Cuffe was a family man. The following is one of several letters to his brother John about bringing up their children. At the time it was written, Paul, Jr., was sixteen years old and had already sailed with his father on a trip to Sweden.

Westport, October 8, 1808

Dear Brother and Sister John & Jenny Cuffe:

I observe that my son Paul has brought home a gun that he borrowed of his Uncle John which I dare say his good uncle lent unto him out of pure love and good will, for the want of due consideration. In the first place I have two guns and make but little use of them, which is enough, as Christ said unto Peter, by the sword.

It is but little time since Paul got my powder and loaded a log and Charles fired it. It was wonderful that he had not been killed. Again, he has lately sold his trunk to be able to gratify himself in these unnecessary evils which we both disapprove of.

A word of advice concerning thy son Zacharias. I understand that he is taking or is allowed great liberty of going and coming when he pleases and laying about in low and unbecoming places. This looks unto me to need great watchfulness. Should there have been anything lost it might have labored hard with you to have cleared the boy, although he had not been guilty.

Dear brother and sister, this I mention out of pure love and regard for the welfare of us, here and hereafter.

Your affectionate brother, Paul Cuffe

P.S. I do not wish you to take any great trouble to recall the gun immediately but have mentioned it for our mutual advantage and due consideration.

Some blacks were not as honest as Paul Cuffe. One clever rascal dined well for months by passing himself off as Richard Allen's or Paul Cuffe's son. In a letter to James Forten, Cuffe traced the imposter's grand tour:

January 23, 1817

Respected friend James Forten:

Some months ago a colored man came to New Bedford. Called on my son-in-law, saying he was Richard Allen's son and was a minister. He left New Bedford, went to Boston and with false letters of recommendation, stating to be brother-in-law to P. Cuffe, he succeeded in getting $900 worth of goods packed for New York.

He next appeared in New York with false letters of credit to amount of $10,000. He was had before the authority and acquitted on condition of his leaving the state. He went to Albany and got into the employ of Ira Porter. Stole Porter's horse valued at $200.

He arrived at York in Pennsylvania. There he was P. Cuffe. After staying at Joseph Jessup 3 nights, Joseph grew suspicious of him. Jesse Talbot of Baltimore wrote me saying this hypocritical man was in Baltimore and had illy made use of my name, being bound to Congress with plans for civilizing Africa &c. On examination, he was P. Cuffe, Jr., and then a son-in-law to P. Cuffe. Should he make his appearance in Philadelphia, please to stop his mad career. Beware of wolves in sheep's clothing are the advice of thy affectionate and ever well-wishing friend

Paul Cuffe

Jailed at last, the imposter boldly called on Cuffe for help:

York Jail, January 13, 1817

To Paul Cuffe
Dear Father:

This is to inform thee that in my journey to Alexandria I have been confined in prison for an imposter. They say I am not your son. I wish thee come on immediately or send some of the neighbors and by that means I can get released. They say that I must prove that I am thy son or else must stand trial at the next court which is in April. This from thy son,

John Cuffe

Free Public Library, New Bedford, Massachusetts

Replying, Cuffe told him that he was disgracing "the

"Negro Governor" on Election Day

whole community of the African race. If nothing better can be obtained from thee, let me entreat thee to petition for a prison for life."

In the eighteenth century, Election Day was an important holiday in New England. The slaves, not permitted to vote in the general election, held elections of their own to chose a "Negro Governor" and his aides. The "Nigger 'Lection" was encouraged by whites who vied with others—and sometimes bought votes—each to have his own slave win. With few opportunities to have fun or to feel pride in themselves, the slaves cooperated willingly. Even after they won freedom, elections for a "Negro Governor" were held in many places until the mid-nineteenth century. A New England historian collected contemporary accounts of the elections. The first came from a white resident of Connecticut:

The person selected for office was usually one of much note among themselves, of imposing presence, strength, firmness and volubility, who was quick to decide, ready to command and able to flog. When elected he had his aides, his parade and appointed military officers, sheriffs and justices of peace. He settled all grave disputes, questioned conduct and imposed penalties and punishments. He was respected as "Governor" by the Negroes throughout the state and obeyed almost implicitly.

A troop of blacks, an hundred in number, marching sometimes on foot, sometimes mounted in true military style and dress on horseback, escorted him through the streets, with drums beating, colors flying and fifes, fiddles, clarinets uttering martial sound. After marching, they would retire to some large room which they would engage for the purpose, for refreshments and deliberations. This was all done with the greatest regard for ceremony.

A proclamation from a Negro Governor in 1776:

I, Governor Cuff of the Negroes in the province of Connecticut, do Resign my governmentship to John Anderson, Negro Man to Governor Skene. I hope that you will obey him as you have done me for this ten years past.

I, John Anderson, having the honor to be appointed Governor over you, I will do my utmost to serve you in Every Respect, and I hope you will obey me accordingly.

John Anderson, Governor over the Negroes in Connecticut

A later newspaper advertisement. Fiddlers who played at dances used catgut for the strings of their violins and rosin for rubbing on their bows.

ATTENTION FREEMEN!
There will be a general election of the colored gentlemen of Connecticut, October first, twelve o'clock noon. The day will be celebrated in the evening by a dance at Qarner's tavern, when it will be shown that there is some power in muscle, catgut and rosin.

By order of the Governor

Ebenezer Bassett, school principal and later U. S. Minister to Haiti, recalled his father's election as Governor:

My father was the great-grandson of an African prince. His father was "raised" in the family of Capt. Wooster of Derby, fought in the War of Independence and was recognized as a man of tact, courage, and intelligence. [My father] was of the very finest physical mold, being over six feet tall. He was besides, ready of speech and considered quite witty. Indeed, his sayings are even still quoted.

Under the circumstances, it was altogether natural that he should be "elected" one of the so-called "Negro Governors" of Connecticut. I remember that he held the office two or three terms. Sundays and nights he used to pore over books on military tactics and study up on the politics of the state.

In my day I think that the election was more by *viva voce* [voice] vote than by ballot. The affair was always accompanied by a military display, a big dinner and a ball. It generally ran through two days. These features certainly existed much later than 1837 for I was born in 1833.

Orville Platt, "Negro Governors," *New Haven Historical Society Papers*, Vol. VI (1900)

As time passed, blacks tended to ignore white holidays. Instead, they turned out to mark notable dates in the anti-slavery calendar. January 1 was celebrated after the African slave trade was abolished on that day in 1808, and July 5 when slavery ended in New York State in 1827. After the British abolished slavery in the West Indies on August 1, 1834, August 1 became a major black holiday.

James McCune Smith, America's first university-trained black doctor, recalled a parade that he had taken part in as a youth:

The great celebration of the Abolition of Slavery in the State of New York was held July 5th, 1827. That was a celebration! A real full-souled, full-voiced shouting for joy, and marching through the crowded streets, with feet jubilant to songs of freedom!

First of all, Grand Marshal of the day was Samuel Hardenburgh, a splendid-looking black man, in cocked hat and drawn sword, mounted on a milk-white steed; then his aids on horseback, dashing up and down the line; then the orator of the day, also mounted, with a handsome scroll, appearing like a baton, in his right hand; then in due order, splendidly dressed in scarfs of silk with gold-edgings, and with colored bands of music, and their banners appropriately lettered and painted, followed, THE NEW YORK AFRICAN SOCIETY FOR MUTUAL RELIEF, THE WILBERFORCE BENEVOLENT SOCIETY, and THE CLARKSON BENEVOLENT SOCIETY; then the people five or six abreast, from grown men to small boys. The sidewalks were crowded with the wives, daughters, sisters, and mothers of the celebrants, representing every state in the Union, and not a few with gay bandanna handkerchiefs, betraying their West Indian birth. Neither was Africa itself unrepresented. Hundreds who had survived the middle passage and a youth in slavery joined in the joyful procession.

> Henry Highland Garnet, *A Memorial Discourse,*
> with an introduction by James McCune Smith
> (Philadelphia, 1865)

William J. Brown described a smaller-scale celebration in Providence when the African Meeting House was dedicated in 1822:

At the time of the church dedication, the colored people made great preparations to celebrate the day. The young colored men formed a military company called the African Greys to escort the African societies to their new house of worship.

The African societies wore their regalias. The president of the societies was dressed to represent an African chief, having on a red pointed cap, and carried an elephant's tusk in his hand. Each end was tipped with gilt. The other officers carrying emblems decked with lemons and oranges, representing the fruits of Africa. The military company wore black belts and carried muskets, and the officers their side arms. After the services, the company paraded the streets.

> *The Life of William J. Brown* (Providence, 1883)

The solidarity that free black people of the North felt for their brothers in slavery, and the sense of African heritage to which they still clung were expressed at a dinner in Boston in 1828. The dinner was given for Abduhl Rahhahman, prince of the African kingdom of Footah Jalloh (in present-day Guinea), who had been a slave in Mississippi for forty years. When the State Department became interested in him, hoping that his return to Africa would open up trade with his kingdom, his master set him free and allowed him to purchase his wife for a small sum. But he had nine children in slavery. Traveling to major cities in the North, he tried to raise the money to buy them. Freedom's Journal, *the nation's first black newspaper, reported his reception in Boston:*

On Wednesday last the colored inhabitants of this city gave a public dinner to their fellow countryman, Prince Abduhl Rahhahman. A procession was formed at the African

John B. Russwurm, editor of *Freedom's Journal*

School House at 4 o'clock and moved to the African Masonic Hall. After partaking of a well-provided dinner, the following toasts were announced:

Royal Sir— The colored inhabitants of Boston welcome you this day. Their hearts participate with your long sufferings in this land of ours. May the evening of your days be the rising sun which illuminates Footah Jalloh.

May the slaveholders of the world be like the whales in the ocean, with the trasher at their back and the swordfish at their belly, until they rightly understand the difference between freedom and slavery.

Our worthy guest who was torn from his country and doomed to unlawful bondage, may God enable him to obtain so much of the reward of his labor as may purchase the freedom of his offspring.

The following song, written for the occasion by [the] City Marshal, was sung by him with effect:

All hail to the chief from old Africa's shore,
Who forty years' bondage has had to deplore
Huzza for the chieftain—huzza for the chief;
Huzza for the chief from old Africa's shore.

He's bound to the land where his name is held dear,
Where welcome awaits him and people will cheer,
Where friends will receive him with gladness of heart,
And he may be call'd on to act a new part.

Our hearts are quite heavy, our purses are light—
We sympathize with him and throw in our mite.
Our wishes are good but our powers are small—
We thought this treat better than nothing at all.

We'll do our endeavors to let the world see
That Africa's children of right should be free.
Huzza for the chieftain—Huzza for the chief;
Huzza for the chief from old Africa's shore.

Freedom's Journal, October 24, 1828

Prince Abduhl's tour netted $2,500, but the asking price for his children was $7,000. He and his wife returned to Africa; their children remained slaves in Mississippi.

II·COLORED AMERICANS (1830–40)

How unprofitable it is for us to spend our golden moments in long and solemn debate upon the question whether we shall be called *Africans, Colored Americans* or *Africo Americans* or *Blacks*. The question should be, my friends, *shall we arise and act like men, and cast off this terrible yoke?*

Henry Highland Garnet

1. Our Claims Are on America

The United States was fifty years old, going on sixty. The black population, except for a handful of old people, was American-born. To this new generation, ending slavery and winning equal rights in the United States seemed more important, and more possible, than resettling in Africa. At a meeting of the New York African Society for Mutual Relief in 1828, Thomas L. Jennings, a successful New York tailor, said:

Our claims are on America; it is the land that gave us birth. We know no other country. It is a land in which our fathers have suffered and toiled. They have watered it with their tears and fanned it with their sighs.

Our relation with Africa is the same as the white man's is with Europe. We have passed through several generations in this country and consequently we have become naturalized. Our habits, our manners, our passions, our dispositions have become the same. The same mother's milk has nourished us both in infancy; the white child and the colored have both hung on the same breast. I might as well tell the white man about England, France or Spain, the country from whence his forefathers emigrated, and call him a European, as for him to call us Africans. Africa is as foreign to us as Europe is to them.

Freedom's Journal, April 4, 1828

This rejection of Africa stemmed in part from a rejection of the American Colonization Society. Black public opinion in the North now looked on the society as an enemy and branded the men who emigrated to Liberia as traitors. All of Paul Cuffe's old associates had become convinced that colonization served only to strengthen slavery and to widen the gulf between free blacks and whites. James Forten's letter to William Lloyd Garrison who had just started The Liberator, *an antislavery weekly, shows how far the pendulum had swung:*

Philadelphia, February 23, 1831

William Lloyd Garrison
My Esteemed Friend:

A communication in Poulson's *Daily Advertiser* states that Mrs. Stansbury of Trenton, N. Jersey has presented

1,000 Dollars to the Colonization Society. It is greatly to be regretted that this highly generous lady has been induced to make this donation for conveying superannuated slaves to Africa, when objects of much greater importance could be obtained by offering a premium to master mechanics to take colored children as apprentices.

I am greatly astonished that the ministers of the gospel should take so active a part in endeavoring to convey freemen of color to Africa. Instead of doing this, they should endeavor to remove prejudice, improve the condition of the colored people by education and by having their children placed in a situation to learn a trade.

I have never conversed with an intelligent man of color (not swayed by sinister motives) who was not decidedly opposed to leaving his home for the fatal clime of Africa. I am well acquainted with all the masters of vessels belonging to this port who have been to the coast of Africa. They all agree in representing it as one of the most unhealthy countries.

Has anyone in our Southern states given anything like a thousand dollars to promote emigration to Africa? Not one has shown so much compassion for the oppressed slave. General Mercer, the President of the Colonization Society, promised to emancipate his slaves and remove them to Africa. Mr. [Francis Scott] Key and the late Judge [Bushrod] Washington promised to liberate their slaves. Neither of them have performed their promise.

According to Mr. Key, they have removed in 14 years about as many hundred [1,400] emigrants. I venture to say that at least a half million have been born during the same period. We ask not their aid in assisting us to emigrate to Africa. We are contented in the land that gave us birth and for which many of our fathers fought and died.

I well remember that when the New England Regiment marched through this city on their way to attack the English Army under Lord Cornwallis, there were several companies of colored people, as brave men as ever fought. I saw those brave soldiers who fought at the Battle of Red Bank where the Hessians [were] defeated. Now the descendants of these men are to be removed to a distant country while emigrants from every other country are permitted to seek an asylum here, and to enjoy the blessings of civil and religious liberty.

I am much pleased with your paper. It is very popular here. The people of color contemplate a meeting for the purpose of making the paper more generally known.

James Forten

Antislavery Collection, Boston Public Library

The columns of The Liberator *and* The Colored American, *a black newspaper that was started in New York in 1837, were filled with letters, speeches and even poems expressing opposition to emigration:*

Catskill, September 30, 1837.

Mr. Editor,

The following lines are the fruits of my first idle hour's attempt at rhyming. If you think they contain sufficient poetry to entitle them to publication, you will insert them;—if not, I am sure you can light segars with them!

Martin Cross.

Talk not to me of "Colonization"—
For I'm a freeman of this nation;
Then why forsake my native land
For Afric's burning sun and sand?
We hereby make our proclamation,
That we're opposed to emigration.—
This is the land which gave us birth,
Our fathers' graves are freedom's earth;
They won the freedom we enjoy—
How can you freemen's rights destroy?
For we're determin'd, to a man,
Not to forsake our native land!

Where bright Emancipation gleams,
Where Freedom's banner o'er us streams!
We've borne its stripes of crimson hue—
We'll share its stars' proud glory too!

The Colored American, October 7, 1837

But if blacks no longer thought of themselves as Africans, who were they? The question touched off a long debate, which a modern scholar has called "The Namestakes." Samplings of the debate:

"Niger" is a word used by the old Romans to designate inanimate [objects] which were black, such as soot, pot, wood, house, &c. Also, animals which they considered inferior to the human species, as a black horse, cow, hog, &c. The white Americans have applied this term to Africans by way of reproach for our color, to aggravate and heighten our miseries, because they have their feet on our throats.

David Walker's *Appeal to the Colored Citizens of the World*
(Boston, 1829)

Philadelphia, May 25, 1831

To the Editor:
Why do our friends as well as our enemies call us "Negroes?" We feel it to be a term of reproach, and could wish our friends would call us by some other name. If you, Sir, or one of your correspondents would condescend to answer this question, we would esteem it a favor.

Ella

The Liberator, June 4, 1831

To the Editor:
The term "colored" is not a good one. Whenever used, it recalls to mind the offensive distinctions of color. The name "African" is more objectionable yet, and is no more correct than "Englishman" would be to a native-born citizen of the United States.

The colored citizen is an American of African descent. Cannot a name be found that will explain these two facts? I suggest one, and I beg your readers to reflect on it before you reject it as unsuitable. It is "Afric-American" or, written in one word, "Africamerican." It asserts that most important truth, that the colored citizen is as truly a citizen of the United States as the white.

A Subscriber

The Liberator, September 24, 1831

Philadelphia, September 1, 1831

Mr. Editor:

"A Subscriber" has suggested the appropriateness of the term "Afric-American." The suggestion is as absurd as the sound of the name is inharmonious. It is true that we should have a distinct appellation—we being the only people in America who feel all the accumulated injury which pride and prejudice can suggest. But sir, since we have been so long distinguished by the title "men of color," why make this change, so uncouth and jargon-like? A change we do want and a change we will have. When it comes, we shall be called *citizens of the United States and Americans.*

A Subscriber and Citizen of the United States

The Liberator, September 24, 1831

The Colored American, founded by the Reverend Samuel E. Cornish and Philip A. Bell, gave the following editorial explanation in its first issue:

The editor, aware of the diversity of opinion in reference to the title of this "Paper" thinks it not amiss to state some reasons for selecting this name. Many would gladly rob us of the endeared name "AMERICAN," a distinction more emphatically belonging to us than five-sixths of this nation and one that we will never yield.

But why colored? Because our circumstances require spe-

Samuel E. Cornish, coeditor of *Freedom's Journal* and *The Colored American*

cial action. We have in view objects peculiar to ourselves and in contradistinction from the mass. How, then, shall we be known and our interests presented but by some distinct, specific name—and what appellation is so inoffensive, so acceptable as COLORED PEOPLE—COLORED AMERICANS?

The Colored American, March 4, 1837

The Namestakes was more than a quibble over words. It was the beginning of a long debate to choose a name that would fully express the special position of black people in the United States—a debate that still continues. Its real issue might be stated thus:

"Has our history and our way of life made us a separate people, with our own traditions, problems and program, or are we really no different than the whites except for the 'accident' of skin color?"

For the first time in their history on this continent, black people had allies. With the appearance of The Liberator *in*

*1831 and the formation of the American Anti-Slavery So-
ciety two years later, blacks no longer felt alone in their
struggle for freedom. Earlier abolitionist groups had worked
for the "poor Africans." Garrison and his associates invited
black people to join with them to combat slavery and discrimination.*

*Starting in 1830, blacks had held annual Conventions of
Colored Men, to discuss mutual problems and to plan for action. After they were invited to join the "white" antislavery
societies, some began to question the need for separate Colored Conventions, separate African Societies. If all men
were brothers, as the Garrisonians said, then why not work
with the whites for the good of the human race?*

*The chief spokesman for integration was William Whip-
per, a black businessman from Pennsylvania. At the Fifth
Annual Colored Convention, he offered a resolution:*

That we recommend as far as possible to our people to
abandon the use of the word "colored" when either speaking or writing concerning themselves; and especially to remove the title of African from their institutions, the marbles
of churches, &c.

William Whipper's resolution in relation to using the
words "colored" and "Africans" was called up, and after an
animated and interesting discussion, it was unanimously
adopted.

"Minutes of the Fifth Annual Convention for
the Improvement of The Free People of Color
In the United States" (Philadelphia, 1835)

*This vote did not end the debate. Although the national
Colored Conventions came to a halt and were not resumed
again until 1843, only a small number of black people
agreed with William Whipper. The majority opinion was expressed by "Sidney," a young New Yorker, who wrote a
series of letters to* The Colored American:

William Whipper

We do not think that by watering and preserving the plant that perfumes our room that *therefore* we dislike all other plants in the world. We do not believe that in loving our own mother's sons, our brothers, that therefore we exclude mankind. In fine we have no sympathy with that cosmopoliting disposition which tramples upon all nationality.

And pray, for what are we to turn around and bay the whole human family? Why are we to act different from all others in this important matter? Why, because we *happen* to be—COLORED.

That we are colored is a fact, an undeniable fact. That we are descendants of Africans is true. We affirm there is nothing in it that we need to be ashamed of, yea, rather much that we may be proud of.

For ourselves we are quite well satisfied. And we intend, in all our public efforts, to go to the power-holding body and tell them, "Colored as we are, *black* though we may be, yet we demand our rights, the same rights other citizens have."

The Colored American, March 6, 13, 1841

2. "Wash Me White"

White abolitionists proposed to end slavery by "moral suasion"—by hammering away at its evils until the hearts of the slaveholders were changed. Blacks were to do their part by demonstrating that they were the equals of whites in every way. Going along with this thinking, The Colored American *asked, "What can we do for the poor slave?":*

You can educate your children; cultivate your own mind; be industrious and economical. These will speak volumes in behalf of the liberty of the slave.

Let us but make our whole people as virtuous and intelligent as any other part of the community, and we shall at one stroke break off the whole body of oppression and slavery. Let us make a character of a high order and of a holy kind and the whole work is done.

The Colored American, June 24, 1837

Self-criticism was widespread. At a time when it was considered daring for women to speak to audiences of men Maria Stewart, a young black woman, spoke at the African Masonic Hall in Boston:

I would implore our men, and especially our rising youth, to flee from the gambling board and the dance hall; for we are poor and have no money to throw away. I do not consider dancing as criminal in itself, but it is astonishing to me that our young men are so blind to their own interest as to spend their hard earnings for this frivolous amusement; for it has been carried on among us to such an unbecoming extent, that it has become absolutely disgusting. Had those men turned their attention as assiduously to mental and moral improvement as they have to gambling and dancing,

I might have remained quietly at home, and they stood contending in my place.

Productions of Mrs. Maria W. Stewart (Boston, 1835)

Articles in The Colored American *made similar points:*

THINGS THAT PAIN OUR HEART

Our heart is grieved when we see colored Americans thronging Porter Houses and Taverns, spending their hard earnings for intoxicating drinks.

When we see them standing in crowds at the corners of the streets, and indulging in the loud unmeaning and vulgar laugh.

When we see them puffing segars in the open streets.

When we see them in crowds, following the troops, or surrounding and gazing upon the bands of music.

When we see them congregated in the Park, or cooped up in the Negro seats in the Courtrooms.

These are painful things, and should be avoided by every colored American. Let colored men have keener sensibility, and more holy ambition, than to indulge in these vulgar practices.

The Colored American, April 29, 1837

ON TRAINING

The great reason why we remain so poor is a want of proper training in childhood and youth. A colored boy at eight years of age is sent to school every day, except one or two when he stays home "to fetch water for mother to wash with." This is the first mode of learning boys to be irregular in employment. Instead of making him rise at 6 and render this service, his school hours are broken in upon.

He arrives at twelve or fourteen years and instead of apprenticing him to some handicraft or to farm labor, he is sent out to [domestic] service. Why? Because as a menial he can earn most money immediately. *This is a gross error in conduct.* Perhaps he is sent to a trade, but in a week or two his parents take him away. Why? Because his master or a journeyman had struck him (for impudence, perhaps) or because he did not receive a handsome suit of clothes, or because they gave him coarse food or because someone in the shop called him "nigger."

If your boy be struck, let him be stricken. Buffets and blows without cause have [always] been the share of the youngest apprentice. Is he compelled to do drudgery? Let him do it. Those who are now millionaires have done the same and *train their boys to do the same.* Is he badly clothed? Let him go in rags and live on crusts of bread and cold water, so long as he can learn a trade which in manhood will support him well. But he is called a nigger! Horrible! Take him away from the trade—do not let him stay, no, not for the world. Such an insult! What then? By a parity of conduct you should not let him walk the streets, nor be seen, but should pack the dear sensitive baby boy in a glass case covered with lead where that awful soul-palsying effort-benumbing phrase may never reach his ear!

If we wish our children to grow up efficient, strong-minded, money-making and money-saving men; if we wish them to obtain those rights which are withheld from us, then we must train them for work. Four or five or seven years spent at one employment is the best discipline the mind can receive. It forms character—it makes boys men!

The Colored American, May 11, 1839

Self-criticism was paralleled by action. In the 1830s "self-improvement societies"—literary clubs, debating groups, library companies—sprang up in every city of the North. Freedom's Journal *described the scene in Boston:*

Our colored brethren here have a Grand Masonic Lodge, the African Masonic Lodge of Boston. It is the first institution of the kind among us. They have a fine lodge room

on Cambridge Street. Our brethren here have also three
religious societies, one or two mutual relief societies and
a debating club.

The Debating Club consists of about eighteen or twenty
members who meet once every two weeks for the discussion of extemporaneous subjects. From the debates which
often come before them, a spirit of inquiry is engendered
which leads to profitable reading on many subjects which
otherwise would have escaped our notice. It would be
well if we were to follow the laudable example set by our
Boston friends. Care should be taken that one long-winded
speaker does not occupy too much of the time of such
societies, nor that any member speak more than twice on
any subject.

Freedom's Journal, November 9, 1827

Samuel Cornish reported to The Colored American *from
Philadelphia:*

We visited Monday evening last, the PHILADELPHIA
LIBRARY FOR COLORED PEOPLE founded by Mr.
Hinton and some others of our patriotic brethren, some two
or three years ago. They have in their cases nearly 1,000
vols., neatly labeled and arranged. Their room is a spacious
one, well located and neatly furnished. The institution presents an appearance of respectability and mental enterprise, worthy the young men of Philadelphia.

The young men of this city spend two and three evenings,
weekly, in debating moral and literary questions, highly
calculated to expand the mind and improve the heart. Their
room is ordinarily attended by large audiences of the young
of both sexes, and by many of the aged and patriotic,
without distinction of color.

The Colored American, December 2, 1837

Pittsburgh had its Theban Literary Society, Albany its

Union Society for the Improvement of the Colored People in Morals, Education and Mechanic Arts, and Troy its Mental and Moral Improvement Association. The Phoenix Society *in New York opened a library, started an evening school and encouraged "Mental Feasts" or "Circles of Improvement." A correspondent for* Voice of the Fugitive *explained the workings of a Circle of Improvement:*

Having met, what is to be done? The object of the association is to be stated, officers chosen, a reader appointed, and a subject or conversation upon which the members shall express their opinions at the next meeting in writing, agreed upon. This will be a good exercise for each member. When the composition is read, there will be an opportunity for the friendly criticism of each one.

Let the "circle" collect all items of historical interest. Let them become familiar with the history of our people on this continent and throughout time—their arts, their science, their literature, their laws and religions. Let them extend their acquaintance and the sphere of their influence to the next village, town, state or province until hundreds and thousands of minds shall become awake. These circles could collect funds, procure lecturers and thus be the means of pouring a flood of light on the minds of the whole community.

Undated clipping, Beman Papers, Beinecke Library,
Yale University

But the most important means of self-improvement was education. New York's African Free School was the pride of the black community. Many notables, including John B. Russwurm, Ira Aldridge, Charles Reason, Henry Highland Garnet and Alexander Crummell, received their early education there. It was the boast of the school that none of its graduates was ever convicted of a crime. James McCune Smith, who attended the school in the 1820s, ascribed its success to its teacher:

Studying by candlelight

Charles C. Andrews, an Englishman by birth, a good disciplinarian, and in true sympathy with his scholars. One special habit of his was to find out the bent of his boys and then, by encouragement, instruction, and if need were, employing at his own expense additional teachers, to develop such talent as far as possible.

In spelling, penmanship, grammar, geography and astronomy, he rightly boasted that his boys were equal, if not superior, to any like number of scholars in the city, and freely challenged competition at his Annual Examinations. In Natural Philosophy and Navigation, which were then new studies in a free school, he carried on classes as far as he was able, and then hired more competent teachers at his own expense. To stimulate his pupils, and bring out their varied talents, he instituted periodical fairs at which were exhibited the handiwork of the children.

Mr. Andrews held that his pupils had as much capacity to acquire knowledge as any other children. It was thought by some, that he even regarded his black boys as a little smarter than whites. He taught his boys and girls to look upward; to believe themselves capable of accomplishing

New York's African Free School

as much as any others could, and to regard the higher walks of life as within their reach.

Henry Highland Garnet, *A Memorial Discourse*,
with an introduction by James McCune Smith
(Philadelphia, 1865)

The students' work was shown at annual exhibitions, for the benefit of proud parents and white patrons. One such exhibition included:

1. A map of Turkey in Europe, with a view of the seraglio at Constantinople, executed by Patrick Reason, aged 12 years.

2. A compendious chart, exhibiting the names of about 300 of the principal ports and places in the world, with their bearings per compass, and their distances expressed in geographical miles from the city of Washington, all calculated by several of the Pupils in the navigation class; namely, Isaiah G. Degrass, George W. Moore, Timothy Seaman, and Elwer Reason.

3. George R. Allen's Essay attested by the Teacher and several of the Trustees of the School, as being his genuine, unaided production.

4. George R. Allen and Thomas Sidney's verses on Slavery, and Freedom, produced in a given time.

5. Journal of a voyage from Boston to Madeira, an exercise in the navigation class, by James M. Smith, a remarkably neat production.

Sketch of Benjamin Franklin, drawn by James McCune Smith while a pupil at the African Free School

(New-York Historical Society)

6. A likeness of Benjamin Franklin, by James M. Smith.

7. An address delivered by James M. Smith to General LaFayette, on the day he visited the Institution, September 10, 1824, very neatly written.

A seven-year-old delivered a valedictory speech at another exercise:

This is my first appearance before you my friends, as a public speaker, and it becomes me to say but little. I am but seven years old, and I think I have learned considerable since last examination. I was then entirely ignorant of writing. I now present you with these humble specimens of my attainments in that art. I was then also unacquainted with the use of figures. I have since gone through simple addition, subtraction, multiplication, and division; I have some knowledge also of the compound rules. I say not these things to magnify my little self into something great, but to the credit of the plan of instruction, and for the encouragement of all my schoolmates to improve the time while they have the advantage of an early education.

Charles C. Andrews, *The History of the New-York African Free-Schools* (New York, 1830)

At the African Free School girls were taught separately from boys. While the boys studied navigation and astronomy—practical sciences since many went on to become seamen—the girls learned to sew and knit. When Samuel Cornish visited a private school in Philadelphia run by Sarah Douglass, a young black woman, he found the girls there receiving a broader education:

Wednesday last, we passed two of the most gratifying hours of our life with Miss Douglass and her *interesting, improving scholars.* The school numbers over 40, selected from our best families, where their morals and manners are equally subjects of care, and of deep interest. All the branches of a good and solid female education are taught in Miss Douglass' school, together with many of the more ornamental sciences, calculated to expand the youthful mind, refine the taste, and assist in purifying the heart.

Miss Douglass has a well-selected and valuable cabinet of shells and minerals, well-arranged and labeled. She has, also, a mind richly furnished with a knowledge of these sciences, and she does not fail, through them, to lead up the minds of her pupils, through Nature, to Nature's God.

The Colored American, December 2, 1837

After school hours, boys in many cities formed self-improvement societies. When William Lloyd Garrison left for England for an antislavery speaking tour, the Juvenile Garrison Independent Society of Boston presented him with a medal. The letter accompanying it was written by sixteen-year-old William C. Nell, who later became active in the antislavery fight.

March 25, 1833

Mr. Garrison
Sir:
    At a meeting of the Juvenile Garrison Independent Society, it was unanimously voted that a committee of three

be chosen to furnish a silver medal as a present to you, in commemoration of their high regard for your valuable services in the cause of humanity. They next proceeded to appoint a committee to wait upon you with the most sincere wish that your tour to England may be crowned with the most heart-felt encouragement.

May the God of the seas protect you from harm on your voyage. You have proved yourself a firm and decided friend of the people of color.

William C. Nell, Secretary

Antislavery Collection, Boston Public Library

Young New Yorkers also had a society named after Garrison: the Garrison Literary and Benevolent Association. Its Constitution stated:

The objects of this Society shall be the diffusion of knowledge, mental assistance, moral and intellectual improvement . . . Any boy of good moral character between the ages of 4 and 20 by subscribing to this constitution and paying 12½ cents on admission and 1 cent per week, may become a member and be entitled to vote at its meetings.

Its officers included Henry Highland Garnet, David Ruggles and William H. Day, all future leaders of the black liberation movement. At a meeting held in March 1834, they resolved:

That the officers of this society endeavor to set before its members the heinousness of intemperance and profane swearing.

That this association use every means possible for improvement in literature.

That this association shall act in time of business as *men* and not as *boys* in a schoolyard.

They soon had an opportunity to act as men. At their next meeting, held in a public schoolroom, they were told that

school trustees objected to a society named after as contro-
versial a figure as Garrison. Unless they dropped his name,
they would not be allowed to meet in the school. An ob-
server described what followed:

This information seemed to shade every countenance with
a cloud of gloom. After one or two minutes silence, one of
the members said, "The name of Garrison shall ever be
cherished by me. If you strike it off from the Constitution,
you may strike me off." Every countenance brightened and
the room rung with applause. Said another, "If there is a
trustee so full of corruption as to deprive us of meeting in
this room to improve ourselves, on account of the name of
our Society, let him do so. The name of Garrison shall ever
be our mottto." (Cheers and immense applause.)

After an interesting discussion, the following resolutions
were passed unanimously:

That we, the members of this association, regard it as un-
called for usurpation of authority in any person to ask us
to strike the name of Garrison from our Constitution.

That the name shall be our motto as long as the society
exists.

That the Executive Committee be instructed to rent a
room for the society to meet in.

That the thanks of the society be presented to Mr.
Livingston for his donation of silk for a banner, and that
a committee be appointed to attend to having it painted.

The Liberator, April 19, 1834

Several years later the young New Yorkers organized the
Phoenixonian Literary Society. Alexander Crummell, who
became a noted churchman and scholar, described its ori-
gin:

A few of us met every day after school hours and de-
bated various questions upon the rights of man and the
liberties of our people. During the winter, three or four

lads might have been seen every Saturday evening bending their course to the hall of the Philomathean Society in Duane Street. It was a cold winter, that. The fierce winds often drove the drifted snow against us and dashed the rain like a flood around us. In that hall by a pale light, not unfrequently without fire, did we meet, consult and weigh various opinions. The result of these deliberations was the formation of the [Phoenixonian Literary] Society.

> Alexander Crummell, "Eulogium on the Life and Character of Thomas S. Sidney. Delivered before the Phoenixonian Literary Society, July 4, 1840." Manuscript, Schomburg Collection.

Members of the society read original essays and poetry, held debates and attended lectures on scientific and literary subjects. Of the fourteen men scheduled to lecture in 1841, almost half were black:

PUBLIC LECTURES OF THE NEW YORK PHOE-NIXONIAN LITERARY SOCIETY.

PROGRAMME

Introductory—Mr. Nathaniel Southard.
Subject—"The responsibility of Man to the development of his Intellectual Faculties."

2. Asa Fitz Esq., Boston,
"Music—Its practical influence on Society."

3. Mr. John Peterson,
"Geography."

4. Nathaniel Southard, Esq.
Astronomy

5. Rev. Samuel E. Cornish,
"The incipient measures to a right understanding of the laws that govern mind and matter."

6. Thomas W. Whitley, Paterson, N. J.
The Philosophy of Phrenology.

7. Mr. Charles L. Reason,
False ideas concerning the independence of Genius.

8. Mr. Oliver B. Pierce,
"The Elements of Moral Science."

9. Dr. James McCune Smith, A.M.
Circulation of the Blood.

10. Mr. Samuel V. Berry, (2 lectures)
Duty of Young Men.

10. John Jay, Esq.
Toussaint L'Overture.

11. Mr. Patrick H. Reason,
"Patriots of the American Revolution."

12. Professor Bronson,
"Oratory—Interspersed with recitations."

13. Mr. Alexander Crummell,
"The Influence of Factitious Life."

The Colored American, February 20, 1841

Although women were discouraged from taking part in public affairs, black women were actively engaged in "mental and moral improvement" groups. The Female Benevolent Society of Newport, organized in 1809, was followed by African Dorcas Associations in many towns. Like their biblical namesake who gave clothing to the poor, these groups provided hats, shoes and coats to needy school children. A Female Literary Association was formed in Philadelphia in 1831, its counterpart in Boston, the Afric-American Female Intelligence Society, a year later.

With the growth of the new antislavery movement, black and white women joined together in Female Anti-Slavery Societies. The call to the first Anti-Slavery Convention of American Women contained a poem by Sarah Forten, one of James Forten's daughters:

We are thy sisters. God has truly said,
That of one blood the nations he has made.

O, Christian woman! in a Christian land,
Canst thou unblushing read this great command?
Suffer the wrongs which wring our inmost heart,
To draw one throb of pity on thy part!
Our skins may differ, but from thee we claim
A sister's privilege and a sister's name.

William C. Nell, *The Colored Patriots of
the American Revolution* (Boston, 1855)

*Women also wrote for the black and antislavery papers,
signing their contributions with pen names, in deference to
public opinion. A black New Yorker offered an early comment on women's liberation:*

To the Editors:

Will you allow a female to offer a few remarks upon a
subject that you must allow to be all important? I don't
know that you have said sufficient upon the education of
females. I hope you are not to be classed with those who
think that our mathematical knowledge should be limited to
"fathoming the dish-kettle," and that we have acquired
enough of history if we know that our grandfather's father
lived and died.

'Tis true the time has been, when to darn a stocking, and
cook a pudding well, was considered the end and aim of
a woman's being. But those were days when ignorance
blinded men's eyes. The diffusion of knowledge has destroyed those opinions, and men of the present age allow
that we have minds that are capable and deserving of
culture.

I would address myself to all mothers and say to them,
that while it is necessary to possess a knowledge of cookery
and the various mysteries of pudding-making, something
more is requisite. It is their bounden duty to store their
daughters' minds with useful learning. They should be
made to devote their leisure time to reading books, whence

they would derive valuable information which could never be taken from them. I merely throw out these hints in order that some more able pen will take up the subject.

Matilda

Freedom's Journal, August 10, 1827

Most of the advice about black "self-improvement" boiled down to this: "Be more like white people, in everything. If enough of us (or you—depending on the color of the advisor) succeed in this, whites will see that blacks are equal." Black people may have been willing to accept this as the truth for life on earth, but what about Heaven? In church, black Christians were accustomed to hearing that salvation depended on having their souls washed "white as snow." "H.F.G.," identified simply as a "colored authoress" from Massachusetts, rejected this idea politely but firmly in an ironic poem:

THE BLACK AT CHURCH

God, is thy throne accessible to me—
Me of the Ethiop' skin? may I draw near
Thy sacred shrine, and humbly bend the knee
While thy white worshippers are kneeling here?

May I approach celestial purity,
And not offend thee with my sable face?
This company of saints, so fair to see,
Behold! already, shrink from the disgrace!

And in thine earthly courts I'll gladly bow
Behind my fellow worms, and be denied
Communion with them will my Lord allow
That I may come and touch his bleeding side.

In that blest fount have I an equal claim
To bathe with all who wear the stain of sin?
Or, is salvation by another name
Than thine? or, must the Ethiop change his skin?

Thou art our Maker—and I fain would know
If thou hast different seats prepared above,
To which the master and the servant go,
To sing the praise of thine eternal love.

There, will my buyers urge the price of gold
Which here, for this uncomely clay, he gave,
That he my portion may allot, and hold
In bondage still the trembling helpless slave?

Or will that dearer ransom, paid for all,
A Savior's blood, impress me with the seal
Of everlasting freedom from my thrall—
And wash me white—and this crush'd spirit heal?

Then will I meekly bear these lingering pains
And suffer scorn, and be by man oppressed,
If at the grave I may put off my chains,
And thou will take me where the weary rest.

H.F.G.

The Liberator, May 21, 1831

The following "Dialogue between a Mother and Her Children," by "a young lady of color" who signed herself "Zillah" resembled the "stories" in children's readers—except that the schoolbooks never included stories about black children.

A DIALOGUE BETWEEN A MOTHER
AND HER CHILDREN

MATILDA: Mother, why did you look so sorrowful this morning, when Henry threw away his bread?

MOTHER: Because I was grieved to see Henry so wasteful; and I know that many men would thankfully receive what he threw away. It brought to my mind an anecdote of a poor old slave man. Come here, my naughty little Henry, and listen to what I am going to say. A lady of my acquaintance went to Savannah, in the state of Georgia.

While there, she had some household duty to perform which required a great deal of water. She was preparing to bring it herself, when she was accosted by a female slave—"Not going to bring water yourself!" said she. "Get one of the turned off negroes to carry it for you." The lady, in some surprise, asked what a turned off negro was? "When a slave is too old to work, he is turned off to provide for himself," said she, "and if he can get any thing to eat, it is well—if not, he must starve." She then called an old man, and told him the lady wished him to bring water for her. After he had brought a sufficient quantity, the lady gave him sixpence. A few moments after, she saw the old man with a loaf of wheat bread, which he alternately pressed to his lips and bosom, while floods of grateful tears coursed down his furrowed cheeks. Wondering at the old man's emotion, she asked the female slave why he wept? "Ah," said she, "he may well cry; he has not seen anything like it these six months." Do you now wonder, my daughter, that I looked sad when your brother threw away his nice bread?

MATILDA: No, dear mother, I do not.

HENRY: Mother, I am very sorry I have been so wicked as to waste bread. I will save all the money my grandfather and uncle gave me, and buy some bread to send to the old man.

MOTHER: Your intended kindness to the old man will avail him nothing, as he has long since passed away from this world of care. I would, however, advise you to save your money, and when you have collected a handsome sum, uncle will put it into the funds now preparing to build a College for our youth.

HENRY: (Clapping his hands joyfully)—O yes, mother, I will, I will!

The Liberator, September 1, 1832

3. Striving—for What?

The hope that nurtured the self-improvement societies was often matched by moments of dark despair. Too often, virtue was the only reward for a youngster whose skin was black. A white abolitionist reported:

A bright colored lad belonging to my class in Sunday School said to me sadly, in reply to my efforts to awaken in him an ambition for self-improvement, "What's the use in my attempting to improve myself when, do what I may, I can never be anything but a nigger?"

> Oliver Johnson, *William Lloyd Garrison and His Times*
> (Boston, 1879)

A boy who was graduating from the African Free School asked the same question:

Why should I strive hard, and acquire all the constituents of a man if the prevailing genius of the land admit me not as such? Pardon me if I feel insignificant and weak. Pardon me if I feel discouragement. Am I arrived at the end of my education, on the eve of commencing some pursuit by which to earn a comfortable subsistence? What are my prospects? Shall I be a mechanic? No one will employ me. White boys won't work with me. Drudgery and servitude are my prospective portion. Can you be surprised at my discouragement?

> Charles C. Andrews, *The History of the New-York African Free-Schools* (New York, 1830)

William C. Nell recalled an incident from his boyhood:

In the year 1829 the Mayor accompanied Hon. Samuel T. Armstrong to an examination of the colored school.

Charles A. Battiste, Nancy Woodson and myself were pronounced entitled to the highest reward of merit. In lieu of Franklin Medals, legitimately our due, Mr. Armstrong gave each an order on Loring's Book Store for the *Life of Benjamin Franklin.* The white medal scholars were invited guests to the Faneuil Hall dinner. Having a boy's curiosity to be spectator at the feast, I made good my court with one of the waiters, who allowed me to seem to serve. Mr. Armstrong improved a prudent moment in whispering to me, "*You* ought to be here with the other boys." Of course, the same idea had more than once been mine. His remark while witnessing the honors awarded to white scholars, only augmented my sensitiveness all the more. The inquiry which I eagerly desired to express—"If you think so, why have you not taken steps to bring it about?"

"Proceedings of the Presentation Meeting" (Boston, 1855)

Even the wealthiest and most respected black people felt "heart burnings," as Sarah Forten explained in a letter to Angelina Grimke, a white friend:

Philadelphia, April 15, 1837

Esteemed Friend:

In reply to your question—of the "effect of Prejudice" on myself, I must acknowledge that it has often embittered my feelings. I am peculiarly sensitive on this point. It has often engendered feelings of discontent and mortification when I saw that many were preferred before me, who by education, birth or worldly circumstances were no better than myself, THEIR sole claim depending on being *White*. I am striving to live above such heart burnings.

No doubt there has always existed prejudice in the minds of Americans toward the descendants of Africa. It can be seen in the exclusion of the colored people from their churches or placing them in obscure corners, in their being barred from a participation with others in acquiring any useful knowledge. Public lectures are not usually free to the colored people. They may not avail themselves of the right to drink at the fountain of learning or gain an insight into the arts and science of our land. All this and more do they feel acutely. I only marvel that they are in possession of any knowledge at all.

Even our professed friends have not yet rid themselves of [prejudice]. I recollect the words of one of the best men in the Abolition ranks. "Ah," said he, "I can recall the time when in walking with a colored brother, the darker the night, the better Abolitionist was I." He does not say so now, but my friend, much of this leaven still lingers in the hearts of our white brethren and sisters.

For our own family, we have to thank a kind Providence for placing us in a situation that has prevented us from falling under the weight of this evil. We feel it but in a slight degree compared with others. We are not disturbed in our social relations. We never travel far from home and seldom go to public places unless quite sure that admission is free to all. I would recommend to my colored friends to follow our example and they would be spared some very painful realities.

My Father bids me tell you that white and colored men have worked with him from his first commencement in business. He has usually ten to twenty journeymen, half of whom are white. I am not aware of any white sailmaker who employs colored men. I think it should be reciprocal —do not you?

Sarah T. Forten

Gilbert H. Barnes and Dwight L. Dumond, eds., *Letters of Theodore D. Weld, Angelina Grimke Weld and Sarah Grimke* (New York, 1934)

Successful as they were, the African schools were only grammar schools. There were no high schools that black boys could attend, and no schools at all for girls in many towns. "When we hear you talk of female seminaries, we weep to think our daughters are deprived of such advantages," a black minister told an abolitionist audience. "Not a single high school or female seminary in the land is open to our daughters." Even in Sunday schools black girls faced double discrimination:

ADVANCING! At the Sabbath School Exhibition, held in Park-Street Church on the 4th of July, the colored boys were permitted to occupy pews one fourth of the way up the side aisle. The march of equality has certainly begun in Boston! The colored girls took their seats near the door, as usual.

The Liberator, July 9, 1831

We worshipped with Mr. Barnes' people yesterday morning. Mr. Barnes is pastor of the large Presbyterian church on Washington Square. We saw a colored girl who evidently was a scholar in the Sabbath School placed on a bench, literally covered with dust, and back of all the pews, by herself, while every white scholar was seated in comfortable pews, under the special charge of the teachers.

The Colored American, November 25, 1837

In 1833 Prudence Crandall opened a boarding school for "Young Ladies and Little Misses of Color" in her home in Canterbury, Connecticut. The good citizens of Canterbury reacted quickly. They refused to sell food to Miss Crandall, threw stones and rotten eggs at her pupils and dumped manure in the school's well. Connecticut legislators backed them up with a law that forbade out-of-state blacks from attending schools in Connecticut. Afer a year and a half of persecution an armed mob forced Miss Crandall to close the school.

One black child described her first weeks at school. The "Brooklyn" that she mentioned was a town in Connecticut near Canterbury.

There are thirteen scholars now in the school. The Canterburians are *savage*. They will not sell Mis Crandall an article at their shops. My ride from Hartford to Brooklyn was very unpleasant, being made up of blackguards. I came on foot here from Brooklyn. But the happiness I enjoy here pays me for all. The place is delightful. All that is wanting to complete the scene is *civilized men*.

Last evening the news reached us that the new law had passed. The bell rang, and a cannon was fired for half an hour. Where is justice? In the midst of all this, Miss Crandall is unmoved. When we walk out, horns are blown and pistols fired.

The Liberator, June 22, 1833

Shortly after Miss Crandall's school closed, the trustees of Noyes Academy in Canaan, New Hampshire, decided to admit black students. Alexander Crummell described his stay there. Although his account mentions only boys, at least one girl attended Noyes Academy. She was Julia Williams, a pupil of Miss Crandall's and later the wife of Henry Highland Garnet:

Three of us New York boys, Henry Highland Garnet, Thomas S. Sidney and myself started for Canaan. The difficulties of the journey you can hardly imagine. On the steamboat from New York to Providence no cabin passage was allowed colored people and so [we were] exposed all night, bedless and foodless, to the cold and storm. There were no railroads, and all the way from Providence to Boston, from Boston to Concord, from Concord to Hanover, and from Hanover to Canaan, [we] had to ride night and day on the top of the coach. It was a long and wearisome journey, of some four hundred and more miles. Rarely would an inn or a hotel give us food, and nowhere could we get shelter.

We met a most cordial reception at Canaan from two

score white students and began, with the highest hopes, our studies. But our stay was the briefest. The Democracy of the State could not endure what they called a "Nigger School" on the soil of New Hampshire and so the word went forth, especially from the politicians, that the school must be broken up. Fourteen black boys with books in their hands set the entire Granite State crazy!

On the 4th of July, the farmers from a wide region around assembled at Canaan and resolved to remove the academy as a public nuisance! On the 10th of August they gathered together from the neighboring towns, seized the building and with ninety yoke of oxen carried it off into a swamp about a half mile from its site.

Meanwhile, under Garnet as our leader, the boys in our boardinghouse were molding bullets, expecting an attack upon our dwelling. About 11 o'clock at night the tramp of horses was heard approaching. One rider passed the house and fired at it. Garnet quickly replied by a discharge from a double-barrelled shotgun which blazed away through the window. At once the hills, for many a mile around, reverberated with the sound. Lights were seen in scores of houses, and the towns and villages were in a state of great excitement. But that musket shot by Garnet doubtless saved our lives. The cowardly ruffians dared not to attack us.

Notice, however, was sent us to quit the state within a fortnight. When we left Canaan, the mob assembled on the outskirts of the village and fired a field piece at our wagon.

Alexander Crummell, *Africa and America*
(Springfield, Massachusetts, 1891)

In 1831, the Convention of the People of Color decided to start a "manual labor college," where blacks could learn trades as well as academic subjects. Samuel Cornish was appointed fund raiser, and the following appeal was circulated:

Philadelphia, September 5, 1831

AN APPEAL TO THE BENEVOLENT

The undersigned committee appointed to assist Rev. Samuel E. Cornish in soliciting funds for the establishment of a Collegiate School, on the Manual Labor System, beg leave to call the attention of the enlightened citizens of Philadelphia and its vicinity to this important subject.

All who know the difficult admission of our youths into seminaries of learning, all who wish to see our colored population more prudent, virtuous and useful, will lend us their patronage. The amount of money required to erect buildings, secure apparatus and mechanical instruments is $20,000. Of this sum the colored people intend to contribute as largely as God has given them ability, and for the residue they look to the Christian community.

The contemplated Seminary will be located at New Haven, Conn., and established on the self-supporting system so that the student may cultivate habits of industry and obtain useful mechanical or agricultural professions while pursuing classical studies.

Signed in behalf of the Convention by
James Forten, Joseph Cassey, Robert Douglass, Robert Purvis, Fredk A. Hinton

The Liberator, September 24, 1831

The citizens of New Haven promptly called a town meeting and voted to "resist the establishment of the proposed College in this place, by every lawful means." Only one man voted in favor of the college.

Later attempts to found a college for black students also failed. Meanwhile, individuals tried on their own to acquire college educations. Four or five succeeded, but these were the exceptions, as an article in The Colored American *explained:*

Prejudice, an Anecdote—No. 1

Some 15 or 16 years ago, a colored lad from Charleston, South Carolina, applied for admission into Amherst College. The President broached the delicate subject to the professors and students. From the students he met the most decided opposition: —"What! have a nigger in our college!!!" "He shan't recite in my class!" "Nor mine"—"Nor mine."

The Doctor resorted to an expedient. At the toll of the bell, all the students were summoned, and the President addressed them as follows—"Young Gentlemen, some of you have been members of this college for two, and three years, during which time there has been no attempt to force you into association with any of OUR BLACKS. We would not INSULT you by such an attempt, but here is an EXTRA CASE: Here is one, NOT AT ALL LIKE OUR NEGROES. Gentlemen, he is a-w-a-y *from the South!* Will you not receive this stranger into your family, though his countenance be burnt with a f-a-r Southern sun? Gentlemen, all who are in favor of it, will you please to signify by saying 'I'." "I!"— "I!"—"I!" rang throughout the college halls. Our Charleston brother entered the college, enjoyed all its privileges and received its honors, whilst a Northern colored man could hardly visit its halls, without being abused and insulted!

Anecdote No. 2

In 1827 or 28, two of our brethren, of about the same complexion, one from Connecticut and the other from Massachusetts, made application to enter the Medical College of this city. Our Connecticut friend was honest enough to say that he was a native of New Haven, but the Yankee brother from Massachusetts was cunning enough to hail from India.

What do you think, reader, was the result? Why the Yankee who hailed from India, notwithstanding his frizzled head and colored face, was received and enjoyed all the privileges of the college, freely associating with the students, and parading the streets, cap and gown, on all occasions. He completed his medical studies, and as a learned EAST Indian, came out with all the honors of the school.

But our poor New Havener, who was so UNFORTUNATE as to be a NATIVE CITIZEN could only be received as an attendant on one of the professors. The same brother, who is one of the most intellectual men ever raised in the country, is practising medicine with a mere license. The Christian noblemen of our medical school, being unwilling to STOOP SO LOW as to give *a colored man* a degree from THEIR INSTITUTION!!!

The Colored American, November 4, 1837

Turned down by Columbia and Geneva Medical Colleges, James McCune Smith went to Glasgow University in Scotland for a medical degree. Another New Yorker, Charles B. Ray, entered Wesleyan University in Middletown, Connecticut, but was driven away by student protests.

"Who shall describe his feelings in that bitter hour?" asked Amos G. Beman. Beman's father was minister of the African Church in Middletown, near the Wesleyan campus. His slave grandfather had chosen his last name when he won freedom because, he said, "I always wanted to be a man." Although not enrolled in Wesleyan, young Beman was studying on the campus with a white student hired to tutor him. He described his own experiences after Ray left:

During this period, and for some time afterward, we continued going there to recite. Insults and jeers from the students we frequently encountered, but we were not daunted. The following letter, with an extract which our teacher published in *The Liberator,* speak for themselves:

Middletown, October 5th, 1833

To Beman, Junior:

Young Beman:— A number of the students of this University deeming it derogatory to themselves, as well as to the Uni-

Amos G. Beman
(James Weldon Johnson Memorial Collection, Beinecke Rare Book and Manuscript Library, Yale University)

versity, to have you and other colored students recite here, do hereby warn you to desist from such a course; and if you fail to comply with this peaceable request, we swear, by the Eternal Gods, that we will resort to forcible means to put a stop to it.

Twelve of Us

Frederick Douglass' Paper, October 13, 1854

His tutor reported the pressures on both of them:

Mr. Beman recited 3 times each week. When reproaches did not deter him from his recitations, [the students] resorted to other means. In going out from the university on a certain morning, a quantity of water was thrown on him, by which he was *completely drenched.* The next day one of the party caused a notice to be put up calling a meeting of the students. After the subject before the meeting had been with much warmth discussed, and a request made that the student who instructed Mr. Beman would hear him recite at some other place, the meeting was dissolved. The recitations went on as before till the college vacation. Since Commencement, for the convenience of him who is instructing Mr. Beman, the recitation has not been heard in the university.

Undated clipping from *The Liberator*, Beman Papers,
Beinecke Library, Yale University

Wesleyan opened its doors to male students without regard to race a year later. Oberlin College admitted blacks in 1835, Dartmouth in 1837. But the doors of most schools—including divinity schools—remained closed. Refused admission to the Episcopal Theological Seminary in New York, Alexander Crummell studied at Queen's College in Cambridge, England. Isaiah De Grasse was actually admitted to the Seminary. However, as he explained in a letter to Theodore Weld, a white abolitionist, he was soon asked to leave:

New York, September 1837

Dear Sir:

Having completed my collegiate education, I applied for admission into the Seminary. With the rest of the students I selected my room in the building and became settled as an inmate. After having passed my first examination to the satisfaction of the Professors, I was informed by the Rt. Rev. Bishop of the Diocese that there was great disapprobation expressed in relation to the step I had taken.

There were fears, he said, that my presence there, and especially my eating in common with the *pious* students would give rise to much dissatisfaction and bad feeling. Furthermore, as the Institution received much of its support and many of its students from the South, the reception of a colored young man *might* deprive them of pecuniary benefits and prevent Southern gentlemen from connecting themselves with their school of Divinity. Also, in the agitated state of public feeling, the safety of their edifices might be endangered. My immediate withdrawal was, therefore, earnestly and strenuously recommended.

An opportunity, however, of availing myself of most of the privileges of the institution without considering myself a regular member was graciously offered. But the acceptance of their proffered favor, requiring a greater sacrifice of principle than I could possibly, in justice to my oppressed people or myself, make, I respectfully declined. In the presence of the students and in the sight of God [I] removed from the school of his Holy prophets and commenced a private course of study.

Isaiah G. De Grasse

Barnes and Dumond, eds., Letters of Theodore D. Weld,
Angelina Grimke Weld and Sarah Grimke
(New York, 1934)

Of all the denominations, the Quakers were most sympathetic to blacks. But even they had "black benches" in their meeting houses. Sarah Douglass' letter, which follows, was written to answer an inquiry from William Basset, an English Quaker.

Philadelphia, December 1837

Esteemed Friend:

There is a bench set apart for our people, whether *officially* appointed or not I cannot say, but my mother and myself were told to sit there and a Friend sat at each end of the bench to prevent white persons from sitting there. Even when a child my soul was made sad with hearing five or six times during the course of one meeting, "This bench is for the black people," "This bench is for the people of color." Oftentimes I wept, at other times felt indignant.

I have not been in Arch Street meeting for four years,

but my mother goes once a week and frequently she has a *whole long bench* to herself. The assertion that our people prefer sitting by themselves is not true. A very near friend of ours who has been a constant attender of Friends meeting from his childhood, says "Thou mayest tell William Basset, that several years ago a Friend came to me and told that Friends had appointed a back bench for us. I told him with some warmth that I had just as lief sit on the floor as sit there." Two sons of the person I have just mentioned have left attending Friends meeting. Conversing with one of them today, I asked "Why did you leave Friends?" "Because I do not like to sit on a back bench and be treated with contempt."

In reply to your question "whether there appears to be a diminution of prejudice towards you among Friends" I unhesitatingly answer, no. I have heard it frequently remarked and have observed myself, that in proportion as we become intellectual and respectable, so in proportion does their disgust and prejudice increase.

Yet while I speak this of Friends as a body, I am happy to say there is in this city a "noble few" who have cleansed their garments from the foul stain of prejudice. Some of these are members of Anti-Slavery Societies and others belong to the old abolition school.

Sarah M. Douglass

Barnes and Dumond, eds., Letters of Theodore D. Weld,
Angelina Grimke Weld and Sarah Grimke (New York, 1934)

4.   Tales of Woe

At a meeting of the New York State Anti-Slavery Society in 1837, the Reverend Theodore S. Wright said:

I confess it is somewhat embarrassing for a man to speak of his own degradation. But when, whether at home or abroad, in the parlor, the stage coach, the bar room, or the public mart, he feels the pressure of the chain, how can he be silent? Oh! if we had time we should keep you here till midnight, stating facts and telling tales of woe, the thought of which makes our spirits to sink within us.

Wright went on to describe a trip that he and his wife had made from their home in Schenectady to Princeton, New Jersey:

On our return, between Brunswick and New York, we were overtaken by a tremendous gale. In consequence of being excluded from the ladies' compartment [my wife] caught a violent cold which detained us several days in New York. Now despair almost drank up my spirits. I went from steamboat to steamboat, from line to line, to obtain a place below the deck, so that our lives might not be endangered, but in vain. At length we went on board of the steamboat and were compelled to sit on deck. This was in the fall. Ice was in the river and the weather was cold. At night, my wife was permitted to sleep with the cook, in a dirty apartment near the machinery whilst I was permitted to lie down on the deck. In the morning, we rejoiced for the preservation of our lives. But alas! my wife had received the fatal shaft and she died after a few months, in consequence of the cold she then caught.

How would the men and women of this convention feel and act were they similarly circumstanced? How would the members of this meeting act were they under the disabilities of the colored man?

Undated clipping, Beman Papers,
Beinecke Library, Yale University

Black and antislavery papers published numerous "tales of woe":

Hartford, June 28, 1832

Mr. Editor: On Saturday, 22nd instant, in the city of New York, we went down to the steamboat *McDonough* to take passage for this city. No sooner than we went on board we were asked by one of the officers in an abrupt manner, "Where are you going?" We answered "To Hartford." He said, "We'll allow you no privilege whatever and you must pay one dollar and a half for your passage; you must keep to the forward deck, &c."

Mr. Editor, we see the horse covered and fed with care on board of a steamboat; but a colored man can have no place there to lay his head! We had to walk the deck half of the night and the other part we laid amongst the pots in the kitchen in order to be sheltered from the inclemency of the weather.

Mr. Editor, what evil have our fathers done, or we their children that we should be so evilly treated?

Henry Drayton, Henry Johnson

The Liberator, July 7, 1832

New York, August 3, 1832

Mr. Garrison:

I embarked on board the steamboat *Oliver Ellsworth,* at New York for Hartford a short time since. I was treated with ordinary civility until evening arrived, when, on asking permission to retire to rest, I was informed that no colored person could be allowed to enter the cabin. I expostulated at what I considered illiberal treatment and the end of the matter was, that I was landed on one of the most desolate spots on Long Island (Crane Neck) at midnight, amid wild cattle who had, probably, not seen the face of man for a twelve-month. Capt. Waterman when he landed me said he hoped that I would not get away for a week!

My wife also experienced similar treatment coming from Hartford to New York. She was compelled to sit all of a very stormy day on the deck with two small children!

In consequence of these and similar proceedings at Hartford, I have been obliged to abandon a very flourishing business and locate myself in N. York at a very great loss.

William Saunders

The Liberator, August 11, 1832

At a meeting of the Library Company of Colored Persons in Philadelphia, a speaker gave an instance of "horrible and soul-destroying prejudice":

A friend of mine had occasion to visit a neighboring town during the cold season and was as usual shown the top of the stage as the place most proper for him. A white passenger who had brought with him a dog had it placed on the top of the stage in company with my friend. But the cold became so intense that he (my friend) could scarcely bear it and the master of the dog began to think that his shivering animal was in danger of freezing. And what course do you suppose was pursued at such a crisis? Why, I will tell you. *The dog was taken into the stage,* and MY WORTHY COLORED FRIEND WAS LEFT TO SUFFER ON THE OUTSIDE!

National Enquirer and Constitutional Advocate of Universal Liberty, June 24, 1837

Worcester, December 4, 1838

TO THE PUBLIC and particularly TO THE CITIZENS OF THE TOWN OF WORCESTER:

Here I am in a free state. Here you advertise your coaches, your railroads and cars. I take my trunk and go to the depot, well-dressed as I always am. Although my pockets are well-lined with money and my person civil, you say, "You cannot go in our cars." The car master will then say, "We will show you where you can ride—come ride here."

I answer, "I do not wish to ride in a *dirt car*. I wish to ride with decent and respectable gentlemen." "Ah!" says he, "you are a colored man."

My feelings have been repeatedly wounded in this way. Notwithstanding your boast of free institutions, you grind the colored people in the dust by destroying their spirit of self-respect. You do it. It is true.

In my experience, which has been extended to every southern state but two, there the colored man who travels is treated with more respect and more like a gentleman, than in the free states. I am a citizen of Worcester and have been for about five years. I have paid my taxes and behaved like a gentleman, and yet I have suffered much on account of my color. I have on this account come before you to express my feelings in my own simple way. The public I trust will excuse me for any fault of expression.

Henry Scott

The Colored American, January 12, 1839

In the 1830s, most abolitionists—black as well as white— believed in non-resistance. In line with this philosophy an editorial in The Colored American *recommended "GO BY FOOT, BRETHREN":*

Brethren, you are MEN—If you have not horses and vehicles of your own to travel with, stay at home or travel on foot. Cease giving your money to men who forebear not to degrade you beneath the dogs. A white "black-leg" can travel in our best cars, and have the accommodations of our best steamboat cabins, with their cards, their guns and their dogs—but a colored gentleman of education, wealth and piety cannot visit his friends abroad without being degraded and insulted—Let us, for the time being, hold intercourse through the mail, or go on foot.

The Colored American, June 30, 1838

However, it was difficult to be non-resistant when one's person or home was under attack. From Providence to Pittsburgh, from New York to Ohio, mob outbreaks were common occurrences. A three-day riot in Cincinnati in 1829 forced a thousand black people to seek refuge in Canada. Rioters in New York in 1834 destroyed Peter Williams' church, an African school and a dozen homes where blacks lived.

In Providence, wrote William J. Brown, "Colored people had little or no protection from the law unless they resided with some white gentleman that would take up for them."

It was a common thing for colored people to be disturbed on the street, especially on the Sabbath. If you were well dressed they would insult you for that, and if you were ragged, you would surely be insulted for being so.

One day I was going with another young man to evening school, carrying our lamps which we used in school. Two colored ladies were close behind us followed by two white men, who ordered them off the sidewalk. The females went out into the street and walked until they came near us. The men then ordered us off. My companion gave me the lamp and grappled with one of the men. [The] man threw him into the gangway, where he fell, striking on a joint bone of an ox. He seized the bone and leaped at the man like a tiger, clenched him by the shirt collar and dealt him three or four blows in his face. The man cried, "Murder," which drew around a large crowd of people.

One tall well-dressed man said to the people that surrounded us, "Take these niggers to jail." We would have been locked up had it not been for the timely appearance of Mr. Joseph Balch, who came out of his apothecary shop. Being well acquainted with us both he said, "Where are you going, boys?" We told him, "To evening school." He said, "Go on, and nobody shall trouble you." The man said, "Why, he is beating a white man." Mr. Balch said, "Well he had no business troubling them, and if the white man lets a boy like him beat him he ought to be beat." We went on and the crowd dispersed.

In the northwest part of the city was a place called Addison Hollow, but nicknamed Hardscrabble. A great many colored people purchased land there, because it was some distance from town and hence quite cheap. They put up small houses for themselves and earned their living in various ways. They could be seen almost any time, with their sawhorses, some on the Great Bridge, some on Shingle Bridge, and some on Mill Bridge, waiting for work. As hard coal was not known at that time, everybody used wood. Some men did jobs of gardening and farming.

[The whites] raised a mob, and drove many from their homes, then tore them down, took their furniture—what little they had—and sold it at auction. This was done late in the fall. One colored man named Christopher Hall, a widower with three or four children, a pious man bearing a good character, and supported himself and family by sawing wood, had his house torn down by the roughs and stripped of its contents. He drew the roof over the cellar and lived in it all winter. The people tried in vain to coax him out, and offered him a house to live in. Some white ladies offered to take his children, but he would not let them go. In the spring following he went to Liberia.

The Life of William J. Brown (Providence, 1883)

Ten men were arrested for their part in the Hardscrabble Riot, but all were acquitted at their trial.

Philadelphia, with the largest black population of any city in the North, had four bloody race riots between 1834 and 1842. An anonymous letter writer described the 1835 riot:

My Dear Sir:

Philadelphia has again been the scene of disgraceful riots. On Sunday afternoon an African servant, living with a gentleman in this city, in a fit of insanity, attempted to kill him with an axe. This was the pretext for attacking the colored people. On Monday evening the rioters, more than a thousand strong, attacked and done much violence, driving the defenseless victims of their fury from their homes in the middle of the night. Their homes were plundered by these midnight ruffians, who set fire to a row of buildings occupied by colored persons, and endeavored to prevent its being extinguished. Our firemen were attacked with stones and clubs, the hose cut and every effort made to prevent their putting out the flames.

This is only a manifestation of that spirit which would drive us from the country. The press contents itself with recommending to the colored population meekness and propriety of conduct, keeping within doors, &c. We look in vain for a holy indignation at the base attempts on our lives and property, and a vindication of our rights as a deeply injured and unoffending people.

(Signature withheld)

The Liberator, August 1, 1835

The worst of the riots took place in 1842. After breaking up a parade of blacks who were celebrating West Indian emancipation, a mob swarmed through the black residential section, burning, looting and killing. The home of Robert Purvis, known as an Underground Railroad station, was a main target. Purvis, like his father-in-law, James Forten, was rich, respectable and non-resistant. But with a howling mob outside, he armed himself and prepared to shoot. Saved by a Catholic priest who turned away the mob, Purvis soon afterward moved from Philadelphia and did not return until after the Civil War. He had been a founding member of the American Anti-Slavery Society and a believer in integration. But the riot, and the apathy of white Pennsylvanians afterward, shook him badly. He poured out his feelings in a letter to Henry C. Wright, a white abolitionist:

Philadelphia, August 22, 1842

My dear friend Wright:

I have been absent from the city all of the past week. This I offer in excuse for not acknowledging your letter before this.

I am even now, in every way, disqualified from making proper answers to your [questions] in reference to one of the most ferocious and bloody-spirited mobs that ever cursed a Christian (?) community. I know not where I should

Robert Purvis (*Sophia Smith Collection, Smith College*)

begin, nor how or when to end in a detail of the wantoness, brutality and murderous spirit of the actors in the late riots, nor of the apathy and *inhumanity* of the *whole* community in regard to the matter. Press, Church, Magistrates, Clergymen and Devils are against us. The measure of our sufferings is full.

From the most painful investigation in the feelings and acts of this community in regard to us, I am convinced of our utter and complete nothingness in public estimation. I feel that my life would find no change in death, but a glorious riddance of a life weighed down and cursed by a despotism whose sway makes Hell of earth—we the *tormented*, our persecutors the *tormentors*.

But I must stop. I am sick—miserably sick. Everything around me is as dark as the grave. Here and there the bright countenance of a true friend is to be seen. Save that—nothing redeeming, nothing hopeful. Despair black as the face of death hangs over us—and the bloody *will* of the community [is] to destroy us.

In a few days perhaps I will write you again. To attempt a reply to your letter now is impossible.

Your brother,
Robert Purvis

Antislavery Collection, Boston Public Library

III · WE ARE MEN (1840–50)

We need more radicalism among us. We have been altogether too fearful of martyrdom—too indefinite in our views and sentiments—too slow in our movements. Let every case where legal rights are withheld be legally investigated. Let every colored man called upon to pay taxes to an institution in which he is denied its privileges, withhold his taxes, though it costs imprisonment.

Charles Lenox Remond

1. We Need More Radicalism

A favorite song at Colored Conventions was:

Ours is not the tented field—

We no earthly weapons wield
Light and love our sword and shield,
Truth our panoply.

After almost ten years of "moral suasion" black people were beginning to wonder if "light and love" alone would get them anywhere. Garrison and his friends did not believe in voting or political action, but a group of antislavery men broke away from the Garrisonians in 1840 to form a Liberty Party and to run abolitionist candidates in elections. Many black men, particularly in New York, allied themselves with the "voting abolitionists."

Working through an Association for the Political Elevation and Improvement of People of Color, the New Yorkers hoped to change the state constitution which gave white men the right to vote but said:

No man of color, unless he shall be possessed of a freehold estate of the value of $250 shall be entitled to vote at any election.

Connecticut had a similar law that required $325 worth of property and blacks were not allowed to vote at all in Pennsylvania, New Jersey and the western states.

Two hundred and fifty dollars was a large sum of money and the restriction kept all but a small minority from the polls. The Political Association circulated petitions asking for equal voting rights and called a State Convention of Colored Citizens. The Convention was immediately attacked by the Garrisonians, who not only opposed political action but also separate Colored Conventions:

We see by *The Colored American* that a Convention of colored citizens is proposed. If our friends who are taking the lead in this will allow a word or two, we will just say to them, do not hold such a Convention. Everything that tends to separate the colored people from the whites aids in building up an impassable barrier to their progress.

Be not impatient! In your desire to become freemen, to

feel the spirit of manhood come over you, be careful that you do not tear down what you build up. You cannot be free until the community shall see and feel that you are *men*. They do not feel it yet.

As long as there are colored churches there will be no room for colored people in white churches. As long as colored people hold conventions made up *exclusively* of men and women of their own complexion, the white slaveite will let them hold them in peace.

Call, then, a Convention for the proposed purpose. Tell every abolitionist to attend. Teach them to make common cause with you. Teach them to forget and forget yourselves as fast as possible, that you are colored men and women.

The National Anti-Slavery Standard, June 18, 1840

Blacks reacted sharply to this paternalism. Two editorials in The Colored American, *the first by a temporary editor and the second by Editor Charles B. Ray, were a declaration of independence from the Garrisonians:*

As long as we attend the Conventions called by our white friends we will be looked upon as playing second fiddle to them. They will always form the majority of such Conven-

Charles B. Ray
  (*Moorland-Spingarn Collection, Howard University Library*)

tions and the sentiments and opinions thus promulgated will go forth as the sentiments and opinions of white men. But when *we act* then they will see that the worm is turning.

We have called the convention. Come on then. Let everyone who is in favor of removing the disabilities under which we groan and suffer attend. True the call is to colored men, and our thoughts must be put forth, our wrongs made known and our wishes represented. The Convention is ours but we will not shut the door against our white friends.

The Colored American, June 27, 1840

This article is dictatorial in spirit. The writer thereof feels himself the colored man's superior and advisor. I agree and yet I disagree with the call for our [white] friends to meet with us. I hope they will be present, but they must remember it is our Convention. While we shall be gratified for their suggestions, they must be less prominent than ourselves. If not, such is the public disposition, they will regard the proceedings of the Convention as theirs, and not as ours.

The Colored American, July 18, 1840

The New York Convention of Colored Citizens was followed by similar meetings in Connecticut, New Jersey, Rhode Island, Pennsylvania and Ohio. After New York's convention, Henry Highland Garnet led a delegation to the state capitol in Albany. Garnet, who was then studying for the ministry, reported on his apparent success:

Gentlemen:

As chairman of the Central Committee I appeared before the judiciary committee of the legislature, on the evening of the 18th February. The chairman of the committee has told us that we may look for a favorable report during the present week. And there is no doubt but that it will be a favorable one. It is the general sentiment about the capitol that the bill will pass the House by a great majority and will get through the Senate almost unanimously, the members of both parties being decidedly in favor of the measure.

Perhaps it is too much for one so young and humble as myself to say that my remarks produced any effect upon the wise and learned judiciary committee, yet in humility, I think I may say that God blessed *the truth for its own sake.*

H. H. Garnet

The Colored American, March 13, 1841

But the law repealing the restriction on black voters did not pass. The petition campaign continued and Dr. James McCune Smith led a second delegation to Albany. In 1846 New York voters were asked whether they wanted to drop the property qualification for blacks. Their answer—224,000 to 85,000—was "No!" In a letter to Gerrit Smith, a white "voting abolitionist," Dr. Smith expressed deep discouragement. The "earth-owning oath" he mentioned was the oath required of would-be black voters who owned property.

December 28, 1846

Gerrit Smith, Esq.
Dear friend:

Each succeeding day, that terrible majority falls sadder, heavier, more crushingly on my soul. At times I am so weaned from hope that I could lay me down and die. There is in that majority a hate deeper than I had imagined. The heart of the whites must be changed, thoroughly, entirely, permanently changed. This must be done, but how?

Of course it is mind work. Physical force has no place in it. The possession of votes simply states the question. My personal influence, manhood-presence at the ballot box is utterly destroyed when the earth-owning oath is thrust at me. The Negro *Man* is merged into the Negro Landowner. It is established by the solemnity of an oath that the vile earth has rights superior to Manhood!

Dr. James McCune Smith

What horrible mockery! Is it right to be a party in such blasphemy?

James McCune Smith

Gerrit Smith Miller Collection, George Arents Research Library at Syracuse University

Fourteen years later the question of repealing the property qualification was again placed before the voters of New York. Dr. Smith was then chairman of the New York City Suffrage Committee, one of a number of black-led suffrage organizations in the state. The Suffrage Committee made a special appeal to recent immigrants from Europe who could vote after a short residence in the state, although native blacks could not:

New York, October 20, 1860

Hon. Gerrit Smith
Dear friend:

Your additional donation of $50 came very opportunely and was received with cheers by the Committee. We sent you per express 6,000 tracts with ballots enclosed, in English, and about 300 in German. We sent 25,000 tracts to Frederick Douglass who is pledged to spread them through the state west of and including Rochester.

We have printed 8,000 tracts in German. They have been

received with enthusiasm and more demanded by our German friends in this city & Brooklyn. We would like to print some in French, could we afford it.

Whatever the result, the movement is getting up a fine tone of thought and action, especially among our young men. We are hard put to it for funds yet labor cheerfully.

James McCune Smith

Gerrit Smith Miller Collection, George Arents Research Library at Syracuse University

But New York voters again refused to repeal the property qualification. In most of the states of the North and West black men did not win equal voting rights until after the passage of the Fifteenth Amendment in 1870.

The denial of the vote was only one of many discriminatory laws that hemmed in black people. John Malvin, who became a successful canal-boat operator in Ohio, told of his first encounter with Ohio's "Black Laws":

In the year 1827, a spirit of adventure, natural to most young men, took possession of me, and I concluded to leave Virginia.

I affectionately took leave of my parents, with nothing but my clothes on my back, and an extra shirt, and started on

Receipt for contribution to Suffrage Committee, signed by James McCune Smith

(Gerrit Smith Miller Collection, George Arents Research Library at Syracuse University)

my journey. I walked a distance of 300 miles to Marietta, Ohio, in the short space of six days. At Marietta, I got aboard of a flat boat on the Ohio River and worked my passage to Cincinnati, then a growing town. I thought upon coming to a free state like Ohio, that I would find every door thrown open to receive me, but from the treatment I received by the people generally, I found it little better than in Virginia.

I had not been long in Cincinnati, before I became acquainted with a statute of Ohio, in which I read substantially these words: "That no Negro should be permitted to emigrate to this State without first entering into bonds of $500, conditioned that he would never become a town charge." I read a little further: "That no Negro shall testify in a Court of Justice where a party in a case there pending was white. No Negro child shall enter into any of the public schools, or receive the benefit of the school fund. No Negro shall be permitted to enter any of the institutions of this state: lunatic asylum, deaf and dumb asylum, nor even the poor house."

Thus I found every door closed against the colored man excepting the jails and penitentiaries, the doors of which were thrown wide open to receive him.

Allan Peskin, ed., *North Into Freedom.*
The Autobiography of John Malvin (Cleveland, 1966)

Nevertheless, black emigrants continued to pour into Ohio. Some, like the runaway slave who wrote the following song, went on to Canada:

> Ohio's not the place for me:
> For I was much surprised
> So many of her sons to see
> In garments of disguise.
> Her name has gone throughout the world,
> Free Labor-Soil-and men-

But slaves had better far be hurled
Into the lion's den.
Farewell, Ohio!
I cannot stop in thee.
I'll travel on to Canada,
Where colored men are free.

> Allan Peskin, ed., *North Into Freedom.*
> *The Autobiography of John Malvin* (Cleveland, 1966)

Others organized to protest the laws. A Convention of the Colored Citizens of Ohio, in 1849, appealed to voters to remove "the curse of the Black Laws." Their appeal won them the right to testify in court and—in 1852—a fair share of school tax money. But the other laws remained in force until the Civil War.

All of the Midwestern states had similar restrictions. A prosperous ex-slave explained why he left Indiana. The "oath" he referred to was the law that kept blacks from testifying against whites:

I was dissatisfied with the laws. I had a good deal of property there. It was not safe, for any loafing white might destroy or steal, and unless a white man were to see it, I could get no redress. One time seven white fellows threw brickbats at my house and broke my windows. I was so mad that I seized my gun and pursued them, and put some small shot in the backs of two of them. I afterward made it known that, as my oath was good for nothing, if any white man interfered with me, or trespassed on my property, I would *make him* a witness.

I removed to Canada where I would have an equal oath with any man. Excepting for the oppressive laws, I would rather have remained in Indiana. I left one of the most beautiful places in that country. I had a two-story frame house, with piazza—good stable—abundance of apples, peaches, quinces, plums and grapes. I paid my taxes and felt hurt and angry too that I was not allowed my oath. The road tax I would not work out. They threatened to sue me. I told them I would take it to the Supreme Court.

"What!" said I. "Shall a white man drive against me on this very road, and break my wagon, and I get no redress? No! When you give me my oath, I'll work on the roads." They never sued me. I suffered oppression in being obliged to leave my place to claim my rights as a man.

Benjamin Drew, *The Refugee: A North-side View of Slavery* (Boston, 1856)

Families who made the long trip to the West Coast found Black Laws there too. Abner H. Francis, a native of New Jersey, wrote to Frederick Douglass from Oregon Territory:

My Dear Friend:

After a two months tour from New York I concluded, in connection with my brother, to locate in Oregon.

We rented a store and commenced business. I was called away for three weeks. Shortly after my departure, my brother was arrested. And what do you suppose was the crime? That he was a Negro and that one of the laws forbid any colored person who had a preponderance of African blood from settling in the territory. He was tried before a Justice of the Peace and, I must say, very generously given six months to leave the territory. The law says thirty days.

The people declare we shall not leave whether the Legislature repeal the law or not. Petitions are now being circulated for its repeal. Thus you see, my dear sir, that even in the so-called *free* territory of Oregon, the colored American citizen is driven out like a beast in the forest.

Yours for equal rights, equal laws and equal justice to all men.

A. H. Francis

Frederick Douglass' Paper, November 13, 1851

A letter to The Pacific Appeal, *a black newspaper published in San Francisco, reported from Idaho:*

Dalles City, Idaho, April 9, 1863

Mr. Editor:

I am proud to inform you of my arrival in this new Territory of Idaho. This Territory was formed by the people of Eastern Washington Territory, with a view of enhancing their chance of forming a State. I am sorry to inform you that all colored persons and Chinamen must pay a road tax of $5 on entering this Territory, or work it out upon the roads at 50 cts. per day, under pain of imprisonment. Like Oregon, you cannot own any real estate in your own name. Thus, you see, the iron heel of oppression has worked this virgin soil ere it arrived at maturity.

Persons coming up this way should have some coin in their pockets, as board is $10 per week. Several gentlemen of color are employed as stewards upon boats. More in my next.

J. G. Wilson

The Pacific Appeal, April 25, 1863

Mifflin Gibbs left Philadelphia for San Francisco in 1850. Co-owner of an "Emporium for fine boots and shoes" he quickly became involved in the civil rights struggle in California:

In 1851, Jonas P. Townsend, W. H. Newby and other colored men with myself, drew up and published in the leading paper of the State, resolutions protesting against being disfranchised, and denied the right of oath, and our determination to secure all the rights and privileges of American citizens.

The committee above named the same year formed a company and published the *Mirror of the Times,* the first periodical issued in the State for the advocacy of equal rights for all Americans. State conventions were held in 1854, '55 and '57, resolutions and petitions passed and presented to

Mifflin W. Gibbs

the Legislature. We had friends to offer them and foes to move they be thrown out the window.

Mifflin Gibbs, *Shadow and Light* (Washington, 1902)

A poll tax required of all voters was levied on blacks, even though they were not allowed to vote. When Gibbs and his partner refused to pay it, the tax collector confiscated some of their merchandise to sell at auction. Gibbs sent a notice to the newspapers:

During a residence of seven years in California, we, with hundreds of other colored men, have cheerfully paid city, state and county taxes, and every other species of tax, save only the poll tax. On the day before yesterday the tax collector called on us and lugged off twenty or thirty dollars' worth of goods, in payment, as he said, of this tax.

Now, while we cannot understand how a white man can refuse to pay each and every tax for the support of the government under which he enjoys every privilege—from the right to rob a Negro up to that of being Governor—we regard it as low and despicable, to pay [the poll tax,] situated as we are politically. However, if there is no redress, the great State of California may come around annually and rob us of twenty or thirty dollars worth of goods. We will never willingly pay three dollars as poll tax as long as we remain disfranchised, oath-denied, outlawed colored Americans.

Lester & Gibbs

The Liberator, July 3, 1857

Gibbs's story had a happy ending:

We learned that we had several good friends at the sale, one in particular a Southern man. This friend quietly moved through the crowd, telling them why our goods were there and advising to give them a "terrible letting alone." The auctioneer asked for bidders, winked his eye, and said "no bidders." Our goods were sent back to our store. No further attempts to enforce [this law] on colored men were made.

Mifflin Gibbs, *Shadow and Light* (Washington, 1902)

The law that black Californians hated most was the one that prohibited anyone with one-eighth or more "Negro blood" from giving legal testimony. Light-skinned blacks who attempted to give evidence in court were subjected to humiliating examinations. Worse, whites could kill blacks almost with impunity, as the following newspaper story reported:

The trial of Schell for the murder of George W. Gordon, the colored barber, was a complete mockery of justice. The fact is well known that it was one of the most deliberate, cold-blooded murders that ever disgraced California, even in her rudest and most lawless days.

And what was the result? The only witness for the prosecution was, by direction of the Court, subjected to a private examination by two pretended *experts* in the new-fangled science of hairology (we know no other name by which to designate it) which professes to trace the descent of an individual from an examination of the hair and nails, and to determine the race from which his ancestors sprang. This witness was excluded from giving his evidence because two M.D.s, both from the Sunny South, *believed* he had one-eighth Negro blood in his veins.

After that the trial was a mere farce. The only witnesses were for the defence, personal friends of the murderer, upon whose testimony the jury found a verdict of manslaughter in the second degree.

The Pacific Appeal, April 5, 1862

After more than a decade of protests, the testimony law was repealed.

2. On the Antislavery Circuit

In the 1840s dozens of black men and women criss-crossed the Northern states to lecture on the evils of slavery and to raise money for various causes. Some were agents of the antislavery societies. Others traveled on behalf of black newspapers or sold copies of books they had written. Many of these speakers were former slaves who gave first-hand accounts of life in the South. Frederick Douglass who escaped from slavery in 1838 told of his first months as a lecturer:

In the summer of 1841, a grand antislavery convention was held in Nantucket, under the auspices of Mr. Garrison and his friends. I was induced to speak out the feelings inspired by the occasion, and the fresh recollection of the scenes through which I had passed as a slave. At the close of this meeting, I was duly waited on by Mr. John A. Collins—then the general agent of the Massachusetts Anti-Slavery Society —and urgently solicited by him to become an agent of that society. I was reluctant to take the position. I had not been quite three years from slavery—was honestly distrustful of my ability—but I finally consented to go out for three months.

Among the first duties assigned me was to secure subscribers to *The National Anti-Slavery Standard* and *The Liberator*. I traveled and lectured through the eastern counties of Massachusetts. Much interest was awakened—large meetings assembled. Many came, no doubt, from curiosity to hear what a Negro could say in his own cause. Fugitive slaves, at that time, were not so plentiful as now; and as a fugitive slave lecturer, I had the advantage of being a "brand new fact"—the first one out. Up to that time, a colored man was deemed a fool who confessed himself a run-

Frederick Douglass

away slave, not only because of the danger to which he exposed himself of being retaken, but because it was a confession of a very *low* origin!

During the first three or four months, my speeches were almost exclusively made up of narrations of my own personal experience as a slave. "Give us the facts," said Collins. "We will take care of the philosophy." "Tell your story, Frederick" would whisper William Lloyd Garrison, as I stepped upon the platform.

I could not always obey, for I was now reading and thinking. New views of the subject were presented to my mind. It did not entirely satisfy me to *narrate* wrongs; I felt like *denouncing* them. Besides I was growing, and needed room.

"Be yourself," said Collins "and tell your story. Better have a *little* of the plantation manner of speech than not; 'tis not best that you seem too learned." These excellent friends were actuated by the best of motives, and were not altogether wrong in their advice. Still I must speak just the word that seemed to *me* the word to be spoken.

Frederick Douglass, *My Bondage and My Freedom*
(New York, 1855)

From his first speeches, Douglass brought new vigor to the antislavery platform. "I appear before this assembly as a thief and robber," he would say. "I stole this head, these limbs, this body from my master and ran off with them." His audiences wept as he told of his separation from his mother and roared with laughter when he sang a parody of a Methodist hymn. But Douglass was far more than a showman. He soon gave up "the plantation manner of speech" to become one of the most powerful orators of his time.

Other ex-slaves followed. Henry Bibb, a runaway from Kentucky, was editor of Voice of the Fugitive, *a black weekly published in Canada. In his autobiography, he told about life on the antislavery circuit:*

The first time that I ever spoke before a public audience was to give a narration of my own sufferings and adventures, connected with slavery. I commenced in Michigan, May 1844, in a section of country where abolitionists were few and far between. Our meetings were generally in small log cabins, schoolhouses, among the farmers. Where they had no horse teams there would be four or five ox teams come, loaded down with men, women and children, to attend our meetings.

The people were poor, and in many places not able to give us a decent night's lodging. We most generally carried a few pounds of candles to light up the houses where we held our meetings after night; for in many places they had neither candles nor candlesticks.

I have traveled for miles over swamps, where the roads were covered with logs, which sometimes shook and jostled the wagon to pieces. We would have to tie it up with bark, or take the lines to tie it with and lead the horse by the bridle. At other times we were in mud up to the hubs of the wheels.

Narrative of the Life and Adventures of Henry Bibb, an American Slave (New York, 1849)

William Wells Brown, another ex-slave, lectured for the Massachusetts and American Anti-Slavery Societies. In a letter to William Lloyd Garrison, he described a hazard that public speakers faced in those premicrophone days:

Linesville, October 20, 1857

Dear Mr. Garrison:

After attending the New York State Fair at Buffalo, I made my way to western Pennsylvania. The people are generally hospitable, but the oddest feature in our meetings is the swarms of little ones.

O, the children! At one meeting last week, I counted twenty-seven babies in their mothers' arms or in their laps. And such music I never before heard. Take an untuned piano, a cornstalk fiddle, a Swiss hurdy-gurdy, and a Scotchman with his bagpipes. Put them all in one room, and set them agoing, and you will have but a faint idea of the juvenile concert we had that evening.

I waited till a late hour before commencing, with the hope that the little ones would stop; but in vain. After being reminded by the dusty clock on the wall that it was ten minutes past seven, I raised my voice to the highest note, and the little ones and I had it, "which and tother," for some time. I was about giving it up as a bad job, when an elderly gentleman near me said, "Keep on, sir, the babies will get tired by and by, and will go to sleep." This encouraged me, and sure enough as the clock struck 8, I found the babies all asleep, and I master of the field.

At Linesville, we found another large crop of children. O, the noise! Some babies were crowing, some crying and some snoring. One [mother] was throwing her child up and catching it, another singing "bi-lo-baby." My head aches now from the great exertion I made to be heard. But they give us rice pudding out here for breakfast, and that gives me strength to meet the babies.

William Wells Brown

The Liberator, October 30, 1857

William Wells Brown
(*Historical Society of Pennsylvania*)

Author of novels, plays, histories and biographies, Brown became America's first black man of letters. While travel-ing, he gave dramatic readings as well as lectures. His plays were Experience, or How to Give a Northern Man a Backbone, *a satirical account of a proslavery minister who was sold into slavery, and* The Escape, or A Leap for Freedom, *a tale of runaway slaves. The following letter was addressed to Marius Robinson, editor of the* Anti-Slavery Bugle:

Hartford, November 29, 1857

Dear friend Robinson:

Your note was duly received. You appear not to compre-hend my meaning about the Drama. There are some places where it would take better than a lecture. People will pay to hear the Drama that would not give a cent in an anti-slavery meeting. In Hartford last Sunday, after three speeches [we] took up *Ninety-Five Cents.* On Wednesday evening I read the Drama in the same place, charging 10 cents at the door. Paid $2 for the hall and had $5 over ex-penses. This is more than [we] have taken up in collections for the last ten days.

Please put in the *Bugle* the following notice:

"Mr. William Wells Brown will lecture during the month of December in Youngstown, Lowell, Middletown, Poland, Boardman, Petersburgh, Darlington. Friends of the cause in the above places will please see that places are secured to hold the meetings in, and give general notice when they are informed of the days when the lectures are to be given."

William Wells Brown

Schomburg Collection

Although unschooled, Sojourner Truth's eloquence and wit made her a favorite on the antislavery circuit. An excerpt from one of her speeches:

When I was a slave I hated the white people. I was born in the state of New York, among the Low Dutch. When I was ten years old, I couldn't speak a word of English. My master died and we was all brought up to be sold. My mother took my hand and she says, "Look up to the moon and stars that shine upon your father and mother when you [are] sold far away. I asked her who made the moon and the stars and she says, "God." And says I, "Where is God?" "Oh," says she, "He sits in the sky and he hears you when you ask him to make your master and mistress good and he will do it."

When we were sold I did what my mother told me. I said, "O God, my mother told me if I asked you to make my master and mistress good, you'd do it. They didn't get good. God, maybe you can't do it. Kill them."

After I made such wishes my conscience burned me. Then I would say, "O God, don't be mad. My master makes me wicked." You see, I was in want. I know what it is to be taken in the barn and tied up and the blood drawed out of your bare back.

But I got no good master until the last time I was sold. And then I found one and his name was Jesus. When God give me that master, he healed all the wounds up. I used to

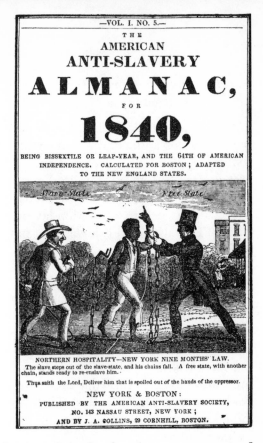

—VOL. I. NO. 5.—

THE

AMERICAN

ANTI-SLAVERY

ALMANAC,

FOR

1840,

BEING BISSEXTILE OR LEAP-YEAR, AND THE 64TH OF AMERICAN
INDEPENDENCE. CALCULATED FOR BOSTON; ADAPTED
TO THE NEW ENGLAND STATES.

NORTHERN HOSPITALITY—NEW YORK NINE MONTHS' LAW.
The slave steps out of the slave-state, and his chains fall. A free state, with another
chain, stands ready to re-enslave him.

Thus saith the Lord, Deliver him that is spoiled out of the hands of the oppressor.

NEW YORK & BOSTON:
PUBLISHED BY THE AMERICAN ANTI-SLAVERY SOCIETY,
NO. 143 NASSAU STREET, NEW YORK;
AND BY J. A. COLLINS, 29 CORNHILL, BOSTON.

hate the white people so. I thought that love was too good for them. Then I said, "Yes, God, I'll love everybody, and the white people too." Ain't it wonderful that God gives love enough to the Ethiopians to love you?

Olive Gilbert, *Narrative of Sojourner Truth*
(Battle Creek, Michigan, 1878)

"Miss Watkins left our house yesterday" wrote the Reverend Jeremiah W. Loguen, a former slave. "We think much of her indeed. She is such a good and glorious speaker that we are all charmed with her."

Born free in Maryland, Frances Ellen Watkins (later Mrs. Harper) was a schoolteacher and poet before she decided to devote her time and talents to the antislavery cause. Selections from three of her letters tell of her experiences as a lecturer:

Well, I am out lecturing. I have lectured every night this week, besides addressed a Sunday school, and I shall speak tonight. Last night I lectured in a white church in Providence [to] about six hundred persons. My voice is not wanting in strength to reach pretty well over the house. My maiden lecture was Monday night in New Bedford, on the "Elevation and Education of our People."

The agent of the State Anti-Slavery Society of Maine travels with me and she is a pleasant, dear, sweet lady. We travel together, eat together and sleep together. (She is a white woman.) In fact I have not been in one colored person's house since I left Massachusetts, but I have a pleasant time.

I have lectured three times this week. Some of the people are Anti-Slavery, Anti-rum and Anti-Catholic. And if you could see our Maine ladies! They are for sending men to Congress who will plead for our oppressed brethren, our helpless sisters.

William Still, *The Underground Railroad*
(Philadelphia, 1872)

Frances Ellen Watkins Harper

Now let me tell you about Pennsylvania. I have been traveling nearly four years and have been in every New England State, in New York, Canada and Ohio. Of all these places, this is about the meanest, as far as the treatment of colored people is concerned. The other day I attempt[ed] to ride in one of the city cars. After I had entered, the conductor wanted me to go out on the platform. I did not move but kept the same seat. When I was about to leave, he refused my money. I threw it down on the car floor and got out. Such impudence!

On the Carlisle road I was insulted several times. Two men came after me in one day. I have met, of course, with kindness among individuals. All is not dark in Pennsylvania, but the shadow of slavery, oh, how drearily it hangs!

The Liberator, April 23, 1858

For the ex-slave speakers, there was always the fear of capture. James Lindsey Smith told of the petty persecution he encountered while touring Connecticut with a white doctor:

In Saybrook we stopped at a tavern. There was an old sea captain there and while in conversation with the Doctor, the captain asked, "What do you know about slavery? All you know is what this fellow (meaning me) has told you. If I knew who his master was, I would write him to come and take him."

This frightened me very much. I feared I should be taken out of my room before morning, so I barred my door with chairs and other furniture before I went to bed. I did not sleep much that night.

The next morning, we went about two miles to the house of a friend. We gave out notice that there would be an antislavery lecture in the schoolhouse that night. When it was time, word came that we could not have the school for such a lecture. The man at whose house we were stopping told us we might use his house. We had a good meeting. At the close of the lecture we retired, feeling that we had the victory.

The next morning the Doctor went to the barn to feed his horse and found that someone had shaved his horse's mane and tail close to the skin and had cut our buffalo robe all in pieces. Besides shaving the horse, the villains had cut his ears off. It was the most distressed-looking animal you every saw.

The Autobiography of James Lindsey Smith
(Norwich, 1881)

Sometimes meetings were broken up by proslavery mobs. Frederick Douglass was speaking in a courthouse in Pennsylvania when the room filled with "Slavery's choice incense"—rotten eggs:

I spoke only for a few moments when through the windows was poured a volley of unmerchantable eggs, scattering the contents on the desk and upon the wall behind me, and filling the room with the most disgusting stench. The audience appeared alarmed, but disposed to stay, though greatly at the expense of their olfactory nerves. I proceeded with my speech but in a very few moments we were startled by the explosion of a pack of [fire] crackers, which kept up a noise similar to the discharge of pistols, and being on the ladies' side, created much excitement. When this subsided I was at once interrupted by another volley of addled eggs, which again scented the house with Slavery's choice incense. Cayenne pepper and snuff were freely used, and produced their natural results among the audience.

At this point a general tumult ensued. The doorway was completely wedged with people. I could hear fierce and bloody cries, *"throw out the nigger,* THROW OUT THE NIGGER." I took the arm of a colored gentleman and several colored friends filling up the rear, we walked out.

As soon as I reached the steps I was discovered by the mob.

"Give it to him, give it to him," they cried. "Let the d—d nigger have it." Two friends behind me received heavy blows. One of them was quite stunned, but they stood around me and received the blows intended for me. By turning a corner I succeeded in eluding my pursuers.

The National Anti-Slavery Standard, August 19, 1847

Frederick Douglass defending himself against an Indiana mob

When Douglass started his weekly paper, The North Star, Martin R. Delany was its coeditor. Delany's assignment was to lecture and sell subscriptions in Ohio and Michigan. Few black men lived in the small towns of the Midwest in those days, and Delany was shocked by the hostility he met as he traveled along the federal highway which ran from Maryland to Missouri:

I cannot permit myself to believe that there is in either Asia or Africa a tribe of heathen among whom a stranger would not meet with more civility than I received upon the National Road, one of the greatest highway thoroughfares in the country.

Aged men and women, youngsters and maidens, all along the road, hallowing, disparaging, pointing a finger in one's face and even throwing stones. Respectable-looking women standing in the doors of fine-looking houses would call out in one's hearing, "Come, here goes a *nigger*."

The North Star, May 12, 1848

In no part of Europe are children known to insult persons as they pass. We well remember a few years ago when the foreign news reported that some children in a German town stoned and cast mud upon a Jew as he passed. Every American journal invited the persecuted Jews to the United States, where humanity, friendship and Christianity stood with extended arms to receive them, where insult was unknown and abuse a stranger.

Not a place is there in the United States in which a colored person may go that they are not subject to abuse. If not adults, the children faithfully keep up the persecution. And though this abuse may not be physical, yet it is an abuse of the feelings.

The North Star, March 30, 1849

Delany's worst encounter took place in the village of Marseilles in western Ohio, where a mob broke up his

*meeting, then followed him and his companion, Charles
Langston, to their hotel. From an upstairs window, the
two men watched and listened. Delany believed in non-
resistance, but before the long night was over, he had
armed himself with a hatchet and butcher knife. A portion
of his letter to* The North Star:

All the men and boys in the neighborhood who were able
to throw a brickbat being now assembled, tar and feathers
were demanded. A tar barrel was procured and after many
yelps and howls, they succeeded in staving in the head.
Failing to find tar sufficient to saturate us, a torch was
brought and the tar barrel set aflame. Store boxes were
piled upon it which produced a fire that must have been
seen several miles around. The fire was in the middle of the
street, directly opposite the hotel in which we stayed.

Then came the cry, "Burn them alive—bring them out—
Niggers! come out, or we will burn down the hotel over
your heads." A consultation was held, the result of which
was that they would drag us out, tie and bind us, and take
us to the South and sell us! declaring that I would bring
fifteen hundred dollars cash.

Our position was such that we could look down upon
them and hear all that was said. This position we occupied
with coolness and deliberation, fully determined not to
leave it [alive]. Under no circumstances could [we] submit
to personal violence. My friends may censure me—even both
of us—for this, but we cannot help it. We are not slaves,
nor will we tamely suffer the treatment of slaves.

The most horrible howling and yelling, cursing and
blasphemy kept up from nine until one o'clock at night—
the roaring of drums, beating of tambourines, blowing of
horns, smashing of boxes and boards for the fire, all going
on at the same time, incessantly, for four hours. During
all this midnight outrage, the proprietor of the hotel acted
like a man. I have no doubt but his influence contributed
toward bringing them to a sober reflection.

The mob eventually concluded to retire until morning, but not without giving strict instructions to the hostler boy who slept in the barroom of the hotel that should we attempt to flee, to give speedy notice. In the morning there were six only of them who howled and yelped as we left. Two stoned us, striking the horse and buggy, fortunately without injury to either. We left that place untarred and even unfrightened, as we were reconciled to the course we should pursue.

The North Star, July 14, 1848

3.   Hug Those Gentlemen!

*With black lecturers traveling tens of thousands of miles
each year, they could no longer follow Samuel Cornish's
advice to "Go by foot, brethren." Instead, they began a
vigorous fight against segregated accommodations.*

*On the railroads, they were forced to ride in separate
"Jim Crow cars" or "Jimmys," a name made popular by
Thomas D. Rice, a white entertainer who performed a
"Jim Crow" song and dance in black face. Blacks re-
sented his caricature as bitterly as they resented the cars
themselves. The following was one of many protests against
Rice:*

Albeit I may differ from those who regard theatres as a
perversion of the morals of a community, there ought to be
but one sentiment concerning those plays which hold up to
ridicule an already too much oppressed people and towards
those actors who represent characters in their most ridicu-
lous light, and pretend that they are the characteristics of
the whole people.

I have been led to those remarks by the following speech
from that most contemptible of all Buffoons, Thomas D.
Rice, alias "Jim Crow." I hope after reading the following no
colored American will ever disgrace himself by patronizing
such performances.

"Ladies and Gentlemen: It is now two years since I had
the honor of appearing before a Baltimore audience. Within
that period I made the tour of England and Ireland.
Before I went to England the British people were under
the impression that Negroes were equal to whites. But I
effectually proved that Negroes are essentially an inferior
species of the human family and they ought to remain
slaves. I have studied the Negro character on Southern

Thomas D. Rice in black face

plantations. The British people acknowledged that I was a fair representative of the great body of our slaves.

"Ladies and Gentlemen—It will ever be a source of pride to me that in my humble line, I have been of such signal service to my country."

The Colored American, December 9, 1837

One of the first fights against the "Jimmys" took place in Massachusetts when two white abolitionists, John A. Collins and James Buffum, were traveling with Frederick Douglass. Collins told the story:

Douglass and myself occupied one seat and Buffum sat behind. We had scarcely exchanged salutations before the conductor made his appearance, greatly enraged. He was pale as death. His lips quivered. He forced up his courage sufficiently to collar Douglass and ordered him out.

"If you will give me any good reason why I should leave this car, I'll go willingly, but without such reason, I do not feel at liberty to leave," said Douglass. "Though," he continued, "you can do with me as you please, I shall not resist."

"You have asked that question before," quoth the trembling conductor.

"I mean to continue asking the question over and over again," said my colored friend, "as long as you continue to assault me in this manner."

"Give him the reason," cried one voice after another.

The conductor finally made up his mind to say, in a half-suppressed half-audible voice, "Because you are black."

The little pale man again collared Douglass but finding him inflexible called some eight or ten of the Company's minions to his aid.

"Snake out the d—d nigger," cried one. "Out with him," responded another. The word was given, "Take him out!"

Five or six, like so many tigers, laid hold of Douglass, but he happened to be exceedingly heavy, as the laws of gravity were in full force. Our seat gave way, and we, with five or six of these villains laying hold of our head, arms and legs were dragged out and deposited upon the ground in no very gentle manner.

The Liberator, October 15, 1841

Public pressure forced the railroads of Massachusetts to abandon their separate cars in 1843. The fight against Jim Crow moved on to other states. Henry Highland Garnet was a leader in the struggle, despite a serious physical handicap—he had had a leg amputated and got about on crutches. At a protest meeting in Rhode Island, he said:

The railroad company, through its servants, treats our wives and daughters worse than they do brutes. I have seen ladies in the cars with poodle dogs in their arms, but respectable, intelligent colored people are thrust out and are sometimes beaten.

I would advise my brethren always to remonstrate and resist when abused in this manner. *Resistance* would secure respect from friends and foes. For my part, I generally hug the seats and sometimes they go with me as a whole or in part. If every colored man molested on our railroads would give his assailants an affectionate embrace, after the mode of the grizzly bear, these upstarts would become weary of such manifestations of brotherly love. I wouldn't say that it would be well to fight, but simply say, "Hug those gentlemen!"

The North Star, April 14, 1848

Three months later, Garnet was manhandled on a train in New York State:

I attempted to take the cars for Niagara Falls this morning, but the conductor insultingly ordered me to leave. He said, "Colored people cannot be permitted to ride with the whites, for Southern ladies and gentlemen will not tolerate it." Not being accustomed to yield up my rights without making at least a semblance of lawful resistance, I quietly returned to my seat. I was prevented by the conductor who seized me violently by the throat and choked me severely. I have been for many years a cripple. I made no resistance further than was necessary to save myself from injury, but nevertheless this conductor and another person continued to choke and to assault me. A part of the time my leg was under the cars, near the wheel, and several persons were crying out—"Don't kill him—don't kill him."

An officer of the road said that they would put me or any other person out whenever they pleased and no law could interfere and that I might as well attempt to sue the state of New York as to prosecute that company. I am suffering greatly from my wounds and bruises, so much so that I called in a physician. My eyes, temples and breasts are severely injured.

The North Star, July 7, 1848

Women too did battle. Like Rosa Parks in Montgomery a hundred years later, Elizabeth Jennings refused to leave a New York horsecar when told to by a conductor. These

streetcars pulled by horses were the only public transpor-
tation within cities. Some horsecar lines refused all black
riders; others ran Jim Crow cars at infrequent intervals.
The conductors of the horsecars were usually European
immigrants who had only been in the United States a few
years. Miss Jennings, a schoolteacher and church organist,
could boast of a grandfather who had fought in the Revo-
lution and a father, Thomas Jennings, who was a leader in
the black community. Her report, read at a mass meeting
of black citizens:

Sarah E. Adams and myself walked down to the corner
of Pearl and Chatham Sts. to take the Third-Av. cars. We
got on the platform when the conductor told us to wait
for the next car. I told him I could not wait, as I was in
a hurry to go to church.

He then told me that the other car had my people in it,
that it was appropriated for "my people." I told him I had
no people. I wished to go to church and I did not wish to be
detained. He still kept driving me off the car; said he had
as much time as I had and could wait just as long. I replied,
"Very well, we'll see." He waited some few minutes, when
the driver becoming impatient, he said, "Well, you may
go in, but remember, if the passengers raise any objections
you shall go out, whether or no, or I'll put you out."

I told him I was a respectable person, born and raised in
New York, did not know where he was born, and that he
was a good-for-nothing impudent fellow for insulting decent persons while on their way to church. He then said he
would put me out. I told him not to lay hands on me. He
took hold of me and I took hold of the window sash. He
pulled me until he broke my grasp. I took hold of his coat
and held on to that. He also broke my grasp from that. He
then ordered the driver to fasten his horses and come and
help him put me out of the cars. Both seized hold of me
by the arms and pulled and dragged me down on the

bottom of the platform, so that my feet hung one way and my head the other, nearly on the ground.

I screamed, "Murder," with all my voice and my companion screamed out, "You'll kill her. Don't kill her." The driver then let go of me and went to his horses. I went again in the car and the conductor said, "You shall sweat for this." Then told the driver to drive until he saw an officer or a Station House. They got an officer on the corner of Walker and Bower.

The officer, without listening to anything I had to say, thrust me out and then tauntingly told me to get redress if I could. This the conductor also told me. He wrote his name, Moss, and the car, No. 7, but I looked and saw No. 6 on the back of the car. After dragging me off the car he drove me away like a dog, saying not to be talking there and raising a mob or fight.

When I told the conductor I did not know where he was born, he answered, "I was born in Ireland." I made answer it made no difference where a man was born, provided he behaved himself and did not insult genteel persons.

I would have come myself but am quite sore and stiff from the treatment I received from those monsters in human form yesterday afternoon. This statement I believe to be correct and it is respectfully submitted.

Elizabeth Jennings

Frederick Douglass' Paper, July 28, 1854

Miss Jennings sued the Third Avenue Railroad Company and won damages of $225. The judge, in his charge to the jury, said that "colored persons, if sober, well-behaved and free from disease, had the same rights as others" on the horsecars. To make sure that this ruling was enforced on all the lines in the city, black New Yorkers formed a Legal Rights League and sent the following NOTICE to the newspapers. During "anniversary week"

James W. C. Pennington
(*Moorland-Spingarn Collection, Howard University Library*)

*in May antislavery societies, womens' rights and temper-
ance groups held their annual meetings in New York.*

To the numerous colored ladies and gentlemen who may
visit this city during the coming anniversary week, let me
say:

1. That all our public carrier-conveyances are now open
to them upon equal terms.

2. No policeman will now, as formerly, assist in assaulting
you.

3. If any driver or conductor molests you, by laying the
weight of his finger upon your person have him arrested,
or call upon Dr. Smith, 55 West Broadway, Mr. T. L.
Jennings, 167 Church St., or myself, 29 Sixth-Av., and we
will enter your complaint at the Mayor's office.

4. You can take the conveyances at any of the Ferries or
stopping places. Ask no questions, but get in and have your
five cents ready to pay. Don't let them frighten you with
words; the law is right and so is the public sentiment.

J. W. C. Pennington

Frederick Douglass' Paper, May 11, 1855

*The right to ride in horsecars was contested in city after
city, from Philadelphia to San Francisco. Sojourner Truth*

Runaway slave resists capture

and a white companion, Laura Haviland, helped to de-segregate the cars in wartime Washington:

As Mrs. Haviland signaled the car, I ran and jumped aboard. The conductor pushed me back, saying, "Get out of the way and let this lady come in." "Whoop!" said I, "I am a lady too." We met with no further opposition till we were obliged to change cars. A man coming out as we were going into the next car, asked the conductor if "niggers were allowed to ride." The conductor grabbed me by the shoulder and jerking me around, ordered me to get out. I told him I would not. Mrs. Haviland took hold of my other arm and said, "Don't put her out." The conductor asked if I belonged to her. "No," replied Mrs. Haviland. "She belongs to humanity." "Then take her and go," said he, and giving me another push slammed me against the door. I complained to the president of the road, who advised me to arrest the man for assault and battery. The [Freedmen's] Bureau furnished me a lawyer. Before the trial was ended, the inside of the cars looked like pepper and salt.

Olive Gilbert, *Narrative of Sojourner Truth*
(Battle Creek, Michigan, 1878)

4. Kidnappers!

From the eighteenth century until the Civil War, the word "Kidnappers!" sent a thrill of fear through black communities. The kidnappers were professional people-hunters who carried blacks to the South to sell as slaves. Some of their victims were runaways who had lived in the North for years; others were freeborn.

Advertisements in black newspapers frequently announced the disappearance of children. Occasionally they were found and brought back, but many remained slaves for life. Even if a kidnapped child could be located, Southern authorities would not accept the testimony of black claimants. In the following account, Lewis Williamson, an Ohio farmer, described his six years' search for his children:

Three miles below Gallipolis [Ohio] I once possessed a farm of rich soil, that yielded seventy-five bushels to the acre. I lived in comfort with my family and there I might have been living now, had not my prosperity raised the envy of a neighbor whose land joined mine. He employed me to assist in rebuilding a corn crib that had fallen five miles below. We could easily have done the work and returned home the same day, but [the other workmen] loitered and I, with one or two others, were sent to stay at his brother's.

At dead of night they entered my little habitation and dragged my wife and three small children from their beds. With savage brutality, they were driven over frozen ground to the river and thrown into a canoe. Two hundred and forty miles below, my wife was set ashore. With a heart burning with anguish she got on board of a steamboat and returned home.

But to return to myself. I arose early. I set about finishing the work. When the business was accomplished, we set out for home. On the way a neighbor came running to tell me the state in which he had seen my house. The horrible conviction flashed on my mind. I turned to my employer and said, "Did you get me away to sell my wife and children?"

He swore he knew nothing of it, but he looked like a monster to me. If a weapon had been at hand, I fear I should have taken his life.

But I had no time to lose. The thought that I might overtake and regain my dearest earthly treasures spurred me on. I took passage on a steamboat for Louisville, but could hear nothing of them. I then procured handbills and had them distributed in every steamboat. My name was called by a Capt. Buckner, who had one of my handbills. I soon found that he had conveyed my children to Natchez, whither I pursued with all possible speed. On my arrival, I learned they had been resold and taken three days before, no one, alas! knew whither.

I now wandered about in Mississippi, Alabama, Georgia, Tennessee, and Louisiana in the forlorn hope of lighting upon them. I then learned the name of the second purchaser. I found that he resided in Louisiana, about 80 miles from Natchez. I immediately went to his plantation and saw my children, but did not make myself known to them or their master, for it might have prevented forever their return to liberty.

I returned home to procure one of my white neighbors for evidence. As compensation, I gave him my farm, besides handsome suit of broadcloth, traveling expenses, &c. When we arrived [in Louisiana] the master was from home and the mistress, who heard of our coming, had sent the children 100 miles farther into the country.

But when the master came home, he sent for them. About midnight, I heard voices approaching. The people began to arouse and said, "Wake up, Williamson." Ah! they thought a father could sleep.

I fell back from the light of the door and saw them enter. Tears ran down my cheeks to see their famished and miserable appearance. The man whom I had brought as witness kept his face from them for a time. When he turned around, the boy rushed to him, exclaiming, "Oh, Mr. Gibson. Where's my father—my mother?"

I approached the door and said, "Beck, are you here?"

My daughter dashed through the crowd crying, "That's my father—Oh, father, where's mother?" and sunk into my arms.

After this the owner said, "Old man, come in. These children are yours and you must have them." Thus joyfully ended my six years' search.

The Liberator, December 10, 1841

In the cities, blacks banded together to protect themselves. The New York Committee of Vigilance brought kidnappers to court and attempted to arouse sympathy for their victims. More than three hundred people were rescued from slave hunters during the Vigilance Committee's first year of work. But cases were often lost because judges and policemen sided with the kidnappers. David Ruggles, the Committee's energetic secretary, told of one:

A West Indian named Ayres imported an apprentice from the island of Jamaica to this city, [then] shipped him on board the brig *Buenos-Ayres* for South Carolina, to sell him.

After collecting sufficient proof, application was made to Judge Irving for a writ of *habeas corpus* to liberate the boy. But His Honor declined issuing it upon the ground that he was sick and should leave his office and go to bed.

Application was then made to Judge Ulshoeffer, who refused to allow the writ as he wanted his dinner and could not attend to it. When the counsel stated that the vessel was about to sail and that delay was dangerous, the Judge advanced to the door, opened it with all the authority of a Judge and said, "There's the door—this is my house." The applicants could not succeed in obtaining the writ until the next day when it was too late.

The Colored American, September 15, 1837

Police Constable Tobias Boudinot often provided the cover of law for Nash and Waddy, a team of slave catchers. George Thompson, a runaway slave who had been in New York for five years, was arrested in a midnight raid by the trio. He dictated his story while he was in Bridewell prison:

I had gone to bed and was asleep. Was aroused by a knocking at the door. Got up and drew aside the curtain of the window. Saw there a colored man. Asked him what he wanted. He asked if a man named George Thompson lived there. I said, "Yes." He then wanted to come in, as he was cold. I opened the door to let him in. As the door bolt was lifted, several men rushed in. A person they called Nash grabbed me. Another person they called Boudinot had two pistols in his hand and said, "Now raise a hand and I'll see who will shoot the strongest." I had a gun in the room but could not get to it. Another person called Waddy took my gun, but my wife told him it was not paid for, so he let it remain.

They pulled me out of doors and handcuffed me before I was allowed to put on my trousers. I was put in a hack. Outside on the box [were] two persons, one of whom drove. There were in a wagon three others. The black man was about 25 or 30 years old. Like a fool, I had a feeling for him and so let him into the house.

One of them said to Waddy when he was getting out of the carriage at the prison, "Ned, you must not be seen here. Keep out of the way." In the course of the conversation between them, heard Waddy say, "I will take $1,200 for him, but shall take him back first."

The Colored American, May 9, 1840

Being a runaway was not sufficient grounds for an arrest like this one. Thompson therefore was charged with robbery—because he had stolen the boat in which he and sixteen others escaped from their masters. And as a thief he was returned to slavery.

After the decision, the prisoner was shipped for the South in charge of D. D. Nash, who on his return said that Ben, as he called the man, was tried for stealing the boat and found guilty; that he was sentenced to be whipped and burned in the hands and that he assisted in the same by applying the iron himself!

The Colored American, May 9, 1840

David Ruggles' aggressive fight against kidnapping made him a target of the slave hunters. After he visited the Brazilian slave ship, Brilliante, *in New York harbor, he too was awakened by a late-night knock on the door.*

January 4, 1836

Mr. Editor:

On Wednesday morning, between one and two o'clock, several notorious slave catchers made an attack upon the house in which I board. I stepped to the door and inquired, "Who's there?" "Is Mr. Ruggles in?" "Yes." "I wish to see you, sir." "Who are you?" "A friend—David, open the door." "What is your name?" "Why—it is Nash. I have come to see you on business of importance." "What's the matter?" "Nothing—I only wish to see you on some private business." "This is rather an unseasonable hour Mr. Nash, to settle private business. Call in the morning at eight o'clock."

Nash did not call to see me at 8 o'clock. At 12 I proceeded

to make a statement of the facts in the case before the Mayor. As I entered City Hall, I was pounced upon by Boudinot who dragged me to the Police Office. I desired him to show his authority to arrest me. He refused to do so and jammed me against one of the marble pillars. Said he, "I was after you last night!"

When I appeared before the magistrate, he said that I had been engaged in a riot on board the brig *Brilliante* and that I must appear to answer to the charge. Boudinot immediately dragged me to the city prison and gave the jailor a paper, who said, "I have no right to lock up. That is not a commitment." "Yes it is," said Boudinot. "Shut the fellow up!"

In less than 20 minutes, they had me on the way to Bellevue Prison. They said, "We have got him now. We will learn him to publish us as kidnappers!" Boudinot [had a] warrant which he informed a gentleman he obtained from Governor Marcy in 1832 or '33, by which he can arrest any colored person that Waddy may point out to him named Jesse, Abraham, Peter or Silvia, and send him or her South, without taking such person before a magistrate.

David Ruggles

Weekly Advocate, January 14, 1837

Ruggles was released, but was arrested again and again in subsequent years. His health impaired by bad living conditions in prison, he later lost his sight.

The Vigilant Committee of Philadelphia was organized in 1837 "to aid colored persons in distress." Headed by Robert Purvis, its agent was Jacob C. White, a barber. A selection from White's "Record of Cases Attended to by the Vigilant Committee" shows that much of his time was spent in forwarding runaway slaves further North:

No. 1 June 4, 1839. Man arrested by Constable Hogg and

Jacob C. White, Sr.

committed to prison at Woodbury, N.J., without trial, or without any hearing whatever. Mr. Browning, procured as counsel, obtained a writ of *habeas corpus* from Judge Ford. We have made arrangements for prosecuting the case.

No. 2 & 3, June 27th. Two men. One sent to the Committee by William Whipper, Columbia, from Virginia, light complexion, an interesting young man, sent to Morrisville, from thence to N.Y. for Canada. The other was employed some few weeks, since left for Canada. The expense attending these two cases was $4.83

No. 6. July 6th. Man from Virginia, reported by S. H. Gloucester, sent to Vigilant Committee of N.Y. Expenses $3.25.

No. 17. August 15th. Boy. A letter intercepted, directed to the number of a house on Shippen St. in which resided a man by the name of Day. From the contents of the letter there is no doubt he intended selling the boy. We had this man taken before Alderman Hutton, who, at once, decided that this man had no right to send the boy out of this state.

No. 33–40. Nov. 5th. Eight persons from Virginia, a very interesting family, sent to Canada accompanied by the agent.

No. 49. Dec. 4th. Samuel Williams from Columbia, imposter. This man was brought to E. H. Coates and feigned himself deaf & dumb, but not succeeding to his satisfaction, he made a second call representing himself a slave. He was, however, detected and finally acknowledged the fraud, but believing him in want, we gave 20 cts. to help him on his way and furnished him with some food.

Historical Society of Pennsylvania

While the New York and Philadelphia committees used legal means to fight the kidnappers, black Bostonians sometimes tried more direct methods:

The colored people who were in the courthouse sprang from their seats in every direction, gathered round the two slaves, rushed to the nearest door, burst it open, and bore them away in a carriage which was at hand. The Deputy Sheriff interfered, but the mob seized him by the throat and threw him aside. Judge Shaw commanded the rioters to *stop,* but they pressed on till in the space of not more than two minutes not a colored person was in court.

African Repository, August 1836

When New Yorkers attempted a similar rescue the following year, an editorial by Samuel Cornish deplored their action:

TO THE THOUGHTLESS PART OF OUR FELLOW CITIZENS

Brethren, my heart is grieved at your conduct yesterday, and on all occasions of fugitive trials. We have an intelligent and efficient Vigilance Committee who have eminent lawyers in their employ so that everything that can be done for those unhappy victims of our slave system will be faithfully attended to. We must here enter our SOLEMN PROTEST against your going to the Courts or assembling in the Park on the occasion of fugitive trials.

You can do no good but much harm. You degrade yourselves and if you do not desist, you will be forsaken by
all your friends. Everlasting shame and remorse seize upon
those females that so degraded themselves yesterday. We
beg their husbands to keep them at home and find some
better occupation for them.

We ask the pardon of our municipal authorities and the
Court, in behalf of the ignorant part of our colored citizens
who act so inconsiderately. *We assure them that such
doings are in opposition to the judgment, wishes and feelings
of all the intelligence and piety among us.*

The Colored American, April 13, 1837

*But Cornish's was soon a minority voice on this point.
In towns and villages all over the North, the war against
slave catchers became increasingly militant. A minister described the rescue of a runaway who had been living in a
small Ohio town:*

While engaged in his daily avocation, by which he made
an honest and respectable living for his family, three men
came suddenly upon him, put a rope around his neck and
unceremoniously dragged him beyond the limits of the
Town authorities and on to his former place of slavery.

The news spread, almost with lightning speed through the
colored community. We rallied 200 strong in little or no
time. Men and women were much excited, some of the
latter consoling the bereaved wife and children, others
following the accumulating multitude. We came upon those
man-stealers three miles from the town. One end of the
rope was connected to the neck of a horse, and the fugitive
was walking or running, while the men were riding.

The advancing crowd raised a shout. The slave looked
behind and motioned his hand for them to hasten their
speed. When it became apparent to [the slave catchers]
that their own liberty and security were in danger, they

cut the rope from the neck of the steed and spurring their horses, were soon out of sight. The fugitive was borne back on the shoulders of his friends, with triumphant shouts, "A man saved from Slavery!".

William Mitchell, *The Underground Railroad* (London, 1860)

Martin R. Delany reported on the resistance of a community in Michigan:

On the 27th of January 1847, early in the morning, Troutman [a Kentucky lawyer], David Giltner and Francis Lee went to the house of the Crosswait family—the old man, his wife and four children—forced their way in, asserting their intention of taking them back to Kentucky. The old man cried out, "kidnappers! kidnappers!" This had the effect of rousing the neighborhood. A colored man was the first who came to their aid. An old gentleman mounted his horse, rode through the streets ringing a bell, crying, "Kidnappers—the Crosswait family," until the whole town was gathered about the house of the fugitives. The family was very well thought of by all the people of Marshall.

Dr. Comstock, addressing Troutman, remarked, "My good sir, you must see that you cannot take these people by moral, legal or physical force." Troutman insolently inquired, "What—do you say I shall not take them?" To which Dr. Comstock replied, "According to the excited crowd around you, you must see the impossibility of taking them by force."

The Kentuckians as a last resort endeavored to get them before a Justice of the Peace. But before its accomplishment, the ever-vigilant colored men spirited away the whole family on the Underground.

The North Star, July 28, 1848

In Cincinnati, housewives bested a party of slave catchers:

For the last three or four days our colored community has been thrown into somewhat of an excitement. Some eight or ten slaves landed on the Ohio banks on Friday morning and immediately struck for the [Underground Railroad]. On Saturday, hot and heavy, came the blood-hounds in quest of their prey—bowie knives in their pockets and revolvers in their hats.

The women began to gather about from adjoining houses until the Amazons were about equal to the [slave catchers] —the former with shovels, tongs, washboards and rolling pins; the latter with revolvers, sword-canes and bowie knives. Finally the besiegers decamped, leaving the Amazons in possession of the field, amid the jeers and loud huzzahs of the crowd.

The North Star, August 11, 1848

Even with help from the Underground Railroad, the road to freedom was long and hard. A runaway described his trip to Canada:

Kentucky was my home. I was not far from the Ohio River, and at Madison, Indiana, lived a man named Mason, a preacher. That was the beginning of the Underground Railroad for Canada. I traveled at night. In the day I would hide in the woods. I lived on raw potatoes, turnips and anything I could get. I had money but a runaway nigger was worth $50, them days, and they watched for them mighty close. My old master paid $1,200 for me, so I knowed he would follow me hard. I went to the stable of preacher Mason in Madison, and he had a man start with me and two other niggers for a point thirty miles north. It took us two nights to make it. Then we was in an old cave for more than a week.

A man comes one night when we was nearly starved and give us some apples and says the officers were watching for us. I was scared to death. Then t'other man comes and says, "It will take a lot of money to get you niggers out of here. Has you got any?" The other niggers said "no," but I says "yes." The white man says, "How much you got?" I says "$25." I had more but I knowed too much to tell him. You see, I was a horse trader for my master and mighty cunning.

"Give me that $25," says that white man, "and I will get you away from here." I asked him how far, and he says, "To Detroit." I knowed that was right across the river from Canada but the Kentuckians used to tell us that the river between Detroit and Canada was a thousand miles wide.

So I give him $25. We walked two nights, sleeping all day in a hollow tree. Then we got to a big place and the man says, "This is Indianapolis. You got a long way to go yet." Then he brought another man to where I was staying in a cellar with lots of other runaway niggers and he loaded us all in a big covered wagon and we started again. In the day he covered us with bedclothes, and I heard him telling folks he met, he was moving. In about a week we comes to a big town and a big river, and the man told us to get out. It was night, and a man on a long boat with big paddles told us to get in quick, and he fetched us across and says, "This is Canada and you niggers is free." I just hollered.

Hamilton, Ontario, Public Library

Slaves in the Deep South rarely had contact with Underground Railroad workers. Those who escaped were dependent on their own courage and ingenuity. None were more ingenious than William and Ellen Craft, a young couple from Georgia, who made their way, unaided, to Philadelphia. A dozen years after their escape, William Craft told their story:

Knowing that slaveholders have the privilege of taking their slaves to any part of the country, it occurred to me that, as my wife was nearly white, I might get her to dis-

Runaway slave

guise herself as an invalid gentleman, while I could attend as his slave, and that in this manner we might effect our escape. I suggested it to my wife, but at first she shrank from the idea. She thought it almost impossible for her to assume that disguise and travel a distance of 1,000 miles across the slave states. However, the more she contemplated her helpless condition, the more anxious she was to escape. So she said, "If you will purchase the disguise, I will try to carry out the plan."

I went to different parts of the town, at odd times, and purchased things piece by piece (except the trousers which she found necessary to make). Some slaveholders sometimes give their favorite slaves a few days holiday at Christmas. She obtained a pass from her mistress allowing her to be away for a few days. The cabinetmaker with whom I worked gave me a similar paper. At first we were delighted at the idea of having gained permission to be absent, but when the thought flashed across my wife's mind that it was customary for travellers to register their names in the visitors' book at hotels it made our spirits droop within us.

William Craft

Ellen Craft, many years after her escape

All at once my wife raised her head, and with a smile upon her face, which was a moment before bathed in tears, said, "I think I have it! I can make a poultice [bandage] and bind up my right hand in a sling and ask the officers to register for me." I thought that would do.

My wife, knowing that she would be thrown a good deal into the company of gentlemen, fancied she could get on better if she had something to go over her eyes so I went to a shop and bought a pair of green spectacles. Just before the time arrived for us to leave, I cut off my wife's hair square at the back of the head. In the disguise, she made a most respectable looking gentleman.

We said farewell and started in different directions for the railway station. I got into the Negro car but my *master* (as I will now call my wife) obtained a ticket for himself and one for his slave and stepped into one of the best carriages. We arrived at Savannah early in the evening and got into an omnibus which took us to the steamer bound for Charleston, South Carolina.

*Traveling by steamboat and train, the Crafts made their
way to the North. Although they came close to being discovered several times, their worst moments were in Baltimore:*

After I had seen my master into one of the carriages
and was just about to step into mine, an officer saw me.
"Where are you going, boy?" "To Philadelphia, sir," I
humbly replied. "Well, what are you going there for?" "I
am traveling with my master who is in the next carriage,
sir." "Well, you had better get him out and be mighty quick
about it. It is against my rules to let any man take a slave
past here, unless he can satisfy them in the office that he
has a right to take him along."

On entering the room we found the principal man, to
whom my master said, "Do you wish to see me, sir?" "Yes,"
said this eagle-eyed officer. "It is against our rules, sir, to
allow any person to take a slave out of Baltimore into
Philadelphia unless he can satisfy us that he has a right to
take him along."

This conversation attracted the attention of the large
number of bustling passengers. After the officer had finished,
a few of them said, "Chit, chit," not because they thought
we were slaves endeavoring to escape, but because they
thought my master was a slaveholder and invalid gentleman, and therefore it was wrong to detain him. The officer,
observing that the passengers sympathized with my master,
asked him if he was not acquainted with some gentleman
in Baltimore that he could get to endorse for him, to show
that I was his property. He said, "No," and added, "I bought
tickets in Charleston to pass us through to Philadelphia, and
therefore you have no right to detain us here." "Well, sir,"
said the man, "right or no right, we shan't let you go."

These words fell upon our hearts like the crack of doom.
My master looked at me and I at him, but neither of us
dared to speak. Just then the bell rang for the train to
leave. The sound of the bell caused every eye to be fixed

upon us. The officer all at once thrust his fingers through his hair and said, "I really don't know what to do. I calculate it is all right." He then told the clerk to run and tell the conductor to "let this gentleman and slave pass" adding, "As he is not well, it is a pity to stop him here."

My master thanked him and hobbled across the platform as quickly as possible. I tumbled him into one of the carriages and leaped into mine just as the train was gliding off towards our destination.

Early in the morning I heard a fearful whistling of the steam engine and heard a passenger say to his companion, "Wake up, old horse, we are at Philadelphia!" As soon as the train had reached the platform, I hurried to my master, whom I got at once into a cab. On leaving the station, my master—or rather my wife, as I may now say—said, "Thank God, William, we are safe!" then burst into tears and wept like a child.

> William Craft, *Running a Thousand Miles for Freedom; or,*
> *the Escape of William and Ellen Craft from Slavery*
> (London, 1860)

Vigilance Committee members in Philadelphia sent the Crafts to Boston. There they lived and worked until 1850 when their masters discovered their whereabouts and sent agents North to capture them. An aroused community drove the slave hunters away, and the Crafts went to England until after the Civil War.

5.   Time for a Change

In the struggles of the 1840s, black people lost the optimism that had sustained them ten years earlier. Even in Pennsylvania where black leaders had remained loyal to Garrison, a State Convention of Colored Citizens, in 1848, rejected the idea that good behavior on their part would convert prejudiced whites:

We hope that our friends will cease to place any faith in the doctrine that our religious, literary and moral improvement will be the means of enfranchising us. We are not asking the voters of Pennsylvania to elevate us. They cannot do it. All we ask of them is that they "take their feet from off our necks" that we may stand free and erect like themselves.

No, if we had colored men who could write like Paul, preach like Peter, pray like Aminadab, iron-hearted prejudice would cry out, "He is black." Our political elevation is more depending on the improvement of the white man's heart than on the colored man's mind.

"Minutes of the State Convention of the Colored Citizens
of Pennsylvania" (Philadelphia, 1849)

This change in direction had been building for a long time. There had always been some men who did not believe in moral suasion. In 1829 David Walker, proprietor of a clothing store in Boston, had published an "Appeal to the Colored Citizens of the World" in which he called on slaves "to kill or be killed." People were still discussing Walker's pamphlet when Nat Turner led a slave rebellion in Virginia. As slaveowners put down the rebellion, they also drove hundreds of free blacks from the South. Some went to Liberia; others settled in northern cities. Mifflin

Gibbs recalled the impact of the rebellion on black North-erners:

At eight years of age, two events occurred which had much to do in giving direction to my life. The one the death of my father; the other the insurrection of Nat Turner in August 1831. Nat Turner was a Baptist preacher, who with four others, concocted plans for an uprising of slaves. The whole state was aroused and soldiers sent from every part. The blacks fought hand to hand with the whites but were soon overpowered by numbers and the superior implements of warfare.

Foolhardy and unpromising as the attempt may have been, it had the ring of an heroic purpose that gave a Bossarius to Greece and a Washington to America. A purpose "not born to die" but to live on, stimulating endeavors to attain the blessings of civil liberty.

In Philadelphia, so near the line, excitement ran high. The intense interest in the face of my mother and her colored neighbors; the guarded whisperings, the denunciation of slavery, the hope defeated of a successful revolution keenly affected my juvenile mind, and stamped my soul with hatred to slavery.

Mifflin Gibbs, *Shadow and Light* (Washington, 1902)

While Nat Turner was spoken of in "guarded whisper-ings," the revolt of 54 Africans aboard the slave ship Amistad *in 1839 was openly applauded by whites as well as blacks. Leading abolitionists took over the Africans' defense and John Quincy Adams argued for their freedom before the Supreme Court. An anonymous "Colored American," in a pamphlet about slave rebellions, summed up the story of the* Amistad:

After being out from Havana about four days, the African slaves, captives on board, led by Joseph Cinque, a fellow slave, rose and killed the captain and cook with canes, knives and clubs. Two passengers, Spaniards, dealers in the slaves on board, were made prisoners by the mutineers in order to navigate the vessel to some port in Africa. This they did not do. On the contrary the vessel was steered for the United States and entered the port of New London, Connecticut, where she was easily recaptured by the United States sloop of war *Washington*. The brave Cinque and his compatriots were consigned to the prison-house, with gloomy prospects of death on the scaffold staring them in the face.

Through the instrumentality of Mr. Lewis Tappan and other gentlemen of New York, New Haven and elsewhere, Cinque and his band were highly honored during their stay in this country. Through the philanthropic gentlemen, their imprisonment was softened. They were instructed not merely in the English language but in the Bible. In New Haven, professors and people were interested to impart a knowledge of the truth to the benighted sons of Africa.

The Supreme Court in Washington before whom the African prisoners were cited for mutiny, murder, and piracy on the high seas, after a patient hearing, and notwithstanding the influence of the President against the Africans, honorably acquitted [them]. After which a committee of gentlemen sent them to their homes in the Mendi country, to meet their friends from whom they had been torn by the ruthless hands of the kidnapper.

The Late Contemplated Insurrection in Charleston
(New York, 1850)

During the Africans' two-year stay in the United States, their leader, Joseph Cinque, became a popular hero. Copies of his portrait, which had been commissioned by Robert Purvis, were sold to raise money for his return to Africa.

PORTRAIT OF CINQUE—We acknowledge with many thanks to Mr. Purvis, the receipt of a mezzotinto likeness of

Cinque, the chief of the *Amistad* captives. This is a true likeness taken from a painted one from real life by N. Jocelyn, Esq., of New Haven, and now in the possession of Mr. Purvis. We shall be proud to have our apartments graced with the portrait of the noble Cinque and shall regard it as a favor to our descendants to transmit to them his likeness. For sale at the Anti-Slavery Offices, 143 Nassau Street. Price. $1.00.

The Colored American, February 27, 1841

Madison Washington followed in Cinque's footsteps. An American slave, he led a revolt aboard the Creole, *which was carrying slaves from Virginia to New Orleans. Speaking years after the event, Frederick Douglass expressed his pride in Washington:*

Let me refer to the story of Madison Washington. We see him at the head of a gang of one hundred slaves destined for the Southern market. He [was] driven aboard the brig *Creole* and placed beneath the hatchway in irons. The slave dealer—I sometimes think I see him—walking the deck of that ship quietly smoking his segar, and calculating the value of human flesh beneath the hatchway.

The first day passed, the second, and there was nothing to disturb the repose of this iron-hearted monster. On the eighth day, Madison Washington succeeded in getting off his irons [and those] of some seventeen or eighteen others. About twilight on the ninth day, Madison leaped from beneath the hatchway, gave a cry like an eagle to his comrades. In an instant, his master was prostrate on the deck. In a very few minutes, Madison Washington, a black man with woolly head, high cheekbones, protruding lips, distended nostril and retreating forehead, had the mastery of the ship. Under his direction, that brig was brought safely into the port of Nassau.

The North Star, May 11, 1849

Nevertheless, the idea that armed rebellion was the way to end slavery was still a startling one when Henry Highland Garnet spoke at the National Convention of Colored Citizens in 1843. The twenty-eight-year-old minister had written "An Address to the Slaves of the United States" which he wanted the convention to print and distribute. The "Address" said, in part:

Brethren and Fellow Citizens: Your brethren of the North, East and West have been accustomed to meet together in National Conventions, to sympathize with each other and to weep over your unhappy condition. In these meetings we have addressed all classes of the free, but we have never, until this time, sent a word of advice and consolation to you.

Brethren, the time has come when you must act for yourselves. Go to your lordly enslavers and tell them plainly that you *are determined to be free.* Do this, and for ever after cease to toil for the heartless tyrants. If they then commence the work of death, they, and not you, will be responsible for the consequences. You had better all die—*die immediately,* than live slaves. However much you and all of us may desire it, there is not much hope of redemption without the shedding of blood. *Rather die freemen, than live to be slaves.*

Brethren, arise, arise! Strike for your lives and liberties. Now is the day and the hour. Let your motto be resistance! *resistance!* RESISTANCE! No oppressed people have ever secured their liberty without resistance. Trust in the living God. Labor for the peace of the human race, and remember that you are FOUR MILLIONS.

Henry Highland Garnet, *A Memorial Discourse,*
with an introduction by James McCune Smith
(Philadelphia, 1865)

Garnet's "Address" touched off days of debate. Frederick Douglass, still a Garrisonian at that time, led the opposition. From the minutes of the convention:

Henry Highland Garnet
(*Library of Congress*)

Charles B. Ray moved its reference to a select committee of five of which he hoped Mr. Garnet would be the chairman. Mr. Ray remarked that his object in moving its reference to a committee was that it might pass through a close and critical examination, and, perceiving some points in it that might in print appear objectionable, to have it somewhat modified.

H. H. Garnet arose to oppose the motion and proceeded to give his reasons why the address should be adopted by the Convention and sent out with its sanction. He reviewed the abominable system of slavery, showed how it robbed parents of children, and children of parents, husbands of wives; how it prostituted the daughters of the slaves; how it murdered the colored man. He referred to what had been done to move the slaveholders and asked if we have not waited long enough—if it were not time to speak louder and longer—to take higher ground and other steps. Mr. Garnet, in this speech, occupied nearly one hour and a half. It was a masterly effort, and the whole Convention was literally infused with tears. Mr. Garnet concluded amidst great applause.

Frederick Douglass arose to reply to Mr. Garnet. Mr. Douglass remarked that there was too much physical force, both in the address and the remarks of the speaker last up. He was for trying the moral means a little longer. The address, could it reach the slaves, would be the occasion of an insurrection; and that was what he wished in no way to have any agency in bringing about, and what we were called upon to avoid. Therefore, he hoped the motion to refer would prevail.

Mr. Garnet said that the address advised the slaves to go to their masters and tell them they wanted their liberty and if the master refused, to tell them, "Then we shall take it."

Mr. Douglass said that would lead to an insurrection, and we were called upon to avoid such a catastrophe. He wanted emancipation in a better way, as he expected to have it.

The convention voted to refer the address to a committee headed by Garnet, with Douglass as one of its members. Making only minor changes, the committee reported back with a resolution:

That each member of the Convention who is friendly to the sentiments contained in this address, come forward and sign it in the name of the ever-living God, and that measures be taken to print 1,000 copies for circulation.

But the delegates were not ready to recommend an armed rebellion of the slaves. The resolution was defeated by one vote.

"Minutes of the National Convention of Colored
Citizens Held At Buffalo, August 15–19, 1843"
(New York, 1843)

In its report on the convention, The Liberator *was sharply critical of Garnet. Maria W. Chapman, a leader of the Boston Female Anti-Slavery Society, who was acting as editor in Garrison's absence, wrote that "bad counsels" from white men had led Garnet astray. "But we fervently hope that Mr. Garnet had no other intentions than merely to write what he thought a high-sounding address" her editorial concluded. Stung by her condescending tone, Garnet replied:*

Troy, New York, November 17, 1843

Respected Madam:

You say that I have received bad counsel. You are not the only person who has told your humble servant that his productions have been produced by the *"counsel"* of some Anglo-Saxon. I have expected no more from ignorant slaveholders and their apologists, but I really looked for better things from Mrs. Maria W. Chapman, an antislavery poetess and editor *pro tem* of the Boston *Liberator*. I can think on the subject of human rights without "counsel" either from the men of the West, or the women of the East.

My address was read to but two persons, previous to its presentation. One was a colored brother, who did not give me a single word of counsel, and the other was my wife; and if she did counsel me, it is no matter for "we twain are one flesh."

In a few days I hope to publish the address. Then you can judge how much treason there is in it. In the meantime, be assured that there is one black American who dares to speak boldly on the subject of universal liberty.

Henry Highland Garnet

The Liberator, December 3, 1843

Garnet did not succeed in publishing the "Address" until 1848. Then he brought it out as a pamphlet, along with David Walker's "Appeal to the Colored Citizens of the World." Part of the money for the publication came from a white man named John Brown.

IV·SOME PEOPLE, ORDINARY AND EXTRAORDINARY

Our residents in the free states toiled, had ambitions for their offspring, took ventures, made sacrifices, much after the fashion of other Americans.

Maritcha Remond Lyons

1. The Black Family

Historians have written more about the very real tragedies of black family life under slavery than they have about its great strength, which was equally real. It is true that slaves could marry only with permission and that masters broke up countless marriages by selling husbands, wives and children separately to new owners. But separation could

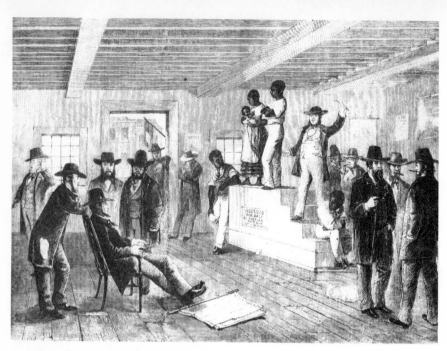

Family on auction block

not wipe out blood ties and family feelings. The struggle of the black family to keep itself together and to protect its members was a basic and powerful form of resistance to slavery. And for many individuals, the self-sacrificing loyalty of their families produced the only ways and means of winning freedom.

These selections, from a mass of neglected information on this subject, begin with Charity Bowery's story, as taken down by Lydia Maria Child, a white writer:

Sixteen children I've had, first and last. From the time my first baby was born, I always set my heart upon buying freedom for some of my children. I used to do the washings of [mistress'] family. The public road run right by my little hut, and I thought I might just as well be earning something to buy my children. So I set up a little oyster-board and when anybody come along that wanted a few oysters and a cracker, I left my washtub and waited upon him. When I got a little money laid up, I went to my mistress and tried to buy one of my children. She knew how hard I had worked for it. But she wouldn't let me have one! She wouldn't let me have one! So, I went to work again and I set up late o'nights, in hopes I could earn enough to tempt her. When I had two hundred dollars, I went to her again but what do you think that women did? She sold me and five of my children to the speculators!

While I kept my oyster-board, there was a thin, peaked-looking man used to come and buy of me. I always made something good for him and if he didn't happen to have any change, I trusted him. Now, who do you think that should turn out to be, but the very speculator that bought me! He come to me, and says he, "Aunt Charity, you've been very good to me, and now you shall have your freedom for it, and I'll give you your youngest child."

Well, after that, I concluded I'd come to the Free States. But mistress McKinley had one child of mine; a boy about twelve years old. I had always set my heart upon buying Richard. He was the image of his father, and my husband was a nice good man and we set stores by one another.

I carried all my money to my mistress, and told her I had more due to me and if all of it wasn't enough to buy my poor boy, I'd work hard and send her all my earnings, till she said I had paid enough. But she was a hard-hearted woman. She wouldn't let me have my boy.

One day, she sent me of an errand. When I come back, mistress was counting a heap of bills in her lap. My little girl stood behind her chair and as mistress counted the money—ten dollars—twenty dollars—fifty dollars—she kept crying. I thought maybe mistress had struck her. But when I see the tears keep rolling down her cheeks I went up to her, and whispered, "What's the matter?" She pointed to mistress's lap, and said, "Brother's money! Brother's money!" Oh, then I understood! I said to mistress McKinley, "Have you sold my boy?" "Yes, Charity; and I got a great price for him!"

Then I had nothing more to wait for, so I come on to the Free States.

The Liberty Bell (Boston, 1839)

Slave mother who ran away with her seven children to prevent them from being sent to Mississippi

Sojourner Truth told of a similar experience:

Well, you know, the [New York State] law had passed that the colored folk was all free. My old mistress, she had a daughter married about this time who went to live in Alabama—and what did she do but give her my son to take to Alabama? When I got back to the old place, I went right up to see old mistress and says I, "Missis, have you sent my son away down to Alabama?"

"Yes," she says. "He's gone to live with your young mistress."

"Oh, Missis," says I, "how could you do it?"

"Pooh!" says she, "what a fuss you make about a little nigger! Got more of 'em now than you know what to do with."

I tell you, I stretched up. I felt as tall as the world! "Missis," says I, "*I'll have my son back again!*"

"*You* will, you nigger? How you going to do it?"

Oh, but I was angry to have her speak to me so haughty and scornful, as if my child wasn't worth anything. I said to God, "Oh Lord, render unto her double!" It was a dreadful prayer and I didn't know how true it would come.

Well, I talked with people and they said I must get the case before a grand jury. So I went into town when they was holding a court to see if I could find any grand jury. And I stood round the courthouse and when they was a-coming out I walked right up to the grandest-looking one I could see, and says I to him, "Sir, be you a grand jury?"

He wanted to know why I asked and I told him all about it. He asked me all sorts of questions, and finally he says, "If you pay me ten dollars, I'd agree to get your son." And says he, pointing to a house over the way, "You go tell your story to the folks in that house, and I guess they'll give you the money."

Well, I went and they gave me twenty dollars. Then I thought, if ten dollars will get him, twenty dollars will get him certain. So I carried it to the man and said, "Take it all —only be sure and get him."

Finally, they got the boy back. They tried to make him say that I wasn't his mamma, and that he didn't know me, but they couldn't make it out. They gave him to me and I carried him home. When I came to take off his clothes, there was his poor little back all covered with scars and hard lumps where they'd flogged him.

I told you how I prayed the Lord to render unto her double. I was up at old mistress' house not long after, and I heard them reading a letter to her how her daughter's husband had murdered her when he was in liquor. Then says I, "O Lord, I didn't mean all that! You took me up too quick!"

Harriet Beecher Stowe, "Sojourner Truth, the Libyan Sibyl," in *Atlantic Monthly* (April 1863)

Sojourner Truth (about 1864)

(*Sophia Smith Collection, Smith College*)

When runaway slaves reached the North, their first thoughts were for the families they had left behind. They did not dare communicate directly with their relatives in the slave states for fear of incriminating them. But for those fugitives who traveled on the Underground Railroad by way of Philadelphia and New York, William Still acted as an intermediary. Chairman of the Philadelphia Vigilance Committee from 1852 until the Civil War, Still kept records of all of the runaways who passed through his hands. Through Underground Railroad workers in the South, he forwarded mes-

sages to the slave states and arranged innumerable family reunions. The following letters are typical of hundreds that Still received:

Toronto, March 6, 1854

Dear Mr. Still:

I arrived safe into Canada on Friday last. I must request of you to write a few lines to my wife and state to her that her friend arrived safe in this glorious land of liberty and she will make very short her time in Virginia. Tell her that I likes here very well and hopes to like it better when I gets to work. I don't mean for you to write the same words that are written above, but I wish you give her a clear understanding where I am and shall remain until she comes or I hears from her.

John Clayton

Toronto, May 7, 1854

Mr. W. Still:—Dear Sir:

I take this opportunity of writing you these few lines. My soul is vexed. My troubles are inexpressible. I often feel as if I were willing to die. I must see my wife, in short. What would I not give just to gaze on her one moment? If I had known as much before I left, as I do now, I would never have left until I could have found means to have brought her with me. You have never suffered from being absent from a wife as I have. I consider that to be nearly superior to death.

You will oblige me by seeing Mr. Brown and ask him if he would go to Richmond and see my wife and see what arrangements he could make with her. I would be willing to pay all his expenses there and back.

What is freedom to me, when I know that my wife is in slavery? Please write in haste.

Isaac Forman

Syracuse, January 6th

Mr. Still: You will oblige me if you will direct this letter to Virginia to my Mother.

John Thompson

William Still

My dear Mother:

I am now a free man, living by the sweat of my own brow, not serving another man & giving him all I earn. What I make is mine and if one place do not suit me I am at liberty to leave and go somewhere else. I think highly of freedom. I am waiting [on table] in a hotel

When I leave you, my heart was full, but I knew there was a better day ahead & I have live to see it. I hear when I was on the Underground R. Road that the hounds was on my track, but it was no go. I was too far out of their reach where they could never smell my track.

Remember me to your husband and all inquiring friends & say to Miss Rosa that I am as free as she is & more happier. I am getting $12 per month for what little work I am doing.

Your son, John Thompson

Salford, 1857

Dear Sir:

I take my pen in hand to request a favor. I received a letter that states that my father has been betrayed in the act of helping some friend to Canada and the law has convicted and sentenced him to state prison for 10 years. If you can get any intelligence from Baltimore about this please write all the information as regards the event and the best method to redeem him. Direct your letter to Salford post office, Canada West.

Samuel Green

Samuel Green

Auburn, June 10, 1858

Mr. William Still:—Sir, Will you be so kind as to write a letter to Affey White in Strawberry Alley in Baltimore. Please tell Affey White to let me know where Joseph and Henry Ambie is. They was eleven of us children and I feel interested about my brothers. I have never heard from them since I left home.

Nat Ambie

William Still, *The Underground Railroad* (Philadelphia, 1872)

Free black families were not subject to the pressures that slaves encountered, but Black Laws and the difficulty of earning a living drove many to Canada. Some became Canadian citizens and ardent boosters of their adopted country. Most, however, still felt closely tied to family and friends back home. The following letters were written to Jacob C. White, Jr., who was principal of the Institute for Colored Youth and the leader of a group of young black intellectuals in Philadelphia.

Dresden, Canada West, July 27, 1861

Dear Friend:

We arrived safe in Chatham on the 5th inst. Dresden is a small village, 16 or 20 miles from Chatham, and as fine a little place as ever the sun shone upon. I have been at work for two weeks and have entered into partnership with my father-in-law and we have 3 men working for us. I pay half the expenses and get half the proceeds. You never saw a gladder set of people in your life than my father-in-law's family were when we got here. Such kissing!

There is the nicest water here that I ever drank, so cold that it almost makes your teeth ache to drink it, and everything is correspondingly nice, except the houses, and those we cannot build fast enough. Butter churned and brought immediately to the store brings 10 cts. per lb. and potatoes are selling for 25 cts. per bushel. I have my own cow and my father-in-law has one also, and we have no scarcity of milk. I have so great an appetite that I can eat almost as much as a small family itself. It is a very healthy place.

Everything at present invites me to stay here, and I only need cigars and newpapers to complete my happiness. I would like you to send me 500 cigars. The cigars that I want are branded DeUndia and I used to pay 55 cts. per hundred for them. Write as soon as convenient and tell me all you know.

Parker T. Smith

Dresden, Canada West, November 1861

My dear Sir:

Everyone was extremely glad to hear from Philadelphia, especially Margaret who is always glad to hear from what she calls home. I must confess that I am *homesick already myself*. I have never lived in a place where I felt so free. We have a smokehouse well filled with meat, both beef and pork, a plenty of flour, some fifteen or sixteen bushels of wheat ready to grind for winter, a plenty of peas for coffee and wood at hand to keep a good fire.

But you may yet see me in Philadelphia. *I am so lonesome that I cannot content myself here.* These things I say in confidence. I make money and could soon accumulate property, but unless a person is satisfied there is no use of talking about staying in a place.

Give my love to everybody and consider yourself as entitled to the largest share.

Parker T. Smith

Jacob C. White Collection, Moorland-Spingarn Collection, Howard University Library

A small number of well-to-do free blacks in the South were able to send their children North for schooling. John H. Rapier's sons, John, Jr., and James were educated in Canada and Scotland. John, Jr., to whom the following letter was written, became a doctor and James a congressman from Alabama during Reconstruction.

Florence, Alabama, March 17, 1857

My Son:

Your letter dated St. Paul, February 22 was received. We are all well and was glad to hear from you. I hope you are better of your frostbite.

James will quit school soon and will come out to you to try his luck. I hope you and him will be like brothers towards each other, for it very unpleasant to hear that my children are disagreeing with each other.

John, you should settle down and not have a wish to ramble so much. I hope your uncle James will come to the same conclusion. You and your uncle have the capacity of doing well in any country.

Your counsel with regard to me, I felt every word of. I hope I shall carry out your wish, my son, with regard of moving out to some free state. As soon as you and your uncle have found the place that will suit you both, you can calculate on me being your neighbor. The time has come for me to act. My eyes are getting so I cannot see how to shave and to tell the truth I hate the name of barber. A farmer I look on as a superior occupation.

I think you and James—I mean your brother—ought to make sure of some land. It do not require more than fifty dollars to do that. You can save that very soon. I am willing to help if you take one piece of a hundred and sixty acres between you. You should encourage James all you can, my son, as you are calculated to advise him.

John H. Rapier

Rapier Papers, Moorland-Spingarn Collection,
Howard University Library

While black abolitionists traveled in the cause of freedom, their wives stayed at home. Few letters from these women have survived, but Frederick Douglass' daughter, Rosetta, wrote an account of "My Mother as I Recall Her":

She watched with a great deal of interest and no little pride the growth in the public life of my father, and aided him by relieving him of all the management of the home. It was her pleasure to know that when he stood up before an audience his linen was immaculate and that she had made it so. When he was on a long journey she would forward a fresh supply.

Being herself one of the first agents of the Underground Railroad she was an untiring worker along that line. To be able to accommodate the fugitives that passed our way, father enlarged his home where a suite of rooms could be made ready for those fleeing to Canada. It was no unusual occurrence for mother to be called up at all hours of the night, to prepare supper for a hungry lot of fleeing humanity.

She was greatly interested in the publication of *The North Star* or *Frederick Douglass' Paper* as it was called later, and publication day was always a day for extra rejoicing. Mother felt it her duty to have her table well supplied with extra provisions that day, a custom that we, childlike, fully appreciated. During one of the summer vacations the question arose in father's mind as to how his sons should be employed. Mother came to the rescue with the suggestion that they be taken into the office and taught the [type] case. The thought had not occurred to father. He acted upon the suggestion and at the ages of eleven and nine they were perched upon blocks and given their first lesson in printer's ink, besides carrying papers and mailing them.

She also found time to care for four other boys at different times. As they became members of our home circle, the care of their clothing was as carefully seen to as her own children's and they delighted in calling her Mother.

During her wedded life of forty-four years, she was the same faithful ally, guarding every interest connected with my father, his lifework and the home. Unfortunately an opportunity for a knowledge of books had been denied to her, the lack of which she greatly deplored. She was able to read a little. By contact with people of culture and education her improvement was marked. She took a lively interest in every phase of the antislavery movement. I was instructed to read to her. She was a good listener, making comments on passing events which were well worth consideration. Her value was fully appreciated by my father.

Rosetta Douglass Sprague, "My Mother as I Recall Her."
Paper read to Anna Murray Douglass Union, W.C.T.U.
(May 1900)

Maritcha R. Lyons, the daughter of Albro Lyons, a New York businessman and antislavery worker, described her mother and grandmother:

Grandmother Marshall (1780–1860) knew personally or by reputation, every colored person in the city. Also, she had many acquaintances among those of English and Dutch extraction. During her periods of widowhood, she had to work abroad to support herself and family. Five days a week she toiled outside of her home. Saturdays she reserved for domestic duties. On Sunday, she kept the Sabbath. This meant a scrupulous avoidance of all but the most necessary labor.

Going uptown meant for her going about as far as Bond Street, the journey consuming half a day, for the horses had to be fed and rested before the return trip was undertaken.

Up the Hudson to Albany in a sailing vessel was one of her annual recreations. Though she worked hard she always indulged in a vacation once a year. The length of a water trip was always uncertain and preparations included extra garments, bedding, and a full hamper of food of all kinds.

The first day young Lord and Taylor opened a dry goods store on Catherine Street, she hurried over to make an early purchase of a yard of white ribbon, to give the "boys" good luck, for she knew them both very well. When the DeForrests, former employers, found coal in Pottsville, Pennsylvania, she was always sure of a full bin in winter, something to be thankful for as winters then were long and severe. November snow usually remained until the latter part of April. The East River was so regularly frozen over that walking across it was one of the winter recreations. My father rec-

Mrs. Albro Lyons

Maritcha Lyons or one of her sisters

Albro Lyons, Jr.

Family Record
Albro Lyons Born in Fishkill Dutchess County, New York
February 10th 1814 Mary Joseph Marshall Born
in Orange Street City of New York July 20th 1814
Albro Lyons and Mary Joseph Marshall was Married on the
Fourteenth (14) July in the year our lord one thousand
Eight and Fourty (1840) in St Phillips Church by
the Revd Peter Williams Rector of Said Church

Births
Mary Marshall Lyons Born
14 Day of april 1843
Theresa Lyon Born
2d Day March 1847
Marietta Remond Lyons
23 Day of May 1848

Deaths
Mary Marshall Lyons died on the
29 Day of December 1845
age 2 years 8 month and
15 Days

Family Record Continued
Albro Lyons, was married to Mary Joseph.
the daughter of Joseph and Elizabeth Hewlet
Marshall, on the 14 day of May in St Philips
Church by Revd Peter Williams Rector at
4 Oclock P.M. in the year 1840, New York City

Births.

Mary Marshall, first child of Albro
and Mary J. Marshall Lyons was born
April 14 1843 house 144 Centre street
N York City. Physician, James McCune Smith.
Theresa, second child of Albro and Mary J.
M. Lyons was born March 2 1847
house 144 Centre street N York City. Physician McCune Smith

Mariche Remond, third child of Albro and
Mary J. Lyons was born May 23 1848
house 144 Centre Street, N York City. Physician McCune Smith.

Mary Elizabeth Pauline, fourth child of Albro and
Mary J. Lyons was born on the 12 November 1850. house
530 Pearl street. Attending Physician Dr James McCune
Smith. New York City.

Lyons' family records   (*Negro History Associates*)

ollected seeing a barbecue on the ice in celebration of Washington's birthday.

My mother had an extensive acquaintance among the colored people in the city and elsewhere throughout the Northern states. Many colored New Yorkers were more or less closely connected families dating prior to the Revolution. Some of the colored folks in New York City spoke both English and Dutch but none used the corrupt dialect referred so often to them by those who knew nothing about them.

Mother, endowed with a sense of humor, was an accomplished raconteur. She amused us with gossipy, good-natured chat. She was the life of a group of young single and married folks. Her guests were frequent. They danced, played or sung, played games or sewed for charity. Mother's early matronhood saw in New York City colored jewelers, carpenters, undertakers, printers, shoemakers, tinsmiths, crockery and chinaware dealers.

Father's connection with the Underground Railroad brought many strange faces to our house. Refugees were kept long enough to be fed and to have disguises changed. Father used to say humorously this part of his business was "keeping a cake and apple stand." He estimated he had been of help to a thousand persons, thanks to mother's devotion and discretion.

At antislavery meetings and conferences mother was almost invariably present, not to agitate but to learn her duty. My parents were only samples of the great majority of our people in the free states who worked, suffered and prayed, that no one who had the courage to start [toward freedom] should fail to reach the goal.

Lyons-Williamson Papers, Schomburg Collection

Even earnest young abolitionists went to parties, flirted and fell in love. Henry Highland Garnet was twenty-two when the first Anti-Slavery Convention of American Women was held in New York. There he renewed his acquaintance with Julia Williams, a classmate of his at the Canaan School, whom he later married. The following letter was written to Alexander Crummell:

New York, May 13, 1837

Dear Friend:

The ladies would not admit any males [to the Convention] therefore I can tell you nothing about them more than that Miss Julia Williams of Boston was one of the delegates and I had the pleasure of waiting upon her six or seven times, and dined, and supped with her. What a lovely being she is! Modest, susceptible and chaste. She seems to have everything which beautifies a female, a good Christian and a scholar. I don't want you to think that I am in love, yet I shall keep a correspondence with her. I have received a polite invitation from Miss Hannah Lewis to call and see her. Of course I am going. I am quite popular among the people, and were I not so well acquainted with the honesty of the world there would be some danger of being puffed up. I [am] called the poet, and often solicited to write in albums and so on. I never saw so much fashion in all my life as now is.

Your father is very much altered as well as my poor unfortunate Sire. I have not yet seen your mother though I have called several times. Your sister looks well. Very hard times in New York. I am in great haste.

Henry H. Garnet

Crummell Papers, Schomburg Collection

As the son of a hotelkeeper who catered the most important dinners in Washington, William H. Wormley was a leader in black social circles in the capital. The following letter was written to Octavius Catto, a teacher. After the Civil War, Wormley became Commissioner for Washington's Colored Schools and Catto their Superintendent.

Washington, September 11, 1860

My dear old friend:

You don't know what pleasure it gave me to read that some fair young lady had won the gallant heart of our most noble Catto. I tell you, old boy, you may say what you will about that young lady, but old Wormley is in the picture yet and has made up his mind not to run except when I see in the distance a Catto striding toward me. Is there any danger?

I suppose you have heard of the wedding, have you? Jim Johnson-Liz Dogans has been tied together in hymenal tie, to love through all ages and live till they die. Do you think they will, old boy?

Ha! more news yet. Did you know James and Robert Hays? They have put their foot into the noose also. What is the matter with the boys? I think the disease is contagious.

Miss Pet Jones has come home from Oberlin, and I am going out in the spring to stay two years. I wrote to Miss Susie Goines yesterday. Miss Jennie Browne asked me to give her best love to you. The Georgetown ladies are all well and send their love. Mrs. Johnson—alias Dogans—sends her very best love and says she would like very much to see you. Will you come, won't you come, and bring "Blue Dress" with you?

Dear Cat, it is time for me to go to the President's and I must close with great respect,

William H. Wormley

N.B. I heard your father lecture last night in the Presbyterian Church. It was on the "Condition of Our Race" in the United States. It was excellent. Three cheers for Mr. Catto —hip-hip-hip.

Jacob C. White Collection, Moorland-Spingarn Collection,
Howard University

Hattie Purvis, daughter of Robert Purvis and Harriet Forten Purvis, lived a more privileged life than her black contemporaries. The Purvises' spacious country home, fifteen miles from Philadelphia, was both an Underground Railroad station and a gathering place for the nation's leading abolitionists. Hattie grew up with white as well as black friends and had a normal teen-ager's interest in boys. However, even her father's wealth and social position could not protect her family from slights. The following letter was written to Ellen Wright, a white girl who had gone to boarding school with Hattie. Ellen later married William Lloyd Garrison, Jr.

Byberry, January 16, 1856

My lovely Ellen:

I must not defer any longer writing to you. You like Jos. Pierce do you? Well, that's more than I do. He comes to see me sometimes, takes me out sleighing. Ellie, don't you miss your music? I practise two hours every day.

Yesterday was my birthday. I was seventeen. I am getting old. Did you get any Christmas presents? My brother Bob gave me a very pretty ring. George Barker gave me a beautiful bottle. Wasn't George bashful?

Oh! this is such a busy world. I find so many things to do, I am almost discouraged some times. I have been teaching my little brothers and sister this winter, for there is no school here for them to go except a public school and there they are made sit by theirselves, because their faces are not as white as the rest of the scholars. Oh! Ellie how it makes my blood boil when I think of it. Dame Fortune has not been *very good* to us.

So John Plumbly presented you with a quire of note paper. I feel very very jealous! Tell me, who do you room with? Somebody nice. Are your teachers kind and good? How is Eliza Schofield? Tell her to write to me (that is if she wants to).

Now good-bye, dear. As ever your friend,

Hattie Purvis

Garrison Papers, Sophia Smith Collection,
Smith College Archives

*Amelia Loguen's father, the Reverend Jeremiah Loguen,
was an ex-slave and Underground Railroad activist. This
letter, written when she was a schoolgirl, was sent to Lewis
Douglass, Frederick Douglass' son whom she later married:*

Syracuse, April 10th, '62

My Dear Lewis:
Pardon my negligence in allowing so many weeks to pass
away without writing.

Spring has brought with it the ever dreaded, yearly school
examinations, dreaded because they are so very tedious.
Monday I thought of nothing but Chloride of Sodium, Ni-
trate of Silver, detection of arsenic, uses of Zinc, etc. Tues-
day, *Parlez-vous français? Comment-vous appelez-vous?*
Yesterday oh! terrible thought, Plane Trigonometry. Do
you wonder then that last night I dreamed of being in
France? I was alone in some queer place trying to ascertain
the height of a "fort on a distant hill inaccessible on account
of an intervening swamp." Oh! how refreshing on awaking
this morning to know that all such is for a time past and that
vacation is close at hand.

Please let me know when your sister Rosa returns and I
will write to her. Give my love to your mother.

H. Amelia Loguen

Carter Woodson Papers, Library of Congress

*During their struggle for equal rights, blacks were often
charged with wanting "amalgamation," the nineteenth-cen-
tury word for intermarriage. Sometimes they were able to
laugh at the taboo against black man-white woman:*

Mr. Editor—if there be one exhibition of human weakness more degrading than another, it is that sentiment of caste which even the casual juxtaposition of a black man to a white female is sure to call up in the minds of Northern dough-faces. I am not in favor of amalgamation, sir; *tout au con-traire,* I think that the blood of the Negro and the white man have been mingled too largely already. But to our tale—or scene, rather:

Time, 10 o'clock Wednesday morning; place, Flushing Railroad; scene, inside of a car partly filled with passengers.

Enter high-caste lady, and sits down in the seat with black man.

N. Y. Merchant (rising)—Madame, don't sit there beside that nigger. Take a seat here.

Lady—Thank you, sir. I am very well seated.

Merchant (excitedly)—But, madam, you must not sit there by that nigger. You had better take this seat.

Lady—No, I thank you, sir. I prefer to sit where I am.

Merchant, in a state of great excitement goes to the conductor and calls his attention to the awful spectacle. Conductor approaches the lady and requests her to take another seat. Lady adheres to her determination. The merchant continues during the whole trip to direct attention to a stranger who had casually occupied a seat in which there happened to be a black man. I wonder if when he leaves home he locks up his woman folks for fear some Negro may come between the wind and their *whiteness.*

> *Hic et Ubique* [Here and Everywhere]
>
> *The Weekly Anglo-African,* March 23, 1861

Occasionally, of course, a black man and a white woman did take an intimate interest in each other. William G. Allen was a professor of Greek at the newly integrated Central College in upstate New York. When news got around about his impending marriage to Mary King, a white student, a lynch mob forced them to flee to England. Allen described the mob:

Tar, feathers, poles and an empty barrel spoked with shingle nails had been prepared for my special benefit. We first observed some twenty men turning in the direction of the house. Soon the streets were filled with men—some four or five hundred.

A committee, composed of members of the mob, suggested before reaching the house that if we were still unmarried, there should be no violence done as they intended to carry off the lady. A portion of the committee informed us of the intentions of the assembled multitude. This committee was composed of some of the most "respectable" men of Fulton —lawyers, merchants and others of like position. Had we been married, Miss King [was] to be carried off and myself left, to torture and death. Previous to the death which I was to suffer in the spiked barrel, I was to undergo various torturings and mutilations of person.

I was not frightened—was never calmer—prepared for the worst, disposed of my watch and such articles of value as I had about my person. One of the committee drew back the window curtains and bade me look out. Such cursings, such imprecations, such cries of "nigger," "bring him out," "kill him," "down with the house" were never heard before, I hardly think, even in America.

Compelled to make the best of our unfortunate situation, Miss King consented to go with the committee, and I to leave the village—she, however, taking care to assure me in a whisper that she would meet me on the following day in Syracuse.

William Allen, *The American Prejudice Against Color. An Authentic Narrative Showing How Easily the Nation Got Into an Uproar* (London, 1853)

2.   Making It in the North

*Problem number one for black men and women was earn-
ing a living. In most northern cities, skilled workmen refused
to accept blacks as apprentices or to work alongside of them.
William J. Brown, who grew up in Providence, Rhode Island, recalled the rebuffs he met when he tried to learn a
trade:*

My first call was on a Mr. Knowles, a first-class carpenter,
to see if he would take me as an apprentice. His excuse was
that he had but little work and that he was going to close
up business. I next applied to a Mr. Langley, a shoemaker,
but he refused without giving me an excuse. I next called on
Mr. Ira B. Winsor, a grocery man. His promise to hire me as
a clerk encouraged me very much. He had first to consult his
uncle, who was his guardian. His uncle bitterly opposed hir-
ing a black boy while there were so many white boys he
could get.

Other [white] boys of my acquaintance with little or no
education, were learning trades and getting employments,
and I could get nothing. I found it was on account of my
color, for no colored men except barbers had trades. I was
now seventeen years old and was at a loss to know what
steps to take to get a living, for if I possessed the knowledge
of a Demosthenes or Cicero, it would not bring to me flatter-
ing prospects for the future. To drive carriage, carry a market basket after the boss, brush his boots, or saw wood and
run errands was as high as a colored man could rise.

The Life of William J. Brown (Providence, 1883)

*In the South, slaves were trained to do all the skilled work
on the plantations. When they came North, however, their
trades were useless. The experience of Henry Boyd, an ex-*

slave who tried to find work in Ohio as a carpenter, was typical:

There was work enough in his line, but no master-workman would employ "a nigger." At last he found the shop of an Englishman, too recently arrived to understand the peculiarity of American feeling.

"You may go to work," said the master of the shop. The words had no sooner left his mouth than his American journeymen, unbuttoning their aprons, called, as one man, for the settlement of their wages.

"What?" said the amazed Englishman, "what does this mean?"

"It means that we will not work with a nigger," replied the journeymen.

"But he is a first-rate workman."

"But we won't stay in the same shop with a nigger. We are not in the habit of working with niggers."

"Then I will build a shanty outside, and he shall work in that."

"No, no; we won't work for a boss who employs niggers. Pay us up, and we'll be off."

The poor master of the shop turned, with a despairing look, to Boyd—"You see how it is, my workmen will all leave me. I am sorry for it, but I can't hire you."

> William C. Nell, *Colored Patriots of*
> *the American Revolution* (Boston, 1855)

Nor were blacks barred only from skilled trades. The Colored American *campaigned for years because the city of New York refused to grant licenses to black cartmen. An article headed "Henry Graves and His Hand Cart" said:*

Here was a worthy gray-headed man arraigned and fined, not for driving a horse with a cart, but for being his own horse, and drawing his own cart, for the accommodation of his friends and neighbors, and as a means to furnish himself and family with bread—fined because he had no license to do so when the City would not grant him a license. One reason urged is, the other cartmen, if they should license a colored man, would push horse, cart, and driver all into the dock. Such an outbreak on the part of the cartmen would be a violation of all law. Does the Mayor presume to suppose that the cartmen are lost to all respect for law?

The Colored American, May 30, 1840

In a biting editorial, Frederick Douglass condemned packing-house workers in Chicago for their refusal to work with blacks:

The human form is often called divine and many other agreeable names, but man is worked upon by what he works on. Vile and loathsome beasts often get themselves better expressed in the human form than in the forms appropriated to them by nature. This train of thought was suggested by reading the following preamble and resolution:

"Whereas, It has come to the knowledge of this meeting that it is the intention of one or more of the leading packers of this town to bring Negro labor into competition with that of the white man, for the purpose of reducing the wages of the latter to the lowest possible standard.

"Resolved, That we, the packing-house men of the town of South Chicago, pledge ourselves not to work for any packer, under any consideration, who will, in any manner, bring Negro labor in competition with our labor."

In all this may be seen the veritable swine. This preamble and resolution might have emanated from a body of "porkers," rather than of pork-packers, had the former the gift of speech. A slight change in the wording would bring out the genuine animal:

"Whereas, It has come to the knowledge of the big pigs of this meeting, that it is the intention of one or more of the pig-owners of this town to bring little pigs into competition with big pigs, for the purposes of reducing the amount of swill to the lowest possible standard, therefore,

"Resolved, That we, the big pigs of the town of South Chicago, will do our utmost to drive the little pigs away from the trough, and have all the swill ourselves."

Douglass' Monthly, November 1862

Most black men and women were forced to work as servants, bootblacks, waiters, porters. James McCune Smith wrote a series of sketches of ordinary black New Yorkers at work. "The Washerwoman":

Saturday night! *Dunk!* goes the smoothing-iron, then a swift gliding sound as it passes smoothly over starched bosom and collar of one of the many dozen shirts that hang round the room on chairs, lines and every other thing capable of being hanged on. *Dunk! Dunk!* and that small and delicately formed hand and wrist swell up with knotted muscles and bursting veins!

The apartment is small, hot as an oven, the air in it thick and misty with the steam rising from the ironing table. In the corners, under the tables, and in all out-of-the-way places are stowed tubs of various sizes, some empty, some full of clothes soaking for next week's labor. On the walls hang pictures of old Pappy Thompson, or Brother Paul, or Sammy Cornish; in one corner of the room a newly varnished mahogany table is partly filled with books—Bunyan's *Pilgrim's Progress*, Watts' *Hymns*, the *Life of Christ*, and a nice "greasy novel" just in from the circulating library. Between the windows stand an old bureau, the big drawer of which is the larder, containing sundry slices of cold meat, second-handed toast and the carcass of a turkey, the return cargo of a basket of clothes sent downtown that morning. *Dunk! Dunk!* goes the smoothing-iron. The washerwoman bends again to her task. Her mind is far away in the South, with her sisters and their children who toil as hard but without any pay! And she fancies the smiles which will gladden their faces when receiving the things she sent them in a box by the last Georgetown packet. *Dunk! Dunk! Dunk!!!* goes the iron, this time right swift and cheerily. Oh Freedom! Her tired muscles forget all weariness. The iron flies as a weaver's shuttle, shirts appear and disappear with rapidity and at a quarter to twelve, the groaning table is cleared, and the poor washerwoman sinks upon her knees in prayer for them, that they also may soon partake of that freedom which, however toilsome, is yet so sweet.

Sunday evening! Can it be the same apartment? No sign of toil is there; everything tidy, neat and clean; all the signs of the hard week's work stowed away in drawers or in the cellar. The washerwoman dressed up in neat, even expensive garments; and her boy with his Sunday go-to-meetings on, one of the pockets stuffed with sixpence worth of candy.

Frederick Douglass' Paper, June 17, 1852

Several steps higher in the economic scale were the owners of small businesses—barber shops, restaurants, catering and tailoring establishments. Many black leaders offered their goods and services in advertisements in black newspapers. David Walker was a tailor and David Ruggles the proprietor of a grocery store:

CLOTHING kept constantly on hand for sale by David Walker, No. 42 Brattle Street, Boston. A great variety of New and Second-hand clothing. He also cleans all kinds of woolen clothing in the neatest manner and on the most reasonable terms.

Freedom's Journal, October 30, 1828

GROCERIES

THE Subscriber returns his sincere thanks to his friends and the Public for their liberal patronage, and solicits a continuance of their favours; he has received at his store, No. 1

Courtlandt-Street, near Broadway, a quantity of superior Canton and Porto Rico *Sugars.* ALSO—*Coffee, Teas, Flour,* Goshen *Butter, Cheese, &c. Rum, Gin, Brandy, Wine, Cordials, Porter and Cider, &c.* which will be sold cheap for cash.

David Ruggles

Freedom's Journal, August 22, 1828

William P. Johnson, general agent for The Colored American, *and William J.* Wilson, *a contributor to* Frederick Douglass' Paper, *were shoemakers:*

SWAMP Leather and Finding Store, 64 Frankfort-Street, New York. W. P. Johnson thanks the public for patronage already received, and solicits a continuation of the same. Stock, consisting of an assortment of Sole Leather, Calf Skins, Linings, Findings &c. Johnson being a Boot and Shoemaker flatters himself that he can accommodate his Customers a little better than many in his line. N.B. He always trusts after he gets the cash.

The Colored American, June 10, 1837

William J. Wilson, Boot Maker, has removed to 15 Ann-Street (corner of Theater Alley), basement story, where he continues to manufacture Boots and Shoes in the best manner, and on reasonable terms, for *Cash.*

The Colored American, December 2, 1837

Dr. James McCune Smith owned a drugstore and Martin R. Delany supported his family by cupping and bleeding:

Drugs and Medicines for sale at 93 West Broadway; also fancy articles of every description.

Bleeding, Tooth-drawing, Cupping and Leeching performed by Dr. Smith at his office, 93 West Broadway.

The Colored American, December 9, 1837

(*Schomburg Collection, The New York Public Library, Astor, Lenox and Tilden Foundations*)

M. R. Delany has removed his dwelling and office to Hand St., between Liberty and Penn, where he will always have on hand good, active, healthy Leeches and the best of cupping instruments and will attend calls at all hours, day and night.

The Mystery, December 16, 1846

Patrick Reason, a graduate of the African Free School, made his living as an artist:

PATRICK H. REASON, Historical, Portrait and Landscape Engraver, Draughtsman and Lithographer, No. 148 Church-Street, New York. Address, Visiting and Business Cards, Certificates, Jewelry, &c, neatly engraved.

The Colored American, June 2, 1838

John Jones, spokesman for black Chicago, ran an Intelligence Office and a tailor shop:

John Jones Intelligence Office
No. 60 Dearborn St., Chicago, Ill.

Situations procured for Stewards, Cooks, Waitresses, Seamstresses, Chambermaids, and girls to do general housework both for the City and Country. Persons in the Country or Eastern States wishing information upon any subject in my line can have the same by enclosing $1 to my address. Loans of Money procured on the best terms. Houses to Rent and Rents Collected.

Frederick Douglass' Paper, September 15, 1854

John Malvin, a leader of Cleveland's black community, was a canalboat captain:

ARRANGEMENTS FOR 1840
ON THE OHIO CANAL

The splendid Canal Boats *Bunker Hill,* Capt. R. D. Kenny and *Auburn,* Capt. John Malvin will run from CLEVELAND to PORTSMOUTH on the Ohio Canal.

John Jones (*Chicago Historical Society*)

The above Captains are well known and experienced men.

The Colored American, June 13, 1840

A number of men, including Alexander Du Bois, grand-father of W. E. B. Du Bois, and the Reverend James W. C. Pennington, owned real estate:

FOR SALE—in the city of New Haven, Conn., a HOUSE and LOT, situated on Washington-Street, near Bishop's Hotel. This property has an elevated site, and is surpassed by none for the fine prospect which it presents, both front and rear. It is close in upon town, say eighty rods from the public green. The building is a one and a half story house, three rooms on the floor, finished chambers, and convenient for two small families. The lot is about forty feet wide and 120 feet deep, with several good fruit trees on it, and an excellent well of water.

For terms enquire of the subscriber on the premises.

The Colored American, September 30, 1837

APARTMENTS TO LET TO COLORED PEOPLE—I have taken charge of the fine four-story brick house, 312 West 26th Street, near Tenth Avenue [in New York City]. There is Croton water on each floor, and four rooms on each side of the hall. I am having the house put in the best order, and wish to let it to none but orderly and prompt paying tenants. Apply at 349 West 26th Street, or at the house, from 8 to 10 A.M.

J. W. C. Pennington

The Weekly Anglo-African, April 21, 1860

Thomas Hamilton whose family had lived in New York for generations had extensive real estate holdings. Income from sales and rentals enabled him to publish The Weekly Anglo-African, The Anglo-African Magazine, *and books by black writers. One of many letters concerning his property:*

New York, April 24, 1858

Friend Rantous:

Will you do me the favor to call on Mr. Lynch and ascertain from him

1. Whether the School needs another place to meet in.
2. How much the Trustees pay for the room they now hire.
3. How they hire it—by the month or year.
4. Who the President of the Board is.

If I can get a fair offer from the Trustees, I will commence immediately to make the alterations. In the meantime, if convenient, will you please see Mr. Brown, the carpenter, and get him to make an estimate for taking the partitions and chimney out and placing stairs on the outside. You know exactly what will have to be done. Then let him make another estimate for making all the necessary repairs that it may be occupied as a dwelling.

Thomas Hamilton

Long Island Collection, Queensborough Public Library,
Jamaica, New York

*By the late 1840s a few black men were able to break
through the educational barriers to become lawyers and doctors. George B. Vashon, an Oberlin graduate, was not permitted to take a bar examination in Pennsylvania but was
admitted to practice law in New York. Massachusetts had
two black lawyers, Macon B. Allen and Robert Morris. Morris, who started out as a servant in a lawyer's household,
described his first courtroom appearance:*

There was something in the courtroom that morning that
made me feel like a giant. The courtroom was filled with
colored people, and I could see, expressed on the faces of
every one of them, a wish that I might win the first case that
had ever been tried before a jury by a colored attorney in
this country. At last my case was called; I went to the work
and tried it for all it was worth; and until the evidence was
all in, the argument on both sides made, the judge's charge
concluded, and the case given to the jury, I spared no pains
to win. The jury after being out a short time returned, and
when the foreman in reply to the clerk answered that the
jury had found for the plaintiff [Morris' client] my heart
bounded up and my people in the courtroom acted as if they
would shout for joy.

John Daniels, *In Freedom's Birthplace* (Boston, 1914)

*Among the few black capitalists of the mid-nineteenth
century were Stephen Smith and William Whipper. Martin
Delany described their holdings after visiting their lumber-
yard in Columbia, Pennsylvania:*

In the winter of 1849, these gentlemen had in store several

thousand bushels of coal, two million two hundred and fifty thousand feet of lumber; twenty-two of the finest merchantmen cars running on the railway from Philadelphia to Baltimore; nine thousand dollars' worth of stock in the Columbia Bridge; eighteen thousand dollars in stock in the Columbia bank; and besides this, Mr. Smith was the reputed owner of fifty-two good brick houses in the city of Philadelphia, besides several in Lancaster and Columbia. The principal active business attended to by Mr. S. is that of buying good negotiable paper and speculating in real estate. The business of the firm is attended to by Mr. Whipper. Take Smith and Whipper from Lancaster and Philadelphia counties, and the business community will experience a hiatus that may not be easily filled.

> Martin Delany, *The Condition, Elevation,*
> *Emigration and Destiny of the Colored People*
> *Of the United States* (Philadelphia, 1852)

But Smith and Whipper were exceptions, as the following letter attests:

Mr. Editor:

How differently would colored people be looked upon could our oppressors pass along the principal thoroughfares and read over the doorway of several first-class business houses the firm name of *Blackman & Co?* Or taking up the morning paper read the arrival of a ship consigned to *Negroman & Co?* Or a first-class factory in operation, the door of which read *Black, Son & Co?* If this were so, colored men generally would not be looked upon as a nation of steamboat waiters.

> J. R. Starkey
>
> *The Pacific Appeal*, August 23, 1862

3. Black Pioneers

As black families moved from the eastern seaboard, black settlements were organized in Ohio, Michigan and upstate New York. In a letter to Gerrit Smith, Dr. James McCune Smith reported on the Franklin County Pioneers, who were farming on land that Gerrit Smith had given them:

New York, July 7, 1848

Dear friend,

Last night two footsore and travel-worn Pioneers from Franklin came down to tell of their log houses and cleared acres, pine stumps—and want of a team! It did my soul good to shake their hard hands!

One of the Franklin Pioneers, William H. Smith, said, among other good things, that it is better to suffer two years in Franklin than forever in New York. On Friday last, at home, he said, "Wife! I am going to New York tomorrow. You had better write to some of your friends." She sat down and in a few minutes exclaimed that she did not know the day of the month. "How so?" said he. "Oh, because I am not forced to remember the *landlord's* call."

Willis Hodges is the other returned pioneer. He has purchased some 200 acres and has built a log house. Both complain much of the high charges made for carting luggage or draying logs and I am endeavoring to raise money to buy them a team. They return *home* next week.

James McCune Smith

Gerrit Smith Miller Collection, George Arents Research Library at Syracuse University

The Mercer County Settlement in western Ohio was successful for more than a decade but eventually broke up be-

cause of the hostility of neighboring whites. A letter to Frederick Douglass reported on its achievements:

New Bremer, Ohio, July 4, 1848

Friend Douglass:

The colored people here are giving the lie daily to the old dogma, "The niggers can't take care of themselves." When my father moved here about ten years ago, it was an almost unbroken forest for several miles around. We had to go about thirty miles for provisions, and then pay an uncommonly high price for them.

In 1839 there were only nine families residing here. The land cleared was not more than forty acres and most of this cleared by "squatters" who came to hunt, &c. We boast now of sixty or seventy families of as industrious and intelligent individuals as the surrounding country can afford. There are very few farms less than twenty acres and many twice this amount.

In point of intelligence and mental improvement, the colored people of Mercer County are far in advance of the surrounding whites. We have the best total abstinence society, and the best library of books in northwestern Ohio.

The Randolph excitement has not deterred us from our onward and upward path. The panting fugitive is always a welcome visitor here. God speed the day when life, liberty and the pursuit of happiness shall be extended to all mankind.

Yours for the redemption of the downtrodden and oppressed,

M. P. F. Jones

The North Star, August 11, 1848

"The Randolph excitement" illustrated the difficulties that black settlers faced. John Randolph, Congressman from Virginia, had freed his five hundred slaves at his death in 1833, leaving money for the purchase of land for them in Ohio.

After his executors bought the land, whites drove them away. One citizens' meeting resolved:

That we will not live among Negroes. We have fully determined that we will resist the settlement of blacks and mulattoes in this county to the full extent of our means, *the bayonet not excepted.*

That the blacks of this county be requested to leave on or before the first day of March, 1847; and in the case of their refusal to comply, we pledge ourselves *to remove them, peaceably if we can, forcibly if we must.*

That we pledge ourselves not to employ or trade with any black person, or permit them to have any grinding done at our mills, after the first day of January next.

African Repository, March 1847

Instead of receiving their legacy, "the Randolph people" were scattered through western Ohio. After meeting with some of them Martin Delany reported:

They have been greatly imposed upon by people in Ohio, in buying articles. For instance, in the purchase of a tub which cost but one dollar, the storekeeper received a five dollar note which he kept. Another lost ten dollars in like manner. Old horses and plows and other farming utensils, worn out and good for nothing, are frequently sold to them at high prices. Hence some of them have been known to say that they would rather be back in Virginia again.

The North Star, July 7, 1848

Ignorance and fear, deliberately fostered by their masters, were among the handicaps that ex-slaves faced as they settled in the North. Two black farmers, interviewed in Canada, recounted lies that slaveowners had told them:

I was told before I left Virginia, that the wild geese were so numerous in Canada and so bad, that they would scratch a man's eyes out; that corn wouldn't grow there, nor anything else but rice; that everything they had there was imported.

After we began to hear about Canada our master used to tell us all manner of stories about what a dreadful place it was. When they told us that we must pay half of our wages to the Queen, every day, it didn't seem strange nor wrong; but when they said it was so cold there that men going mowing had to break the ice with their scythes, I didn't believe that, because it was unreasonable. I knew grass wouldn't grow where ice was all the time.

Benjamin Drew, *The Refugee: A North-Side View of Slavery* (Boston, 1856)

By 1860, there were fifty thousand black pioneers in Canada, most of them in rural settlements in southern Ontario. One ex-slave recalled his first years there:

We marched right into the wilderness. At night we made a fire, and cut down a tree, and put up some slats like a wigwam. This was in February, when the snow was two feet deep. We made our bed of cedar boughs. Wolves, as plenty as sheep are now, were howling about us, and bears were numerous.

At last I came to a place where I judged, from the timber, the land was good—and so it proved. Myself and wife built us a little log hut amid the snow, shouldering the logs to bring up to the place. We went to the cedar swamp, and split out boards for the roof. We had plenty of firewood, which served instead of blankets. Wolves were howling about us constantly, night and day—big, savage wolves. We got used to them on our way here, and did not fear them. In the spring, bears came after sheep and hogs. One day my wife and I were walking, and we saw four bears in the cherry-trees eating the fruit. My wife went for my gun, and we killed all four.

I raised that year one hundred and ten bushels of spring wheat, and three hundred bushels of potatoes on land which we had cleared and cultivated without plow or drag.

In the next winter, we went to clearing again. My wife worked right along with me. I did not realize it then, for we were raised slaves, the women accustomed to work, but now I see that she was a brave woman.

It is so often said by slaveholders, that if the "niggers were free, they would starve." I wanted to show the contrary. I have one hundred and fifty acres of land, one hundred and ten of it cleared, and under good cultivation, two span of horses, a yoke of oxen, ten milch cows, twenty head of hogs, forty head of sheep. I have two wagons, two plows and two drags. I would like to show this to that everlasting scoundrel, my former master.

Benjamin Drew, *The Refugee: A North-Side View of Slavery*
(Boston, 1856)

As the frontier moved westward, black pioneers moved too. In 1860, when gold was discovered in the Cariboo mountains of British Columbia, more than four thousand black people were living in California. Many joined the rush to the Cariboo or traveled to Idaho Territory after gold was found there a year later. The Pacific Appeal *printed letters from the gold fields in almost every issue:*

Williams' Creek, Cariboo

Mr. Editor—

We packed our animals and started on foot, moving day after day through nature's solitary wilds. After a wearisome journey of 450 miles on foot, we reached the far-famed Cariboo, where I found many personal friends and acquaintances. There is a population of 3,000 persons, 100 of which are colored men. Everything is bustle and excitement. Many rich claims are being worked. One company of eight men took out in eight hours a hundred pounds of gold dust.

Provisions are high. Flour is $1.25 per pound; sugar, $1.50; bacon, $2; salt, $1.50 per pound; wages, $10 per day. It is a great field for the industrious, enterprising and lucky. Many of the colored miners have fine prospects. The climate is healthy. I trust it will be a blessing to many of our colored Californians.

J. J. Moore

The Pacific Appeal, July 11, 1863

Bannock City, Idaho Territory

Mr. Editor:

After ten days travel through one of the wildest and most unbroken of countries we arrived here safe. Over many of the mountains we crossed, one misstep would have landed us in eternity. A large portion of the country we traveled through is inhabited by the Snake Indians. At night we were compelled to stand watch. As there were but two of us it was

Gold miner in California   (*California State Library*)

hard, after twelve hours of rough riding. We armed ourselves well in case we should be attacked.

Buildings are going up in all directions in this place. Lots
are selling at from $500 to $2,500 cash. There is no question
as to the richness of these mines. I have seen surface diggings that paid $200 per day. $20 and $30 per day are com-
mon. The gold is coarse and is worth $16 per ounce.

Every man seems to have a pile. Provisions are not as high
as one might expect. Bacon is selling at 50 cts.; New Orleans
sugar 35 cts. per pound; washing white shirts $12 per dozen.
Laboring men get from $6 to $7 per day.

I have had the pleasure of seeing some old acquaintances
here. It requires a man to be of good resolution to make
money in this new country. Every man is for himself and
cares but little about his fellow.

T. Detter

The Pacific Appeal, August 1, 1863

Placerville, Idaho Territory

Mr. Editor:

I met with none of the difficulties of locomotion, nor was
I troubled by any of the wild savages that were a source of
so much terror to your Bannock City correspondent. The reports of the richness of the Boise diggings are but little exaggerated. They equal California in her palmier days. The
diggings are located in a sink or basin surrounded by a
chain of mountains. The population of the basin is about
6,000. We have a regular express and a good wagon road to
Salt Lake City which is distant only about 400 miles.

Our colored population are engaged in the "tonsorial"
[barbers]. Some are keeping restaurants, some are mining
and some are jewelers. We all anticipate good and prosperous times in the spring.

Samuel E. Cuney

The Pacific Appeal, January 9, 1864

4. Globetrotters

On whaling ships, coastwise trading vessels and in the Navy, a sizable proportion of the crews and some officers were black. While visiting the whaling port of New Bedford, Charles B. Ray reported to Samuel Cornish:

Dear Brother Cornish:

The people of color here are, perhaps, better off than in any other place, nearly all of them owning their own houses and lots, and many a number of houses and are quite rich.

The brig *Rising States,* owned and commanded by men of color has returned, having sprung her main mast. She has been unsuccessful as to obtaining oil, though they have caught every whale they saw with one exception, and who could have done better? They have been within 1 degree of the Equator and cruised in different longitudes, thus showing that colored men can skillfully navigate vessels over the trackless ocean.

C. B. Ray

The Colored American, July 29, 1837

Although Paul Cuffe, Jr., never achieved his father's eminence, he followed the sea for thirty years. Despite the comparative absence of prejudice aboard ship, Cuffe, Jr., chose to identify himself as an Indian—his mother's race—rather than as a black man when he wrote an account of his voyages. His description of one whaling trip:

About the 25th of June, 1829, I went to sea in the ship *Trident,* of 600 tons. There were sixty of the crew, principally experienced whalemen. We were bound to the Pacific Ocean for Whale. We doubled Cape Horn, and sailed northward off the coast, until we came to the island of Juan Fer-

Seaman's Protection Certificate
> (*Schomburg Collection, The New York Public Library,*
> *Astor, Lenox and Tilden Foundations*)

nandez, famous for being the abode of the celebrated Robinson Crusoe. While here we visited the cave where that noted adventurer is said to have resided. On this island are a great many goats; also peaches which grow wild in the woods.

From this place we sailed for Paita [Peru] where we arrived after more than six months sail from New Bedford. Here we took in potatoes and onions, refitted ship, and made ready for fishing. Then we sailed for the "off shore ground," a famous place for sperm whale. Here we stayed five months, and took but two hundred barrels sperm.

When this was done, we sailed for the Galapagos Islands for Terrapin. The Terrapin very much resembles our large Turtle, only they live wholly on land, and weigh from four to five hundred pounds. In the morning we used to go up into the island, among the bushes, where we usually found them feeding. After finding them two of us used to turn them over upon their backs, then tie their legs, and swing them between us, by lashing them to our backs. We then carry them to the boats, and from thence to the ship. We sometimes keep them alive six months without any food or drink. They make excellent soup, and are esteemed very healthy. They are worth, when brought to a sea-port city, from two hundred to three hundred dollars. We took six hundred of these animals in five days.

Narrative of the Life and Adventures of Paul Cuffe,
a Pequot Indian (Vernon, 1839)

Paul Cuffe's grandson was also a sailor. This letter to his mother came from the Cocos Islands, in the Indian Ocean south of Sumatra. John C. Ross, a Scottish captain, settled on the islands in 1827.

Cocos Islands, October 12, 1849

My dear mother:

You doubtless heard of my leaving the *Junius* here and of my intention to remain here. Now dear mother, I must give you some description of our island home. Fancy a group of islands 25 in number, low and sandy, covered with cocoanut and other trees and inhabited with 300 people, mostly Malays and governed by a fine old man Capt. J. C. Ross, and his son J. C. Ross (who by the by is one of the best of men in this world) and there you have our picture.

It has been so long since I left home I suppose you have almost forgotten how I look. I have grown taller and stronger and my hair curls in ringlets. I am also quite heavy, weighing 150 lbs. and not bad looking either. I will give you my reasons for stopping here. Firstly, because I was tired of the *Junius,* being twenty-one months at sea and taking only 275 barrels of sperm oil. Secondly, if I had remained much longer in that accursed barque I should have been ruined in both soul and body as I was fast verging toward dissipation. And dear Mother, be it some consolation to you to know that the good principles you sought to instill in my mind are remembered and acted by.

And now my third and last reason is because I am contented and that is more than I ever was before. Not that I had reason to be discontented at home, but I was too headstrong and willful. And besides I cannot return if I would as I am over head and ears in love with a beautiful Malay girl, and expect to be married in a short time. I will describe my betrothed. Jemela, for that is her name, is about sixteen years of age, rather taller than myself, well formed with dark piercing eyes and hair the color of the raven's wing, pearly teeth, light complexion and what is better than all, as good as she is lovely.

Dear Mother, do not blame me nor try to persuade me to return. Still I should like to hear from home very much as I have been away better than four years and not received a single line, although I have sent letters and my address. I intend to write every six months regularly and expect to receive the same from home.

Give my love to all inquiring friends and my sisters in particular, Jerusha, Joanna and Freelove. Tell sisters to take care of themselves and you, dear Mother.

I remain your affectionate son,

David Cuffe

P.S. Direct your letters to New Addams & Co., for the Cocos Islands, Batavia in Java.

P.S. Dear Madam. David wishes me to add a P.S. to his letter so that you may not think he is romancing you in this account of these isles. David is really a fine lad, clever, intelligent and above all not lazy, for laziness is the curse of most men.

But the greatest comfort to you I hope will be to know that he is soon to be my brother-in-law. Therefore I believe that I have a right according to the Cocos' fashion to call you mother—therefore, adieu dear mother for the present.

J. C. Ross

Paul Cuffe Papers, Free Public Library, New Bedford

A whaleman from Philadelphia wrote to his friend Jacob C. White, Jr.:

> Hilo, Hawaii
> March 26, 1858

My Dear Sir:

I just received your kind letter of 4th of June, 1857. I am happy to hear that the Colored Brethren are advancing in Literature and Science and hope they are able to show their white friends where the superiority lies.

I have just returned from a cruise off New Zealand. We took 600 barrels of oil making a total 1,600. I hope to be able to start for home next spring and once more see all my old friends. We are now bound to the Okhotsk Sea and Arctic Ocean. If you wish to write you may about the 6th of June and I will be able to get next fall.

> John F. Allan

> Jacob C. White Collection, Moorland-Spingarn Collection,
> Howard University Library

Another correspondent of White's, serving on a U. S. Navy vessel, described the workings of the Negro Seamen Act passed by South Carolina after Denmark Vesey's attempted rebellion in 1822:

> U. S. Steamer *Walker,* Pensacola, Florida
> January 8, 1858

Dear Sir:

I must first tell you of my adventures in Charleston. My duty on board this ship required that I should go on shore. The laws of South Carolina forbade my doing so. The day after I arrived I was ordered ashore and obeyed. When I was walking up King Street I was seized and arraigned before the mayor. Fortunately for me, a young gentleman, an acquaintance of Captain Huger (the Capt. of the *Walker*) saw the arrest and informed him immediately. The Captain rendered securities and I was released.

You, sir, have not perhaps been south of Mason and Dixon line, and judge slavery therefore by the testimony you receive. You must witness it in all its loathsomeness. On the 5th of December I was seated in the stern sheets of one of our boats going on shore. As I neared the wharf I saw a crowd of half-clad, filthy looking men, women and children go on board the Savannah steamer. Poor wretches. In all that vast number, 2 or 300, I did not notice one smile. All were moody, silent, sorrowful. I see in this gang both sexes and all ages from the suckling babe to the decrepit old, all bartered and sold to the rice swamp.

I walked up a large thoroughfare. The first thing that attracted my [attention] was a sign: "Negroes and Land for sale." I passed on a little farther and I see a large open room, over the door "Brokers' office." This means, a Negro Seller. Two or 3 half starved looking wretches were seated around. The very Earth seemed to tremble for the guilt of the oppressor.

A few days after my perambulation about the streets of Charleston I met a young man with whom I had become acquainted in Philadelphia. I invited him to take a cigar with me. He informed me that it was against the law for a colored man to smoke a cigar or walk with a cane in the streets of Charleston. And if the streets (sidewalk) are crowded the Negro must take the middle of the street. I met several white women. They did not move an inch—so I had always to give way to them. If I had run against one of them, they would have had me flogged.

One can witness here what education can effect. The blacks here invariably believe that white men are superior not merely mentally but physically. I had occasion to have some clothes washed and called on an old [slave] woman for that purpose. Several little white children were running about the house, and she called them "Master" or "Mistress." I could not stand this and reprimanded her. She was perfectly astonished, commenced an argument with me to prove that those children were entitled to this distinction. She told me I must not talk this way—some of the people might overhear me and tell master.

G. E. Stevens

Jacob C. White Collection, Moorland-Spingarn Collection, Howard University Library

Black Americans went to sea not only as crewmen but as passengers bound for Europe, to lecture, study and raise money for antislavery causes. Henry Highland Garnet's letter to his wife describes one such voyage:

Liverpool, September 13, 1861

My Dearest Wife:

We arrived in Liverpool yesterday evening. Twelve years ago my treatment on board of an English steamer was very different from that which I have just received. Then I was caged up in the steward's room and not allowed to go into the saloon, or to eat at the table with white humanity.

How changed now. An elegant stateroom with six berths was placed at my disposal and my seat at the table was between two young American gentlemen, educated in Maryland and on their way to Rome. I am happy to say that I did not receive a look or hear a word during the whole voyage that grated upon my very sensitive feelings.

As usual, I was seasick. When I went on board I *resolved* not to be sick, but as soon as we cleared Sandy Hook old Neptune called me to the side of the ship and told me to *throw my resolutions overboard*, which I did in double-quick time.

On the Sabbath after worship we were all gratified to see two whales. They were none of your juveniles or babies but were respectable "old folks" and like most other folks of their color they made a considerable stir. A lady exclaimed as her little under jaw dropped down about an inch, "Oh! why do they make such a noise and commotion? They are the biggest fishes in the sea—and they are black." I said, "Madam, you have accounted for the noise they make."

Henry Highland Garnet

Douglass' Monthly, November 1861

5. Gift of Story and Song

In The Souls of Black Folk *W. E. B. Du Bois wrote of the "gift of story and song . . . the greatest gift of the Negro people" to white America. However, the spirituals and folk songs composed by slaves were not "discovered" in the North until after the Civil War. Blacks knew them, of course. Frederick Douglass sometimes filled in a dull moment at a meeting with a plantation melody. Harriet Tubman sang "Let My People Go" and "Swing Low Sweet Chariot" to Northern friends and Martin Delany included slave songs in his novel, Blake. But most Northerners heard these songs only in the minstrel shows, sung as oddities by whites who performed in black face. As an answer to these caricatures, free black musicians played traditional European-American music. "What induced me more than anything else to appear in public was to give the lie to Negro serenaders [minstrels] and to show the world that colored men and women could sing classical music" one musician explained.*

Probably the first review of the work of black American musicians appeared in Freedom's Journal *in 1827:*

On Friday evening a very respectable audience was assembled in St. Philips Church to attend a Concert of Sacred Music. The singers were the pupils of Mr. Robinson, a teacher of music in this city, who also presided at the organ. The Orchestra was under the direction of Mr. F. Johnson. The ignorant and prejudiced may laugh at the idea of a Concert of Sacred Music being got up by Africans. We know that their laugh is the laugh of fools. The performances of the evening were certainly far from ordinary. The Choruses were well sung and the Duet "O Lovely Peace" was given in fine style. I was much pleased with the young man who sang the solo of "My Song Shall Be." But what shall I say of

The Philadelphia Library Company beg leave to inform their Friends and the Public generally, that by the request of a number of Ladies and Gentlemen who were highly delighted at their late Concert, they will again repeat the same, with the addition of several brilliant and Scientific Pieces, on TUESDAY EVENING, March 30th, 1841; at *St. Thomas's Church*, where they will be happy to greet all the lovers of Music, and those who feel interested in the cultivation and extension of that beautiful and sublime Science.

The proceeds to be appropriated towards extending the Library of said company.

Francis Johnson, leader of the Orchestra.

PART 1st.

1	Overture, the L'Ambassadrice,	Auber
2	Solo, in native worth, M. Brown, Jr.	Haydn.
3	Grand Trio, the Lord my pasture, Mrs. Augustus, Miss M. L. Kenton, and A. J. R. Conner,	A. J. R. Conner.
4	Solo, No more shall the Children of Judah sing, Miss Porter.	
5	Solo, Ruth and Naomi, Mrs. Augustus,	
6	Solo, Go let me weep, Mr. Richards.	
7	Duett, Evening Song to the Virgin, Piano Accompaniments, Mrs. Augustus, and Miss Kenton,	
8	Solo, There's rest for thee in Heaven, A. J. R. Conner,	Bishop,
9	Solo, Most beautiful appear, Miss Porter,	
10	Duett, Arrayed in Clouds, Mrs. Augustus, and T. J. Bowers,	Shaw.

PART 2nd.

1	Overture by the Brass Band,	Mehul,
2	Solo, On mighty wings, Miss Kenton,	Haydn.
3	Grand Fantasia Flute, and Piano J. L. Gordon,	
4	Solo, Lord I believe, A. J. R. Conner,	Barnes,
5	Quintette, Blessed is he that cometh, Mrs. Augustus, Miss Kenton, Messrs Conner, Brown, and Bowers,	
6	The last Rose of Summer,—Brass Band,	
7	Angels ever bright and fair, T. J. Bowers,	
8	Solo, Virgin Goddess, Mrs. Augustus,	
9	Solo, Daughters of Israel, Piano Accompaniments, by T. J. Bowers,	
10	Solo, Sleeping Virgin, Miss Kenton,	Balfe,
11	Grand Trio, Violin, Flute, and Guitar, Messrs Johnson, Anderson, and Gordon,	
12	Finale, Grand Solo, and Chorus Multitude of Angels,	M. P. King.

Previous to the commencement of the Performance, Mr. Robert Douglass, Jr. will, through the earnest solicitation of the Committee, deliver an original Poetical Address, written expressly for the occasion.

In submitting the above Programme, the Committee flatter themselves that their exertions will be duly appreciated; and their anticipations crowned with Success, by receiving the patronage of a generous and benevolent Public.

Tickets of Admittance 25cts, to be had of John Lewis, No. 19, Carpenter Street, John C. Bowers, 71, S. 2nd Street, James M. White, 3rd Street, below Walnut, George A. Collins, 100, N. 4th Street, and at the door on the Evening, of Performance.

Ernest Crozet, Cheap Printer, No. 151, S. Sixth Street, 4 Doors below Pine, Philadelphia.

Handbill for a concert

the young lady who sung "Jubal's Lyre?" No words of mine can add to her merit. It was a charming performance.

Freedom's Journal, October 12, 1827

Frank Johnson, director of the orchestra on that occasion, was a band leader, teacher and composer. William J. Brown described his visit to Providence in the 1820s:

We learned that a [white] military company from Philadelphia were going to pay a visit to our city, accompanied by a colored band, led by Frank Johnson. We were very glad to learn this as we had never seen or heard a full band play. We had a band playing field music—a bugle played by a man named Hamilton—two clarinets, two trombones, one French horn, two fifes, one bass drum and two kettle drums —eleven pieces in all.

The day arrived and the company made their appearance, bringing with them Frank Johnson's band of twenty-six pieces. The company was received by the Rhode Island Infantry at the steamboat wharf. They marched up South Main Street, led by Hamilton's band. Near Market Square Johnson's band opened with music such as never before graced the city of Providence.

Reaching the City Hotel they dismissed and went in to refresh themselves. Some of the gentlemen told Hamilton that he could not begin to play with the colored band's leader. He replied that Johnson's bugle was much better than his. The gentleman wished them to change with each other, which they did. Johnson took his bugle and beat him. This made him so angry that he struck Johnson and threw his bugle on the floor. Johnson immediately knocked him down. The people put a stop to the affray, condemning Hamilton and commending Johnson.

The Life of William J. Brown (Providence, 1883)

Advertisement for a juvenile concert

Martin Delany reported on Johnson's later career:

Captain Frank Johnson of Philadelphia was a master of his profession. In 1838, Johnson went to England with his noble band of musicians where he played to Her Majesty Queen Victoria and His Royal Highness Prince Albert, Captain Johnson receiving a handsome French bugle by order of her Majesty. Returning, he held throughout the Eastern, Northern, and Western States, grand concerts known as "Soirees Musicales." He was a great composer and teacher of music and some of the finest Marches and Cotillions now extant have been composed by Frank Johnson. Captain Johnson died in Philadelphia in 1844.

Andrew J. Conner, one of the members of Captain Johnson's band, also became a distinguished composer and teacher of music. Mr. Conner taught the piano forte in the best families in the city of Philadelphia—among merchants, bankers and professional men. He contributed to the popular literary magazines and many who have read *Music Com-*

posed by A. J. Conner, did not for a moment think that the author was a colored gentleman. Mr. Conner died in Philadelphia in 1850.

> Martin R. Delany, *The Condition, Elevation and Destiny of the Colored People* (Philadelphia, 1852)

Elizabeth Greenfield, who was known as "the Black Swan," also sang before Queen Victoria. Born a slave but educated in the North, she first became fully aware of her talent when she attended a concert given by Jenny Lind, "the Swedish Nightingale." According to Martin Delany:

She went home. She stole an opportunity when no one listened; let out her voice, when [behold!] she found her strains *four* notes *above* Sweden's favored Nightingale. She descended, when lo! she found her tones *three* notes *below!* Now she ranks second to no vocalist in the world. The Black Swan is singing to fine fashionable houses and bids fair to stand unrivalled in the world of song.

> Martin R. Delany, *The Condition, Elevation and Destiny of the Colored People* (Philadelphia, 1852)

A year after Delany's enthusiastic comment Miss Greenfield, under the direction of a white manager, gave concerts in halls which barred black listeners. Wrote Frederick Douglass, "She should be called no longer the Black Swan but the White Raven."

From the days of Newport Gardner, every northern city had black music teachers. Robert Hamilton, co-publisher of The Weekly Anglo-African, *advertised:*

ROBERT HAMILTON, VOCALIST AND CHORISTER of Zion Church respectfully announces to the public that he is prepared to give instructions, day or evening, to such scholars, singing societies, clubs or individuals, as may desire a knowledge of the most beautiful

SCIENCE OF MUSIC

He also offers his services to churches or individuals, to sing at, or conduct for a moderate compensation, the vocal department of concerts or exhibitions, or to act as agent for persons desiring to give concerts.

TERMS, MODERATE

The Weekly Anglo-African, April 21, 1860

The first African Theater opened in New York in the 1820s. Dr. James McCune Smith described its beginnings:

In 1816–17, Mr. Brown, steward of a Liverpool liner, gave up following the sea, hired a house on the north side of

Elizabeth T. Greenfield, "the Black Swan"
(*Moorland-Spingarn Collection, Howard University Library*)

Thomas Street and fitted up a tea garden. In the evening he made the garden attractive by vocal and instrumental music. His brother stewards and their wives and the colored population generally gave him a full share of patronage. Among his *artistes* were Miss Ann Johnson, the mother of an excellent *cantatrice* of the present time, and James Hewlett. These evening entertainments were not dry affairs. Brandy and gin toddies, wine, porter and strong ale, with cakes and meats, enabled the audience to gratify several senses and appetites at the same time.

James Hewlett was quite a character. A very fine singer, he added dramatic exhibitions to the entertainments. His off nights were invariably spent in the gallery of the old Park Theatre, and spent not in vain, for he soon became celebrated for the talent and versatility which enabled him to perform several widely different characters at one exhibition. He followed the fashionable world to Saratoga. When rival singers would scatter their announcements through the hotels there would appear, tastily printed on white satin:

JAMES HEWLETT
Vocalist and Shakespeare's Proud Representative
Will Give an Entertainment
In Singing and Acting
In the large room of the United States Hotel

So great was Mr. Brown's success with his tea garden that in four or five years he built a theater in Mercer Street. The edifice was of wood, roughly built, having capacity for an audience of three or four hundred. The enterprise was quite successful, the audience being composed largely of laughter-loving young clerks, who came to see the sport, but invariably paid their quarter for admission.

The Weekly Anglo-African, October 5, 1861

The white spectators who came to laugh at blacks who dared to play Shakespeare became so riotous that the police closed down the theater. Before its closing, Ira Aldridge, a youngster attending the African Free School, made his first stage appearance there. Because opportunities for black actors were limited, Aldridge went to England in 1824 and never returned to the United States. In Europe, he became one of the great Shakespearean actors of his time. Writing to a French theater manager, Aldridge listed some of his triumphs:

James Hewlett as Richard III, 1821
    (*Raymond Mander and Joe Mitchenson Theatre Collection*)

Ira Aldridge in white face, as King Lear
(*Bakrushin State Central Theatrical Museum, Moscow*)

August 24, 1854

Sir,

For three years I have toured the principal cities of Germany, Austria, Hungary, where my representations have been crowned with the greatest success. It is unheard of that a person of African nationality should play dramatic roles. The success I have had in the greatest theaters of Germany, has increased my desire to make an attempt in the French capital.

His Majesty, the King of Prussia, has condescended to honor me with the Large Gold Medal for Art and Sciences, the Emperor of Austria with the Medal of Ferdinand, and Switzerland with the White Cross.

My intention is to come to France with a troupe of English players to give the following: *Othello, Macbeth, King Lear, Richard III, The Merchant of Venice.* I ask for a guarantee to cover the expenses I will have to bring my troupe to Paris. For each performance I ask for half the net receipts or a fixed salary. Waiting for the favor of your prompt reply,

Ira Aldridge, *African Tragedian*

Herbert Marshall and Mildred Stock, *Ira Aldridge, The Negro Tragedian* (Carbondale, 1958)

Ira Aldridge (around 1865)
(*Mildred Stock*)

Amateur theater groups played in many cities, but it was not until the 1860s that advertisements of black performers appeared regularly in the newspapers. SAM PRIDE'S ORIGINAL COLORED MINSTRELS, probably the first black minstrel show, was praised and then criticized in San Francisco:

We have witnessed the performance of this troupe and can speak favorably of their ability. Their performances are amusing and highly ludicrous—exaggerated of course; all such burlesque must necessarily be, whether of Yankee, Irish or Negro character, but all who like to enjoy a good hearty laugh should go and see them. There is nothing in offense or indelicate in their performance.

Mr. Sam Pride is truly the Champion Banjoist of the world. He produces sounds from his Banjo which we never thought an instrument so crude was capable of expressing. He imitates an entire Band, in fact he almost makes the Banjo play itself. His performances are inimitable.

The Pacific Appeal, April 19, 1862

Mr. Editor:

Those Jim Crow Exhibitions with their burlesque caricature of the Southern plantation slave were gotten up by pernicious men, at the expense of an oppressed, long-outraged and downtrodden people. These pernicious exhibitions exert a powerful influence on the communities where they are tolerated.

Heretofore the work of burlesquing and caricaturing [was] performed by men with white bodies and blackened faces. But recently, to our astonishment and disgust, we learn that men, naturally black, have been induced through ignorance, lack of principle or sheer cupidity, to represent their own degradation and that of their unfortunate race.

J.M.B.

The Pacific Appeal, May 24, 1862

Other showmen included "John E. Smith, the Colored Trainer with his celebrated Trick Pony" and a black magician who promised:

A GREAT GALA NIGHT OF MAGIC
PROF. KELLIES

The unrivalled and only Anglo-African Magician in the World begs most respectfully to announce a *Grand Drawing Room Entertainment* of Astonishing Transformation and Illusions (as presented before QUEEN VICTORIA and the Court at Balmoral Castle, Scotland)

On Monday Evening, April 28th, at the Metropolitan Assembly Rooms

The Extraordinary, Inexplicable MYSTIC, MAGIC PROGRAMME will contain a variety of incredible Feats among which will be The Magic Egg Bag, Enchanted Goblet, Wonderful Bottle Delusion, The Goblet of Fortune Telling. These feats will appear incredible to the senses, impossible to the eye, and improbable to the imagination. Admission 15 cents

The Weekly Anglo-African, April 26, 1862

In 1855, Frederick Douglass said, "The present will be looked to as the age of antislavery literature—when a picture of a Negro on the cover was a help to the sale of a book." Belonging to a people largely denied formal education, a surprising number of black men and women contributed to this literature. Several hundred narratives by ex-slaves sold widely in the United States and abroad. Poets like Frances E. W. Harper, James M. Whitfield, James Madison Bell and George M. Horton published their works and William C. Nell, Martin R. Delany and William Wells Brown tried their hands at history, biography and fiction. Of the latter group, Brown was the most accomplished writer. He was surprised, therefore, when black critics found fault with The Black Man, *a collection of biographies of black notables that he had written. Brown's free-swinging reply to his critics:*

Sir:

No colored man's talents have ever been rewarded by his own class. The narratives of a few escaped slaves have sold rapidly, but principally among the whites. No work written by a colored person in favor of freedom and elevation of his race has ever received their support. Dr. Delany's book stopped with one edition. Mr. Nell's work (*The Colored Patriots of the American Revolution*) has not reached a second edition. In point of numbers, our newspapers have been legion, yet nearly all have died of the same disease, starvation. The *N. Y. Herald* has more subscribers today and gets a larger support from the colored people than *Douglass' Monthly*, *The Anglo-African* and *The Pacific Appeal* put together.

If a colored man publishes a book, every scribbler supposes himself a critic and commences an attack. A friend in Philadelphia says, "the greatest opposition [to *The Black Man*] comes from those who are left out." Not long after the work was published, I met an old friend whom I had not seen for many months. We shook hands and I remarked that I had just been thinking of him. He gave a long sigh and an unearthly groan and said, "You say you were just thinking of me?" "Yes," I replied. "Ah," said he, "You were thinking of me just now, but you could not think of me when you were writing your book." "But," said I, "the book was so small that I could not put in all that I wished." "Yes," replied he, "but you might have left some of the others out, and put me in."

William Wells Brown

The Anglo-African, August 8, 1863

Brown's charge that blacks did not support their writers was unfair. The majority of free blacks were too poor to buy books and too undereducated to be habitual readers. No one knew this better than the editors of black newspapers.

More than two dozen black weeklies were published in the

years before the Civil War. Some lasted only a few months. Others, like The Colored American *and* The Weekly Anglo-African, *survived more than five years.* The North Star, *which became* Frederick Douglass' Paper *and then* Douglass' Monthly, *was issued for almost sixteen years. The editors all had the same goal. "We must plead our own cause," the first issue of* Freedom's Journal *declared. "We alone are the oppressed. We alone must strike the first blow,"* The Weekly Advocate *said ten years later. "Colored men must . . . speak out in THUNDER TONES until the nation repent," wrote the editors of* The Colored American.

In spite of their small readership, the newspapers were an organizing force in the black communities, and a forum for influencing white public opinion. But their editors had to be lecturers, fund raisers, and bill collectors as well as writers. In one of many appeals, Samuel E. Cornish wrote of "The Editor's Difficulties":

If our brethren would see *The Colored American* what it ought to be, they must assist in raising a small salary for the Editor. We have given our services, the last year, for less than one hundred dollars remuneration. The Editor, to do justice to himself, to the subject of human rights, and to the talent of colored men, ought to have some time to read and think. This has not been the case with us. We have had to worry to get our bread and likewise to keep [the paper] in existence.

The Colored American, *December 12, 1837*

When Cornish gave up the editorship after two years, Charles B. Ray toured the Midwest to obtain subscriptions while Philip A. Bell held down the editorial chair in New York:

Dear Ray:
When our last number was ready for the press and I told our workmen I would have no occasion for their services the

following week as we would issue no paper, I folded my hands in utter despondency. Our expenses on the last three numbers were more than $130 over the receipts. I went to the Post Office and, behold, your letter and the draft for $110 from Cincinnati, just in the nick of time. The receipt of news from you, especially such news, buoyed me up.

Since that time our old friend Mason is again in the field. I received a letter from him with a $10 bill showing its pretty face as I opened the missive. Your letter from Circleville and from Columbus, $20 more, put me in good spirits. I re-engaged the workmen, ordered paper, bought a new steel pen, and again *The Colored American* is in the field.

Philip A. Bell

The Colored American, September 28, 1838

Black editors were disappointed by the limited financial support they received from whites. Antislavery men who had a hard time keeping The Liberator *and* The National Anti-Slavery Standard *going discouraged rival papers which might divert energies and readers. Perhaps they also felt that they could do a better job of speaking for blacks than the blacks themselves could do. Certainly this is the way blacks interpreted their attitude.*

When Benjamin F. Roberts, a printer, tried to start a paper in Boston, the Reverend Amos A. Phelps wrote a letter of recommendation for him. A short time later, Phelps asked for the return of the letter. Roberts replied:

Boston, June 17, 1838

Rev. A. A. Phelps—
Dear Sir: I was surprised to learn that you felt dissatisfied with the recommendation you furnished. I return it as requested. But I am aware there has been and *now is,* a combined effort on the part of certain professed abolitionists to muzzle, exterminate and put down the efforts of colored individuals.

I am for *improvement* among this class of people, *mental* and *physical*. If antislavery men will not subscribe to the advancement of these principles but *rail out against* them when took up by those who have a darker skin, why we will go to the *heathen*. It is of no use to say "We are friends of the slave" and not try to encourage and assist the free colored people in raising themselves.

Here is sir! the *first* effort of the colored man of the kind, viz, the paper, *published, printed* and *edited* by colored persons in Massachusetts. Shall this be defeated? But it is contended the individual who started the enterprise has not taken it up from principle. Base misrepresentations, false accusations! I was not aware that so many hypocrites existed in the Anti-Slavery Society.

                                                     B. F. Roberts

                    Antislavery Collection, Boston Public Library

While Frederick Douglass was in England in 1846–47, British admirers gave him $2,175 with which to start a newspaper. On his return to the States he was astonished at the attitude of his white friends, especially William Lloyd Garrison and Wendell Phillips:

I found them earnestly opposed to the idea of my starting a newspaper. First, the paper was not needed; secondly it would interfere with my usefulness as a lecturer; thirdly, I was better fitted to speak than to write; fourthly, the paper could not succeed. This opposition, from a quarter so highly esteemed, and to which I had been accustomed to look for advice and direction, inclined me to abandon the enterprise. I was but nine years from slavery. A slave brought up in the depths of ignorance, assuming to instruct the civilized people of the North in the principles of liberty, justice and humanity!

Nevertheless I persevered. The most distressing thing was the offense which I was about to give my friends by what seemed a reckless disregard of their advice. I labored hard to convince them of the wisdom of my undertaking but without success. From motives of peace, instead of issuing my paper in Boston I came to Rochester, Western New York, where the circulation of my paper could not interfere with the local circulation of *The Liberator* for at that time I was a faithful disciple of William Lloyd Garrison.

Frederick Douglass, *My Bondage and My Freedom*
(Auburn, 1855)

After his escape from slavery, Douglass had spent most of his time in the company of white abolitionists. In his new role as a spokesman for blacks rather than for the American Anti-Slavery Society, his point of view changed rapidly. Dr. James McCune Smith commented on this in a letter to Gerrit Smith who later gave financial help to Douglass' newspaper:

New York, July 28, 1848

Gerrit Smith, Esq.
Dear friend,
    In the matter of a newspaper, I love Frederick Douglass for his whole-souled *outness*. That is the secret of his noble thoughts and far-reaching sympathies. You will be surprised to hear me say that only since his editorial career has he begun to become a *colored man!* I have read his paper very carefully and find phase after phase develop as regularly as in one newly-born among us. The church question, the school question, separate institutions, are questions that he enters upon and argues about as our weary but active young men thought about and argued about years ago, when we had literary societies.
    I earnestly wish that *The North Star* would come down to this city. Here it could do the kind of work alluded to by me as needing a newspaper to accomplish. I have taken up my pen half a dozen times to say as much to F. Douglass; but

there is so little pecuniary support to be relied on that I have shrunk from making the request.

James McCune Smith

Gerrit Smith Miller Collection, George Arents Research Library at Syracuse University

V · IT WAS NATION TIME (1850–60)

We are four-and-a-half millions in number, free and bond. We are a nation within a nation—as the Poles in Russia, the Hungarians in Austria, the Welsh, Irish and Scotch in the British dominions. The claims of no people are respected until they are presented in a national capacity. We must MAKE an ISSUE, CREATE an EVENT, and ESTABLISH A NATIONAL POSITION for OURSELVES.

Martin R. Delany

1. Black Is a Very Pretty Color

The ten years before the Civil War was a disheartening period for black Americans. Congress passed a new Fugitive Slave Law which threatened the freedom of every black in the North and put the federal government squarely in the business of catching slaves. Then came the Dred Scott decision. Speaking for the Supreme Court, Chief Justice Roger Taney said that blacks were not and could never become citizens of the United States and that they "had no rights which a white man was bound to respect."

In response, black people joined together as never before, finding a new pride in themselves and a new feeling of brotherhood. The old Namestakes debate was over. At a convention in 1854 the delegates resolved that:

No people can ever attain to greatness who lose their identity.

We shall ever cherish our identity of origin and race, as preferable, in our estimation, to any other people.

The terms Negro, African, Black, Colored and Mulatto shall ever be held with the same respect and pride with the terms Caucasian, White, Anglo-Saxon and European.

> "Proceedings of the National Emigration Convention"
> (Pittsburgh, 1854)

For years, blacks had been pained by assertions of their inferiority expressed not only by slaveowners but by such liberal thinkers as Thomas Jefferson and Alexis de Tocqueville. In his Democracy in America, *still studied in universities, de Tocqueville had written:*

You may set the Negro free but you cannot make him otherwise than an alien to the European. His physiognomy is to our eyes, hideous, his understanding weak, his tastes low; and we are inclined to look upon him as a being intermediate between man and the brutes.

A series of articles in The Colored American *had attempted to reply to de Tocqueville. One tentatively tackled the question of appearance:*

Preference of color is a matter of taste. Certain it is that there are handsome and ugly persons of every color. If it be allowed that the white has the advantage in youth, it cannot be denied that the black has the advantage in age, as it preserves longer a fresh and wholesome appearance and gives a beauty and dignity to gray hairs. Partial as are the whites to their own complexion, how often do we see them preferring to have statues of their great men sculptured in black marble. They have a grace and grandeur in them which cannot be given to statues wholly white. I make these remarks merely to show that much can be said in favor of the black complexion as well as the white.

The   Colored American, August 19, 1837

By the 1850s, John S. Rock, Massachusetts lawyer and doctor, had a more positive comment to make:

The prejudice which some white men have against my color gives me no pain. If any man does not fancy my color, that is his business. I shall give myself no trouble because he lacks good taste. I admire the talents and noble characters of many white men. But I cannot say that I am particularly pleased with their appearance. When I contrast the fine tough muscular system, the beautiful rich color, the full broad features and the gracefully frizzled hair of the Negro with the delicate physical organization, wan color, sharp features and lank hair of the Caucasian, I am inclined to believe that when the white man was created, nature was pretty well exhausted. She pinched up his features and did the best she could under the circumstances.

In this country, where money is the great sympathetic nerve which ramifies society, and has a ganglia in every man's pocket, a man is respected in proportion to his success. When the avenues to wealth are opened to us, we will then become educated and wealthy, and then the roughest looking colored man will be pleasanter than the harmonies of Orpheus and black will be a very pretty color.

The Liberator, March 12, 1858

At the same time, black commentators more and more often asserted the moral and ethical superiority of their own race. "If you would find real depth of soul, seek a black man," said George T. Downing. In agreement, James McCune Smith wrote:

The pursuit of wealth calls for thrift, punctuality, enterprise and the persistent exercise of energy; all of them characteristics—*drill*—which we greatly need. In the great bulk of the American people, gold is the low goal which incites these habits of mind. This gold pursuit builds houses, nets the land with railroads, tills the soil. [But] it is only a step toward a freer, hopefuller, happier time.

Whilst therefore we need the *drill* which wealth pursuit gives the whites, we must obtain it at less expense of moral excellence. We are here to prove the human to be *one brotherhood*. To stand our ground requires thrift, punctuality, enterprise and persistent energy, such as the pursuit of wealth never stirred up in the human soul.

The North Star, February 26, 1852

The sharpest comment on white morality was a long essay titled, "What Shall We Do With the White People?" Written under the pen name of Ethiop, its author was William J. Wilson, one of the editors of The Anglo-African Magazine. *Selections illustrate Wilson's points:*

They [white people] came to this country in small numbers and began upon a course of wrong-doing. The Aborigines were the first victims. They robbed them of their lands, plundered their wigwams, burned their villages and murdered their wives and children. Thus they advanced, until now they have almost the entire possession of the continent.

One would naturally conclude that with such a condition of things this people would be content. Not so. Restless, grasping, unsatiated, they are ever on the lookout for what they can get. Twice they have quarreled with the mother who gave them origin and once have most unmercifully beaten their weaker and more pacific neighbor [Mexico] and despoiled him of a large portion of his lands.

If we go back to an earlier page in their history, we find them stealing what? Why, men, women and children from abroad and consigning them to a perpetual bondage. The internal slave trade is, today, more actively carried on than was ever the foreign trade and with great pecuniary advantages, which with them is sufficient justification of the business.

Let us turn our attention to another page of their history. Prior to their broil with the English, they framed a form of government which promised well: "We hold these truths to be self-evident, that all men are created free and equal; and endowed with certain unalienable rights; among which are life, liberty and the pursuit of happiness." Scarcely three-fourths of a century has passed since the basis of government was laid, and we find their leaders earnestly engaged in pulling out the foundation stones and anathematizing them as "glittering generalities," gross blunders &c.

What then shall we do with these white people? Plans for removal would be wrong. It is their right to stay. Only they have no right to jeopard the interests or the peace of the country. God has reserved this fair land for higher and nobler purposes than a theater for the exhibition of prejudices, bitter hates, fierce strifes, dissensions, oppressions, frauds.

We find room enough for us in this country. They find its boundaries too circumscribed for their greedy grasp. Possessing acres by the millions, yet they would elbow us off what we possess, to give them room for what they cannot occupy. We want this country, say they, for ourselves alone.

Seriously do we hope that if the peace of the country is to be so continuously disturbed that they would withdraw. They could easily be spared. We give them credit for their material progress. Who knows but that some day, they will make way for a milder and more genial race, or become so blended in it as to lose their own objectionable characteristics? In view of the existing state of things, let our constant thought be, *what for the best good of all shall we do with the white people?*

The Anglo-African Magazine, February 1860

A black man described a contest of wits, in which he bested his opponent:

Mr. Editor:

My main reason [for writing] is to give you an account of a short journey on the Columbia River in the little steamer *Cowlitz*. Soon after we left the wharf, I went into the cabin to read the morning paper. There were a number of gentlemen engaged in conversation. Mr. P., an ex-member of the legislature of Washington Territory, declared that Negroes were ignorant and that God had created them inferior and designed them to be subservient to whites. I slowly folded my paper and asked permission to answer Mr. P.

I commenced by asking his honor if I was not one of the class he referred to? After stammering a while he said, "Yes, I guess so." "Well sir," said I, "I think I will be able to prove that we are not quite so ignorant as you suppose."

Said Mr. P, "Well, you may be an exception. Where do you belong?" "I was born in New Bedford, Massachusetts." Mr. P. then said, "Well, I believe the Negroes there have a better understanding of things than in most places."

The passengers: "Why don't you try him? Perhaps he's only blowing."

"I never mingled with his kind," said Mr. P.

Passengers: "Give him a show." One of the gents got pen, ink and paper and he reluctantly sat down with me to write. After we had each written a given sentence, they were submitted to the passengers for their judgment. The captain and passengers awarded the ignorant Negro the prize.

Mr. P. then suggested the definition of words. To this I agreed. One of the judges gave the word "eleemosynary" to spell and define. Mr. P. could not spell it or define it. Amid cheers and laughter, I proudly bore away the prize. I hope I have convinced Mr. P. that all of the colored race are not so low as he chose to put them.

Tonsor

The Pacific Appeal, October 3, 1863

2. School Days

Schools for black children were still a major issue. In the West, the battle for any kind of school at all was just beginning. The Reverend Jeremiah B. Sanderson noted in his diary, in 1854:

Sacramento, California, April 20. Today I opened a school for colored children. The necessity for this step is evident. There are thirty or more colored children in Sacramento of proper age to attend school and no school provided for them by the board of education. They must no longer be left to grow up in ignorance, with the danger of contracting idle and vicious habits. A school they must have. I am induced to undertake the enterprise by the solicitation of parents. I can do little but with God's blessing I will do what I can.

The following year, he wrote to the Board of Education:

July 10, 1855

Gentlemen:

Allow me to call your attention to the subject of the school for colored children in Sacramento. This school has been operated now about thirteen months. At the time it was commenced no provision whatsoever had been made by the city authorities for the education of colored children.

The school census marshall, though not authorized to include colored, ascertained that there were over eighty colored children in Sacramento. The school kept by the undersigned has numbered 30 pupils during the past two months. The number of children is increasing; the necessity for a permanent public school grows more imperative.

Gentlemen, the parents of the colored children appeal to you. They respectfully and earnestly ask your attention to the school for their children, that they may become upright and worthy men and women.

J. B. Sanderson

Delilah L. Beasley, *The Negro Trail Blazers of California*
(Los Angeles, 1919)

Sacramento's Board of Education opened a school for black children in 1856. San Francisco also had a Public School for Colored Children, but parents filed repeated complaints about its condition to the Board of Education:

There are about fifty pupils in attendance. The room in which they are taught is unsuitable. It is a basement below the grade of the street. It is badly ventilated—the air is foul and unhealthful.

The hall above the schoolroom is occupied by a military company. The loud sounds arising from their exercises greatly disturb the schoolroom. The plastering is broken and falling from the ceiling so that water from above runs upon the desks and floor of the schoolroom below.

The yard appropriated as a playground and for the necessities of the girls has only an area of about 12 by 20 feet. The boys are compelled to go into the street, exposed to dangers from passing horses and vehicles. All [are] continually tempted by the excitements to overstay the half hour of recess or play truant.

There are now upwards of three hundred colored children in this city. To accommodate them we need another, better and larger place. We need a school of a higher grade. We need additional teachers. We feel the same anxiety touching the future of our children that you feel for yours.

Eleven signatures

The Pacific Appeal, September 27, 1862

Some small communities in the East permitted black children to attend the "white" schools but segregated them in the classroom. B. F. Grant recalled his school days in York County, Pennsylvania:

I will mention only a few things which the little Negro had to endure, simply because he was a Negro. He was not permitted to drink from the same bucket or cup as the white children. He was compelled to sit back in the corner from the fire no matter how cold the weather might be. There he must wait until the white children had recited. If the cold became *too* intense to endure, he must ask permission of the teacher, stand by the fire a few minutes to warm and then return to the same cold corner. I have sat in an old log schoolhouse with no chinking between the logs until my heels were frostbitten and cracked open. Sometimes we had a poor white trashy skunk [of a teacher] that would sit in the schoolroom and call us "niggers" or "darkeys." If the little Negro got his lesson at all, he got it; if not, it was all the same.

"Some Undistinguished Negroes," *Journal of Negro History,*
January 1919

Even the children of well-known black families suffered painful rebuffs. Frederick Douglass wrote to H. B. Warner, editor of the Rochester Courier:

Sir:

Desiring to give my daughter, a child between nine and ten years old, the advantages of a good school—and learning that Seward Seminary of this city was an institution of that character, I applied to its principal, Miss Tracy, for the admission of my daughter. The Principal agreed to receive the child into the school at the commencement of the September term.

While absent from home, the term commenced and my daughter was promptly sent to school. On my return I asked, "Well, my daughter, how do you get on at the Seminary?"

Black children turned away from "white" school

She answered with tears in her eyes, "I get along pretty well, but father, Miss Tracy does not allow me to go into the room with the other scholars because I am colored."

Stung to the heart's core, I went immediately to the Seminary to remonstrate with the principal. I was answered that the trustees were opposed to the child's admission, but she thought if I allowed her to be taught separately for a term or more that the prejudice might be overcome.

Before carrying out my determination to withdraw the child, Miss Tracy submitted the question to each scholar personally. They welcomed my child among them and when asked where she should sit if admitted several young ladies shouted, "By me, by me, by me." Each scholar was then told that the question must be submitted to their parents and that if one parent objected, the child would not be received. The next morning my child went to school, as usual, but returned with her books, saying that one person objected and that she was therefore excluded from the Seminary.

You are the person, the only person of all the parents, who was hardened and mean enough to take the responsibility of excluding that child from school. If this were a private affair, only affecting myself and family, I should possibly allow it to pass. But it is a deliberate attempt to injure a large class of persons whose rights and feelings have been the common sport of yourself and such persons as yourself, for ages.

I should like to know how much better you are than me, and how much better your children than mine? We differ in color, it is true, but who is to decide which color is most pleasing to God, or most honorable among men?

Frederick Douglass

The North Star, March 30, 1849

Charlotte Forten, granddaughter of James Forten, boarded with friends in order to attend an integrated school in Salem, Massachusetts. Although the teachers welcomed sixteen-year-old Charlotte, her schoolmates sometimes snubbed her. An entry from her diary:

Wednesday, September 12, 1855. Today school commenced. I wonder that every colored person is not a misanthrope. Surely we have everything to make us hate mankind. I have met girls in the schoolroom. They have been thoroughly kind and cordial to me. Perhaps the next day met them in the street—they feared to recognize me. Others give the most distant recognition possible. I, of course, acknowledge no such recognitions, and they soon cease entirely. These are but trifles, certainly, to the great public wrongs which we as a people are obliged to endure. But to those who experience them, these apparent trifles are most wearing and discouraging. Even to a child's mind, they reveal volumes of deceit and heartlessness, and early teach a lesson of suspicion and distrust. Oh! it is hard to go through life meeting contempt with contempt, hatred with hatred, fearing, with too good reason, to love and trust hardly anyone whose skin is white.

Ray A. Billington, ed., *The Journal of Charlotte Forten* (New York, 1953)

Schools in Philadelphia and New York remained segregated until long after the Civil War. In New England in the

1850s, however, parents were campaigning for integration. George T. Downing, who owned a hotel in Newport and a catering business in Providence, led the fight in Rhode Island. In 1857 he wrote an open letter to the editor of the Providence Journal:

Dear Sir: I was relieved in reading your article in opposition to the admission of colored children to the schools of the respective wards in which they reside because I would rather face an open opponent than a concealed one.

They will learn more in colored schools, says the *Journal*. This wars with experience. There are not held out to the colored child the same incentives in a colored school that there would be in a common school. He feels that there is a wall between him and the white boy; that he is not cared for in community as is the white boy. "Why am I proscribed?" he asks. He feels, in the language of Topsy, "I is nothing but a nigger. Why study, why aim to be anything? Crime and degradation is my portion."

It is clear that this distinction must be done away with. The colored people of today have different ideas and feelings from those they had twenty years ago. We wish our children to be educated with higher ideas, with a nobler dignity than the education of our fathers begat. This, with us, is a test matter. Politically, those *for* us will be our friends; those against us we must know.

George T. Downing

"Abolition of Colored Schools," Handbill, John Hay Library, Brown University

When the Lyons family moved from New York to Rhode Island they joined the campaign. Although schools in the state were not integrated by law until 1866, Maritcha Lyons was permitted to attend high school in Providence. She later wrote:

When mother applied for the admission of her children

into the Providence schools the law prohibited taking a colored child in the high school. The matter was argued before the legislature where I, but sixteen years old, in a trembling voice pleaded for the opening of the door of opportunity. The diehards howled, but the decision was in favor of right and justice.

During the first year I occupied a double desk, the other having been left vacant, though pupils sat in window seats and on corners of the platform for there was an overflow attendance. The second year, the only desk with a single seat was assigned to me. This I held for a month only. A student sitting behind me invited me to share her bench.

Though apparently indifferent to popularity, the iron had entered my soul. I never forgot that I had to sue for a privilege which any but a colored girl could have without asking. Most classmates were more or less friendly. If any girl tried to put on airs, I found a way to inform her of my class record, as I never had less than the highest marks. During the final year, my composition themes were usually chosen from race topics. My sketches of the riots of '63, the Underground Railroad, of episodes on Southern plantations never failed to elicit comment. Sometimes the teacher would question me privately: "Is what you wrote really true, or have you been letting loose your imagination?" My reply was invariably, "The half has never been told."

Lyons-Williamson Papers, Schomburg Collection

Boston's black community fought for more than a decade to close the segregated Smith School, the only school in the city which their children were permitted to attend. In a "Report of a Committee of Parents and others interested in the Smith School" parents pressed charges against Abner Forbes, the school's white principal:

The matters to which the attention of the School Committee was called were,

1. The nature, degree and manner of punishment inflicted at the school.

2. The language and deportment of the Master, both towards scholars and parents.

3. Neglect of duty, such as absence in school hours, reading newspapers, and writing in school hours, and allowing first-class scholars to hear the recitations of junior scholars, when he should have heard them himself.

4. Expressing and entertaining opinions unfavorable to the intellectual capacities of the colored people as a race.

Under the first charge, evidence was introduced of unusual punishments, such as feruling the boys on the soles of their feet; compelling them to stand on one foot; pulling their hair and ears; pinching; and feruling a girl on the back of the hand. The public are requested to bear in mind that not one of the parents opposed corporal punishment in the abstract. They objected to *unusual modes* and *indiscreet application.*

Under the head of improper language to parents there was evidence from Mrs. Angeline B. Gardner. Her child had been kept [at] school until after tea time and lamplighting. She went out in search of him and seeing the schoolhouse door open, she went in. She called her son and told him to come home. Mr. Forbes then came towards her in a violent manner, exclaiming, "Out you vile wretch. If you don't go out I'll put you in the House of Correction."

If a man imbibes a belief that a race of persons are inferior, will he not begin to treat them as such? How can anyone with such views conscientiously retain his situation as a teacher of colored children? Or to put the question in another shape, how can a School Board, being informed on this point, continue him another hour in office?

"Boston Public School for Colored Children,"
Scrapbook, Boston Public Library

The School Committee found Forbes not guilty on all counts, but the fight continued. A petition campaign was followed by a boycott of the Smith School. After attendance had been cut almost in half, the School Committee tried to split the community by appointing a black principal. Supporters of integration called a meeting to protest the appointment:

GREAT SCHOOL RIGHTS MEETING!

Every individual who wears a colored face is called upon to meet at the Belknap street Church, on Monday evening next, at 7 o'clock—then and there to decide the question whether we are satisfied to be humbugged out of our rights in regard to Common School instruction for our children; also to remonstrate against the appointment of any individual as master in the Smith School, to continue it one moment as an exclusive school. Let our motto be, Down with the School!

"Report of a Special Committee of the Grammar School Board"
(Boston, 1849)

The day that the black principal took over the Smith School, protesters gathered in front of the building in order to keep students from entering. A school official reported:

At the hour of assembling, a collection of rude boys, set on by mischievous, misguided men—all of them persons of color —beset the doors in a disorderly manner and sought to intimidate and keep from the school all who repaired to it as pupils. The prompt appearance of a police officer scattered the noisy group and the school opened with comparative quiet. Still, it was found expedient to keep up a patrol about the place for a day or two more.

"Report of a Special Committee of the Grammar School Board"
(Boston, 1849)

Meeting that night, parents voted to continue the boycott and to organize temporary "freedom schools" for their children. In addition, they backed a lawsuit started by Benjamin F. Roberts. Roberts sued the city for damages, claiming that his daughter had been barred from the school nearest her home in violation of the Constitution. The state supreme court rejected his claim, but in 1855 the legislature abolished segregated schools in Massachusetts. At a victory celebration, William C. Nell, one of the leaders of the fight, said:

In the dark hours of our struggle, when betrayed by traitors within and beset by foes without, while some men would become lukewarm and indifferent, then did the women keep the flame alive. Yes Sir, it was the *mothers* of these bright-eyed boys and girls, who, through every step of our progress, were executive and vigilant, even to that memorable Monday morning (September 3, 1855), when the colored children of Boston went up to occupy the long-promised land. It was these mothers who accompanied me to the various schoolhouses, to residences of teachers and committeemen, to see the laws applied in good faith.

On the morning preceding their advent to the public schools, I saw from my window a boy passing the Smith School. Raising his hands, he exultingly exclaimed to his companions, *"Good-bye forever, colored school! Tomorrow we are like other Boston boys."*

"Proceedings of the Presentation Meeting"
(Boston, 1855)

3.   I Intend to Fight

The Fugitive Slave Law passed by Congress in 1850 permitted slave catchers to "seize and arrest" suspected runaway slaves. At hearings before U. S. Commissioners who were the appointed referees in such cases, suspects were denied the right to testify in their own behalf. Since only the slave catcher's word was needed to prove that someone was a runaway, men who were legally free could be captured and sent into slavery.

Within days after the law was passed hundreds of black families in the North fled to Canada. Thousands remained, vowing to defy the law. At a meeting in Boston, men and women put aside their belief in nonviolence and resolved:

To organize a League of Freedom composed of all those who are ready to resist the law, rescue and protect the slave at every hazard.

Joshua B. Smith hoped no one would preach peace, for, as Patrick Henry said, "there is no peace." He advised every fugitive to arm himself with a revolver—if he could not buy one otherwise, to sell his coat for that purpose.

Robert Johnson proclaimed that the meeting was composed of ACTORS and not speakers merely. They were men of overalls, men of the wharf, who could do heavy work in the hour of difficulty. He administered a timely caution to the women who, in pursuit of washing and other work, visited hotels and boardinghouses, [to] be on the constant lookout for the Southern slave catcher and be prepared for any emergency. "We will not go to the depots after the slave hunter, but when he rushes upon our buckler—*kill him.*"

The Liberator, October 11, 1850

In Massachusetts, New York, Pennsylvania, Ohio, Wis-

consin, blacks and whites stormed courthouses and jails to rescue fugitives. When Anthony Burns was arrested in Boston, President Franklin Pierce had to call out the Army and Marines to guard him. Burns was returned to slavery aboard a U.S. revenue cutter, at an estimated cost to the government of $40,000. The Marines were called out again when a group of blacks in Christiana, Pennsylvania, fought a pitched battle with slave catchers, killing one of them. William Parker, an ex-slave, told what happened after the Vigilance Committee in Philadelphia sent word that a party of slave catchers headed by Edward Gorsuch was on its way:

The information spread through the vicinity like a fire in the prairies. When I went home from work I found Pinckney, my brother-in-law, Abraham Johnson, Samuel Thompson and Joshua Kite at my house. They stopped for the night with us. Before daylight, Joshua Kite started for his home. Directly he ran back, burst open the door crying, "O William! kidnappers! kidnappers!"

He said that when he was just beyond the yard, two men crossed before him as if to stop him and others came up on either side. As he said this, they reached the door. I met them at the landing and asked, "Who are you?"

The leader, Kline, replied, "I am the United States Marshal."

I told him to take another step, and I would break his neck. He again said, "I am the United States Marshal."

I told him I did not care for him nor the United States. Mr. Gorsuch then spoke. "Come, Mr. Kline, let's go up and take them. Come, follow me. I'll go up and get my property."

At that he began to ascend the stair, but I said to him—"See here, old man, you can come up, but you can't go down again."

Kline then said, "Stop, Mr. Gorsuch, I will read the warrant and then, I think, they will give up." He read the warrant and said, "Now, you see, we are commanded to take you, dead or alive. So you may as well give up."

Mr. Gorsuch said, "I want my men. They are here and I am bound to have them."

By this time day had begun to dawn and my wife asked if she should blow the horn to bring friends to our assistance. It was a custom with us, when a horn was blown at an unusual hour, to proceed to the spot promptly to see what was the matter. Kline ordered his men to shoot anyone they saw blowing the horn. There was a peach tree at that end of the house. Up it two of the men climbed. When my wife went to the window, they fired as soon as they heard the blast, but missed. My wife then went down on her knees and drawing her body below the range of the window, the horn resting on the sill, blew blast after blast, while the shots poured thick and fast around her. The house was of stone and the windows were deep, which alone preserved her life.

Mr. Gorsuch now said, "Give up and let me have my property."

"Am I your man?" I asked.

"No."

I then called Pinckney forward. "Is that your man?"

"No."

Abraham Johnson I called next, but Gorsuch said he was not his man. Had I called the others, he would have recognized them, for they were his slaves. The whites were coming from all quarters and Kline was enrolling them as fast as they came. I came down and stood in the doorway, my men following behind.

"What do you intend to do?" said Kline.

"I intend to fight," said I.

Gorsuch made a signal to his men and they fell into line. I followed his example. At this time we numbered but ten while there were between thirty and forty white men. While I was talking to Gorsuch, his son said, "Father, will you take all this from a nigger?"

I answered him by saying that if he would repeat that I should knock his teeth down his throat. At this he fired upon me. I ran up to him and knocked the pistol out of his hand. I returned to my men and found Samuel Thompson talking to old Mr. Gorsuch, his master. Thompson took Pinckney's gun, struck Gorsuch and brought him to his knees. All the white men opened fire and we rushed upon them. They turned, threw down their guns and ran away. We clubbed our rifles. We were too closely pressed to fire, but we found a good deal could be done with empty guns. Old Mr. Gorsuch was the bravest of his party. I saw as many as three at a time fighting with him. Sometimes he was on his knees, then on his back and again his feet would be where his head should be.

Having driven the slaveocrats off, our party now turned toward their houses. The riot, so-called, was ended. The elder Gorsuch was dead. His son and nephew were wounded. Of our party only two were wounded. A story was afterwards

Shoot-out at Christiana, Pennsylvania

circulated that Mr. Gorsuch shot his own slave and in retaliation his slave shot him, but it was without foundation. His slave struck him, then three or four sprang upon him. *The women put an end to him.*

William Parker, "The Freedman's Story,"
Atlantic Monthly, March 1866

While U. S. Marines combed the neighborhood, arresting suspects, Parker and the Gorsuch slaves escaped to Canada. Thirty-eight people from Christiana were jailed on the charge of treason against the United States. The charge was so farfetched that a jury acquitted all of them.

In Columbia, Pennsylvania, a short distance from Christiana, William Whipper managed to call off a similar confrontation. A fugitive slave named Dorsey who had been living in Columbia for several years was warned that his master was on his way to capture him. Whipper later wrote:

I went to his house, but was refused admittance, until those inside ascertained who I was. There were several men in the house all armed with deadly weapons, awaiting the approach of the intruders. Had they come the whole party would have been massacred. I advised Dorsey to leave, but he refused, saying he had been taken up once before alive, but never would be again. The men told him to stand his ground, and they would stand by him and defend him. They had lived together, and would die together. He said he had no money, and would rather die with his family, than be killed on the road.

I said, "How much money do you want to start with? Here is one hundred dollars in gold." "That is not enough." "Will two hundred dollars do?" "Yes." I got the money the next morning. When I came, he said he could not leave unless his family was taken care of. I told him I would furnish his family with provisions for the next six months. Then he said he had two small houses, worth four hundred and seventy-five dollars. My reply was, "I will sell them for you, and give the money to your family." He left the next day.

I should state that my sacrifice for the removal of Dorsey was aided by my own desire for self-preservation. I knew that it had been asserted, far down in the slave region, that Smith & Whipper, the Negro lumber merchants, were engaged in secreting fugitive slaves. On two occasions attempts had been made to set fire to their yard for the purpose of punishing them for such illegal acts. I felt that if a collision took place, I should not only lose all I had ever earned, but peril the hopes and property of others, so that I would have freely given one thousand dollars to have been insured against the consequences of such a riot.

I borrowed fourteen hundred dollars and assisted many others to go to a land where the soil was not polluted by the footprints of a slave. The colored population of Columbia, in 1850, was nine hundred and forty-three. In five years they were reduced to four hundred and eighty-seven by emigration to Canada.

I visited Canada for the purpose of ascertaining the condition of those I had assisted. I was much gratified to find them contented, prosperous and happy. I was induced to purchase lands on the Sydenham River, with the intention of making it my future home. In the spring of 1861, when I was preparing to leave, the war broke out, and I concluded to remain and share the fortunes of my hitherto ill-fated country.

William Still, *The Underground Railroad*
(Philadelphia, 1872)

4. The Colored Patriots

The night before the shoot-out at Christiana, a neighbor of William Parker urged him not to resist the Fugitive Slave Law. Parker replied, "The laws are not made for us and we are not bound to obey them. The whites have a country and may obey the laws. But we have no country."

Ever since the death of Crispus Attucks at the Boston Massacre, blacks had had a love-hate relationship with the United States. Speakers at antislavery meetings seldom failed to mention the black soldiers who had fought in the Revolution and the War of 1812. Black Bostonians, led by William C. Nell, had asked the Massachusetts legislature to appropriate money for a monument to Crispus Attucks, and Nell had collected accounts of black military heroes for his book, The Colored Patriots of the American Revolution.

Yet the "colored patriots" were always painfully aware of the gulf between American ideals and American reality. One black orator said of the flag, "Its stars are for the white man and its stripes for the Negro—and it's appropriate that the stripes are red." Parodies of "My Country 'Tis of Thee" and other patriotic songs appeared regularly in the black and abolitionist press:

> My country 'tis for thee,
> Dark land of slavery
> For thee I weep.
> Land where the slave has sighed,
> Land where he toiled and died,
> To serve a tyrant's pride—
> For thee I weep.

> *The Colored American,* July 27, 1838

To black Americans, the Fourth of July was the bitterest

day of the year. An editorial in The North Star *said:*

The anniversary of American hypocrisy passed off in this city with every demonstration of enthusiasm. If the ringing of bells, waving of banners, irregular discharge of firearms, burning powder on the most extravagant scale, confused and tumultuous explosion of crackers, furious driving about the streets in carriages and the uproarious shouts of an apparently purposeless multitude be an evidence of a love of the great principles of human freedom as set forth in the American Declaration of Independence, then are the people of Rochester and vicinity the most devoted of all the lovers of liberty. But out of all the thousands that congregated here, probably not more than a hundred desire to see those principles triumphant in this country—Theirs is a white liberty.

The North Star, July 7, 1848

Blacks were not impressed by the lofty reputations of the founding fathers of the Republic. Had not all of the early Presidents, except for the Adamses, been slaveowners? Jefferson in particular was regarded with disapproval because he was reputed to have fathered slave children and then to have sold them. A popular song to the tune of "Yankee Doodle" commented on his relations with Sally Hemings, one of his slaves:

> Of all the damsels on the green,
>   On mountain or in valley,
> A lass so luscious ne'er was seen
>   As Monticellian Sally.
> Yankee Doodle, who's the noodle?
>   What wife was half so handy?
> To breed a flock of slaves for stock
>   A blackamoor's a dandy.

Richmond *Recorder,* November 17, 1802

Whether or not the story was true, abolitionists—white

as well as black—believed it. When a speaker at a meeting of the Pennsylvania Anti-Slavery Society referred to Thomas Jefferson as "a good antislavery man," he was interrupted by shouts: "He sold his own daughter!" Robert Purvis asked for the floor:

Mr. Chairman, I am astonished at the audacity of the gentleman from Long Island in claiming Thomas Jefferson to be an antislavery man. Sir, Thomas Jefferson was a slaveholder and I hold all slaveholders to be tyrants and robbers. It is said that Thomas Jefferson sold his own daughter. This if true proves him to have been a scoundrel as well as a tyrant!

Sir, I am free to confess that I have no veneration for the founders of this government. I do not share with others in their veneration for the "Father of our country." General Washington was a slaveholder. General Washington as

Robert Purvis (seated at center) at executive meeting of Pennsylvania Anti-Slavery Society. Lucretia Mott is seated at his left.

President of the United States signed the Fugitive Slave bill. General Washington tried, under that bill, to recover a poor woman flying through perils and toils (thereby showing a truer courage than ever he did) that she might escape the yoke of slavery on his plantation.

When a man professing to be an Abolitionist has the—has the—Sir, I don't want to say audacity, but I can't think of any other word—to come here and hold up a slaveholder as a good antislavery man, I forget all my resolutions to be guarded and speak with a vehemence which I afterwards regret.

The National Anti-Slavery Standard, November 3, 1860

Perhaps the saddest statement from a "colored patriot" was a poem written by a member of the Battalion of Free Men of Color who fought under General Andrew Jackson at the Battle of New Orleans in 1814. Written in French, under the pen name of Hippolyte Castra, it circulated by word of mouth in Louisiana and was not published until 1911:

The Campaign of 1814–15

. . . My mother, while sighing,
Said to me: "Child, emblem of innocence,
"You do not know the future that awaits thee.
"You believe that you see your country under this beautiful
    sky
"Renounce thy error, my tender child, . . .
"Here, thou art but an object of scorn."

Ten years later, upon our vast frontiers,
We heard the English cannon,
And then these words: "Come, let us conquer, my brothers,
"We were all born of Louisiana blood" . . .
I followed you, repeating your cries,

Not thinking, in my pursuit of battle,
That I was but an object of scorn.

. . . I fought with great valor
With the hope of serving my country,
Not thinking that for recompense
I would be the object of scorn.
After having gained the victory,
In this terrible and glorious combat,
All of you shared a drink with me
And called me a valiant soldier.
And I, without regret, and with a sincere heart,
Helas! I drank, believing you to be my friends,
Not thinking, in my fleeting joy
That I was but an object of scorn.
But today I sigh sadly
Because I perceive a change in you;
I no longer see that gracious smile
Which showed itself, in other times, so often
Upon your honeyed lips.
Have you become my enemies?
Ah! I see it in your fierce looks,
I am but an object of your scorn.

> Roland McConnell, *Negro Troops of Antebellum Louisiana*
> (Baton Rouge, 1968)

By the 1850s, Castra's gentle reproaches gave way to sterner statements. H. Ford Douglass, also a free black man from New Orleans, spoke at a convention in Ohio:

I can hate this Government without being disloyal because it has stricken down my manhood and treated me as a salable commodity. I can join a foreign enemy and fight against it, without being a traitor, because it treats me as an ALIEN and a STRANGER. When I remember that from Maine to Georgia, from the Atlantic waves to the Pacific shore, I am an alien and an outcast, unprotected by law, proscribed and persecuted by cruel prejudice, I am willing to forget the endearing name of home and country and seek on other shores the freedom which has been denied me in the land of my birth.

"Speech of H. Ford Douglass before the Emigration Convention,"
(Chicago, 1854)

Many disagreed with Douglass and with a Californian who said, "I would hail the advent of a foreign army upon our shores if that army provided liberty to my people in bondage." But the Dred Scott decision had come as a rude shock to people who had always thought of themselves as citizens of the United States. In the past, men like Peter Williams and Robert Purvis had been given passports certifying their citizenship when they traveled abroad. Now every right and privilege associated with citizenship was denied to blacks. The State Department refused them passports and—more important—the Commissioner of the General Land Office barred them from settling on public lands in the West, under the Homestead Laws.

Hurt and angry, the most loyal supporters of Garrison's moral suasion were expressing a new militance. At a Convention of Colored Citizens of Massachusetts, in 1858, Charles Lenox Remond, a lecturer for the American Anti-Slavery Society for twenty-five years, called for a slave rebellion:

Mr. Remond expressed his fervent conviction that the colored people would gain nothing by twaddling and temporizing. They were strong enough to defy American slavery. Mr. Remond announced that he was prepared to spit upon the decision of Judge Taney. He wanted no long resolutions, but a short one saying that we *defy* the Dred Scott decision. He boldly proclaimed himself a traitor to the government and the Union, so long as his rights were denied. Were there a thunderbolt of God which he could

Peter Williams' passport, issued in 1836   (*National Archives*)

invoke to bring destruction upon this nation, he would gladly do it.

Mr. Remond moved that a committee be appointed to prepare an address suggesting to the slaves at the South to create an insurrection. He said he knew his resolution was in one sense revolutionary and, in another, treasonable, but so he meant it. He had counted the cost. If he had one hundred relations at the South, he would rather see them die today, than to live in bondage. The insurrection could be accomplished and the glorious result would be instantaneously attained.

A vote was taken and the motion was lost.

The Liberator, August 23, 1858

In the late 1850s, free blacks began to organize in military companies and to urge state legislatures to repeal the laws that kept them out of state militias. New York had three black military companies—the Hannibal Guards, the Free Soil Guards and the Attucks Guards. A company of Attucks Guards was formed in Cincinnati; the Massasoit Guards drilled in Boston and the Frank Johnson Guards in Phila-delphia. In 1859, General J. J. Simons, an organizer of New York's black militia, addressed a meeting in Philadelphia:

The speaker said, "We have met in conventions and devised plans which have failed to bring us deliverance. We have wept and prayed and sighed." He would suggest that we take the Bible in one hand and the sword in the other, and battle for our rights.

The Frank Johnson Guards made an excursion on Tues-day, in full uniform. Speeches were made by J. J. Simons and others. Mr. Wm. H. Johnson was advertised to speak, but being unable to attend, Mr. Revels read the following letter from him:

To the Frank Johnson Guards:

Soldiers, allow me to congratulate you upon the success-ful completion of your military organization. It is in your power to contribute much towards refuting the calumnies heaped upon our people—that we are not capable of self-government and that we are naturally inferior to the Anglo-Saxon race.

Soldiers, do not trust your arms for the acquirement of

your rights. Believe me, when I tell you that rights are not to be obtained at the point of the bayonet. It will be done by proving the fitness of our people, and the conversion of the American people.

Wm. H. Johnson

The Weekly Anglo-African, August 27, 1859

The contrast between Simons' and Johnson's advice was typical of the conflict that every "colored patriot" faced. For on the same day that the Frank Johnson Guards were on parade in Philadelphia, two black men were traveling toward the city. They were on their way to meet John Brown.

5.   By Any Means Necessary

John Brown was determined to end slavery with "the Bible in one hand and the sword in the other." He proposed to station a guerrilla army in the Allegheny Mountains and slowly move into the heart of the South. At his first meeting with Frederick Douglass in 1848, Brown explained:

"My plan is to take at first about twenty-five picked men, supply them with arms and ammunition and post them in squads of fives on a line of twenty-five miles. The most persuasive and judicious of these shall go down to the fields from time to time and induce the slaves to join them." He thought he could soon gather a force of one hundred hardy men. When these were properly drilled, they would run off the slaves in large numbers, retain the brave and strong ones in the mountains and send the weak to the North by the Underground Railroad.

Frederick Douglass, *Life and Times of Frederick Douglass* (Hartford, 1882)

For ten years, Brown traveled across the country, perfecting his plan. Black Underground Railroad men like George De Baptiste in Detroit, John Jones in Chicago, William Still in Philadelphia, Jeremiah Loguen in Syracuse, told him of escape routes through the South and of blacks there who could be trusted to help. In Kansas, where North and South were battling to decide whether the territory should be slave or free, Brown learned the ways of guerrilla warfare. There he recruited a small band of whites who had sworn to end slavery.

By 1858 he was ready to move. A secret committee of white men had agreed to supply him with money for arms. Scores of black men and women were backing him in every way they could. In February he stayed at Frederick Doug-

lass' home in Rochester. In March he met with Douglass, Henry Highland Garnet and William Still, at the home of Stephen Smith, the lumber dealer, in Philadelphia. In April he went to Canada to enlist men in his guerrilla army. His first recruit there was Harriet Tubman whose trips to Maryland and Virginia had given her an intimate knowledge of the Allegheny Mountains. William H. Day, a black newspaper man working with Brown, wrote:

St. Catherine, C.W., April 17, 1858

Mr. J. Brown
Dear Sir:

Your letter as to Harriet was received about 5 yesterday. I hurried off to her residence and found that Jackson had put her on the cars. From what I could gather, she must have gone to Toronto. I took the liberty to telegraph you for fear you might be over-anxious.

I learned the names of the men at Ingersoll to be as follows: Drennard Hughes, Charles Hall, Josiah Bailey, Peter Pendleton, William Bailey and John Thompson. I asked how you could find them and they said "Go to Patterson's Hotel" and almost any of the waiters will tell you where John Thompson lives. He keeps "Bachelor's Hall" and the rest are all there.

William H. Day

Villard Papers, Columbia University

Jeremiah W. Loguen, one of Brown's closest black friends, accompanied him on the first leg of his Canadian trip. After returning home he wrote:

Syracuse, May 6, 1858

My dear Friend and Brother:

I was glad to learn that you and your brave men had got on to Chatham. I have seen our man Gray and find it as I feared—that he was not ready yet. I do not think he will go to *War,* soon. Others that would go have not the money to get there with and I have concluded to let them rest for the present.

Have you got Isaac Williams with you? Have you got Harriet Tubman? Let me hear from you soon. As I cannot get to Chatham, I should like much to see you and your men before you go to the mountains.

My wife and all unite in wishing you great success in your glorious undertaking. May the Lord be with you is our prayer.

Your friend in the cause,
J. W. Loguen

Kansas State Historical Society

Brown had a double purpose in going to Chatham, which was a center for blacks who had moved from the United States. He had drawn up a constitution for the free state he planned to establish in the Allegheny Mountains and he wanted a representative group of black men to consider and ratify it. Because of the need for secrecy such a meeting could not be held in the United States. In Chatham, Martin Delany, who had moved to Canada two years earlier, helped Brown to call a meeting. Thirty-four black men and the members of Brown's Kansas band formally adopted a "Declaration of Liberty" and a "Provisional Constitution for the proscribed and oppressed people of the United States."

One of the members of the Chatham convention was James M. Jones, a gunsmith and a graduate of Oberlin College. Years later he recalled conversations with Brown:

Mr. Brown called almost daily at my gunshop. One day I told him how utterly hopeless his plans would be if he persisted in making an attack with the few at his command and that we could not afford to spare white men of his stamp. While I was speaking Mr. Brown walked to and fro, with his hands behind his back, as was his custom. He stopped suddenly and bringing down his right hand with great force exclaimed, "Did not Jesus Christ come down from Heaven and sacrifice Himself for the salvation of the race? Should I refuse to sacrifice myself?" With a look of determination he resumed his walk.

J. E. Cook [a member of the Kansas band] worked with me a month, cleaning and repairing the revolvers and other arms belonging to the party. John Brown, never, I think, communicated his whole plan, even to his immediate followers. In his conversations with me he led me to think that he intended to sacrifice himself and a few of his followers for the purpose of arousing the people of the North. He well knew that the sacrifice of any number of Negroes would have no effect. He said, "It is nothing to die in a good cause, but an eternal disgrace to sit still in the presence of the barbarities of American slavery."

J. M. Hamilton, "John Brown in Canada,"
Canadian Magazine, December 1894

After Brown's return to the United States, Delany kept him in touch with his recruits in Chatham. Writing guardedly to John Henry Kagi, Brown's lieutenant, Delany referred to Brown as "Uncle." The other men mentioned in the following letter were blacks, most of whom had been at the Chatham convention.

Chatham, August 16, 1858

J. H. Kagi, Esq.
Lawrence, Kansas Territory
Dear Sir:

I hope ere this reaches you that Uncle will have recovered from his febrile attack. Richardson and Thomas are still here, both of them quite industrious and doing well. I have not seen Richardson since I received your letter today, but have seen Bell, Shadd, Jackson and Thomas. W. H. Day is now here and will be for some days.

Tell Uncle I received his letter dated at Syracuse.

There is nothing new here. I have been anxiously looking and expecting to see something of Uncle's movements in the papers, but as yet have seen nothing, the letter from you being the first intimation of his whereabouts since he wrote me. Please send me any paper which may mention your doings. All are in good spirits here, hoping and waiting the "good time coming."

M. R. Delany

Calendar of Virginia State Papers, Vol. XI
(Richmond, 1893)

The "good time coming" had been postponed. A military man hired to train Brown's troops had betrayed his plan to antislavery Congressmen in Washington. Alarmed, Brown's white backers insisted on a delay. For a year, Brown hid out in Kansas under an assumed name. In the summer of 1859 he came East again. Renting a farm in Maryland, five miles from Harper's Ferry, Virginia, he stationed Kagi nearby in Chambersburg, Pennsylvania, and sent John Brown, Jr., to the North to buy guns and to round up men for the guerrilla army.

The year's delay had scattered Brown's forces. Martin Delany was in Africa, William Day in England; Harriet Tubman was ill someplace in New England, and no one knew where to find her. In response to an urgent summons, Frederick Douglass went to Chambersburg, bringing with him Shields Green, a fugitive slave who had been living in Rochester. There Douglass learned that Brown planned to attack the U.S. arsenal at Harper's Ferry:

Our talk was long and earnest. We spent the most of Saturday and a part of Sunday in debate—Brown for Harper's Ferry and I against it—he for striking a blow which should instantly rouse the country and I for the policy of gradually drawing off the slaves to the mountains, as at first proposed by him. In parting, he put his arms around me and said, "Come with me, Douglass. When I strike, the bees will begin to swarm and I shall want you to help hive them." But my discretion or cowardice made me proof against the old man's eloquence. When about to leave I asked Green what he had decided to do, and was surprised by his coolly saying, "I believe I'll go with the old man."

Frederick Douglass, *Life and Times of Frederick Douglass* (Hartford, 1882)

Douglass brought with him a letter and some money from Mrs. E. A. Gloucester, the wife of a Brooklyn minister:

Brooklyn, August 18, 1859

Esteemed Friend:

I gladly avail myself of the opportunity afforded by our friend, Mr. F. Douglass, to inclose to you for the cause in which you are such a zealous laborer a small amount, which please accept with my most ardent wishes for its and your benefit.

The visit of our mutual friend Douglass has somewhat revived my rather drooping spirits in the cause; but seeing such ambition and enterprise in him, I am again encouraged. With best wishes for your welfare and the good of your cause,

Mrs. E. A. Gloucester

The Anglo-African Magazine, December 1859

Not all black women shared Mrs. Gloucester's enthusiasm for Brown. Mary Jones, the wife of John Jones, met Brown a number of times at her home in Chicago where she helped to run an Underground Railroad station. Interviewed many years later, she said:

The first time I met John Brown he came to our house with Fred Douglass and remained all night. I told Mr. Jones I thought he was a little off on the slavery question

John Brown at Harper's Ferry

and that I did not believe he could ever do what he wanted to do. The next morning I asked him if he had a family.

He said, "Yes, madam. I have quite a large family, besides a million other people I am looking out for and some of these days I'm going to free them." I thought to myself, how are you going to free them?

After that time he dropped into our house most any time. He would talk about slavery and say what might be done in the hills and mountains. Mr. Jones would say, "Why, Mr. Brown, that is all wind. And besides you would lose your life if you undertook to carry out your plans." I remember how Mr. Brown snapped his finger and said, "What do I care for my life—if I can free these Negroes?"

But Mr. Jones told him that he did not believe his ideas would ever be carried out.

Rufus Blanchard, *Discovery and Conquest of the Northwest* (Chicago, 1898)

Doubtless there were other blacks who felt that Brown's mission was "all wind." Enthusiasms had cooled during the long year of waiting. Some who had agreed to go with Brown had married, had children, bought farms. Others had had second thoughts about the venture and were no longer willing to take part. Charles Langston, Brown's chief recruiter in Ohio, was sick and had turned over the work to James H. Harris, a member of the Chatham convention. In a letter to Kagi, who was using the name J. Henrie, Harris told of his difficulties. Of the men mentioned in Harris' letter only Lewis Sherrard Leary joined Brown.

Cleveland, Aug. 22, 1859

My dear J. Henrie:

I went up to Oberlin to see Leary. I saw Smith, Davis and Mitchell. They all promised, and that was all. Leary wants to provide for his family, Mitchell to lay his crops by, and all make such excuses, until I am disgusted with myself and the whole *Negro set*—G-D D-MN 'EM!

If you was here your influence would do something, but the moment you are gone, all my speaking don't amount to anything. I will speak to Smith today. I know that Mitchell hadn't got the money and I tried to sell my farm and everything else to raise money, but have not raised a cent yet. Charlie Langston says, "It is too bad," but what he will do, if anything, I don't know. I wish you would write to him, for I believe he can do more good than I. I will, however, do all I can.

J.H.H.

The Anglo-African Magazine, December 1859

Mary Jones, wife of John Jones (*Chicago Historical Society*)

James Madison Bell, another member of the Chatham convention, was handling recruiting in Canada. Bell's references to "missionaries" and "revivals" in the following letter to John Brown, Jr., were, of course, intended to mislead, in case the letter fell into the wrong hands. Despite Bell's efforts, Osborne Anderson was the only black Canadian to reach Brown's headquarters in time for the raid on Harper's Ferry.

Chatham, September 14, 1859

To J.B., Jr.

Dear Sir:

One hand (Anderson) left here last night and will be found efficient. Richardson is anxious to be at work as a missionary to bring sinners to repentance. He will start in a few days. Another will follow immediately after. More laborers may be looked for shortly. "Slow but sure."

Dull times affect missionary matters here more than anything else. However, a few active laborers may be looked for as certain. I would like to hear of your congregation numbering more than "15 and 2" to commence a good revival. Still, our few will be adding strength to the good work.

J.M.B.

Osborne Anderson, *A Voice from Harper's Ferry*
(Boston, 1861)

Harriet Tubman was located at last in New Bedford, Massachusetts. Lewis Hayden, a black activist from Boston, made arrangements to send her to Brown as soon as she was well enough to travel. "Our friend at Concord," mentioned in Hayden's letter to Kagi, was Franklin Sanborn, one of Brown's white backers.

Boston, September 16, 1859

My dear sir:

I have sent a note to Harriet requesting her to come to Boston, saying that she must come right on, which I think she will do. When she does come we will send her on. I have seen our friend at Concord; he is a true man. I have not yet said anything to anybody except him. I shall, therefore, when Harriet comes, send for our Concord friend, who will attend to the matter. Have you all the hands you wish?

L.H.

New York *Herald*, October 25, 1859

Still ill, Harriet Tubman was unable to leave for several weeks. By the time she reached New York, newspaper headlines were proclaiming "FEARFUL AND EXCITING INTELLIGENCE. NEGRO INSURRECTION AT HARPER'S FERRY."

Of the twenty-one men who fought with John Brown in Virginia, five were black. Shields Green and John A. Copeland were captured. Lewis Leary and Dangerfield Newby were killed in the fighting, and Osborne Anderson escaped. Newby, a former slave, was the first to die. Letters from his

Lewis Sherrard Leary   (*Library of Congress*)

Dangerfield Newby
(*Library of Congress*)

wife, whom he had hoped to rescue from slavery, were found on his body:

Brentwood, August 16, 1859

Dear Husband:

I want you to buy me as soon as possible, for if you do not get me somebody else will. Dear Husband, the last two years has been like a troubled dream to me. It is said Master is in want of money. If so, I know not what time he may sell me, and then all my bright hopes of the future are blasted. There has been one bright hope to cheer me in all my troubles, that is to be with you. If I thought I should never see you, this earth would have no charms for me.

The children are all well. The baby cannot walk yet. It can step around everything by holding on. It is very much like Agnes. Write soon and say when you think you can come.

Your affectionate wife, Harriet Newby

Calendar of Virginia State Papers, Vol. XI
(Richmond, 1893)

Osborne Anderson left the only eyewitness account of the uprising. Writing with the help of Mary Ann Shadd Cary, editor of Chatham's black newspaper, the Provincial Freeman, *he told how the raiders captured a great grandnephew of George Washington, whom they held as a hostage:*

The town being taken, Captain Stevens, Tidd, Cook, Shields Green, Leary and myself went to the country. On the road, we met some colored men to whom we made known our purpose, when they immediately agreed to join us. They said they had been long waiting for an opportunity of the kind. Stevens then asked them to go around among the colored people and circulate the news. Each started off in a different direction. The result was that many colored men gathered to the scene of action.

The first prisoner taken by us was Colonel Lewis Washington. We entered the building and commenced a search for the proprietor. Col. Washington opened his door, and begged us not to kill him. Capt. Stevens replied, "You are our prisoner." Stevens further told him to get ready to go to the Ferry; that he had come to abolish slavery, not to take life but in self-defense.

During this time, Washington was walking the floor, much excited. When the Captain came in, he went to the sideboard, took out his whiskey and offered us something to drink but he was refused. His firearms were next demanded. He brought forth one double-barreled gun, one small rifle, two horse-pistols and a sword. The Colonel appeared taken aback when, on delivering up the famous sword presented by Frederick [the Great] to George Washington, Capt. Stevens told me to step forward and take it.

On the second day of the raid, freed slaves joined Brown's forces:

Monday, the 17th of October was a time of stirring events. Capt. Brown ordered Lewis Sherrard Leary and four slaves and a free man belonging in the neighborhood, to join John Henry Kagi and John Copeland at the rifle factory.

Capt. Brown next ordered me to take the pikes out of the wagon in which he rode to the Ferry and to place them in the hands of the colored men who had come with us from the plantations, and others who had come forward. Among the arms taken from Col. Washington was one double-barreled gun. This weapon was placed in the hands of an elderly slave.

When the Captain received the news that the troops had entered the bridge from the Maryland side, he sent a message to the arsenal for us to come forth. We hastened to the street, when he said, "The troops are on the bridge, coming into town. We will give them a warm reception." He then walked around amongst us, giving us words of encouragement. "Men! Be cool! Don't waste your powder and shot! Take aim and make every shot count!"

The troops soon came up the street facing us. When they got within sixty or seventy yards, Capt. Brown said, "Let go upon them!" which we did. Several of them fell. Again and again the dose was repeated. They beat a confused retreat to the bridge and there stayed under cover until reinforcements came.

Osborne Anderson, *A Voice from Harper's Ferry*
(Boston, 1861)

The next day at dawn, Marines and Cavalry under the command of Colonel Robert E. Lee captured John Brown and the remaining members of his band. Anderson, who had managed to escape, made his way back to Canada. With Brown and their white comrades, Shields Green and John A. Copeland were brought to trial in Charlestown, Virginia.

Osborne P. Anderson
(*Library of Congress*)

The charges against them were: "First. For conspiring with Negroes to produce insurrection. Second. For treason. Third. For murder." With bitter logic, the jury acquitted the black men of treason. Since they were not citizens, they had no country to betray. However, they were convicted on the other charges and sentenced to be hanged. In the days before his execution, twenty-five-year-old John Copeland wrote farewell letters to his family:

Charlestown, Virginia, December 10, 1859

My dear Brother:

I scarcely know how to commence writing. Not that I am terrified by the gallows upon which I am soon to suffer death for doing what George Washington, the so-called father of his slavery-cursed country was made a hero for doing. For having lent my aid to a General no less brave, and engaged in a cause no less honorable and glorious, I am to suffer death.

John A. Copeland
(*Library of Congress*)

It was a sense of the wrongs which we have suffered that prompted the noble Captain Brown and his associates to attempt to give freedom to a small number, at least, of those who are now held by cruel and unjust laws and by cruel and unjust men. Now, dear brother, could I die in a more noble cause?

Believe me when I tell you that though shut up in prison under sentence of death, I have spent very happy hours here. Give my love to all my friends. Good-by.

John Copeland

Charlestown Jail, Virginia, December 16, 1859

Dear Father, Mother, Brothers and Sisters:

The last Sabbath with me on earth has passed away. God's glorious sun I have seen declining behind the western mountains for the last time. I am well, both in body and in mind. If it were not for you—if it were not that I know your hearts will be filled with sorrow at my fate, I could pass from this earth without regret.

Why should you sorrow? I fully believe that not only myself but also all three of my comrades who are to ascend the same scaffold (a scaffold already made sacred to the cause of freedom by the death of John Brown) are prepared to meet our God. I beg of you one and all that you will not grieve about me. And now, dear ones, attach no blame to anyone for my coming here for not any person but myself is to blame.

Dear ones, he who writes this will, in a few hours, be in this world no longer. I bid you that last, long, sad farewell.

Your son and brother to eternity,

John A. Copeland

Handbill, Moorland-Spingarn Collection,
Howard University Library

6.   Where Shall We Go?

Frustrated in their efforts to win equality in the United States, black men and women once again talked of leaving the country. But where should they go? They were generations removed from the home of their ancestors and knew little about the land that Europe and America called the "Dark Continent."

Seeking information, the Reverend Amos G. Beman wrote to Noah Webster, compiler of the famous "American Dictionary of the English Language" to ask what he could read on African history. Webster, one of the most learned men of his day, replied:

New Haven, April 27, 1843

A. G. Beman:

I have your note with a request that I would refer you to such author as may give you some account of the origin of the African race. In answer, I would remark that of the wooly-haired Africans who constitute the principal part of the inhabitants of Africa, there is no history & there can be none. That race has remained in barbarism from the first ages of the world. Their country has never been explored very fully by civilized man & the late efforts of travelers to penetrate to the sources of the Niger have not been very successful.

Of other nations inhabiting the northern part of Africa who are of different origin, viz, the Egyptians, Carthagenians & Numidians, I suppose you will find the best accounts in some Encyclopedia, under the words Copt, Egypt, Carthage & Numidia—and also Morocco.

N. Webster

Beman Papers, Beinecke Library, Yale University

Despite this rebuff, Beman began to read and lecture on African history. Others joined him. After the Colonization Society granted independence to Liberia in 1848, Henry Highland Garnet expressed his pride in the new republic. Criticized for his stand, Garnet defended his position:

You demand an explanation of the change which has taken place in my mind in reference to the American Colonization scheme. My opinion of the Colonizationists has undergone no change. But new developments have been made in relation to the descendants of once glorious but now fallen Africa and these have changed my mind.

1. I believe that the Republic of Liberia will be highly beneficial to Africa.

2. I believe that the new Republic will succeed—and that its success will curtail the slave trade on the coast.

3. I believe that every political and commercial relationship which President Roberts negotiates with European powers goes far to create respect for our race throughout the civilized world.

4. I believe that every colored man who believes that he can never grow to the stature of a man in this country ought to go there immediately, if he desires. I am in favor of colonization in any part of the United States, Mexico or California or in the West Indies or Africa, wherever it promises freedom and enfranchisement. In a word, we ought to go anywhere where we can better our condition.

The North Star, March 2, 1849

By 1854, Martin R. Delany was convinced that blacks must leave the United States. At a National Emigration Convention which he organized, one hundred men and women—the first women to be accepted as delegates at a black convention—discussed plans for leaving the country. A Committee on Foreign Relations was set up to investigate the possibility of forming a black republic in Central America or the Caribbean. Africa was not openly discussed be-

cause the delegates were afraid of being called supporters of the Colonization Society. However, at secret sessions Delany proposed an expedition to Africa to look for land for a settlement. The publication of two books on Africa, by T. J. Bowen and David Livingstone, contributed to the growing interest in the "Dark Continent." Delany recommended the books to friends. Martin H. Freeman, principal of Avery College in Pennsylvania, wrote him in reply:

Alleghany City, April 14, 1858

My Dear Friend:

I have read Bowen's work, and shall today purchase Livingstone's. I am more and more convinced that Africa is the country to which all colored men who wish to attain the full stature of manhood, and bring up their children to be men and not creeping things, should turn their steps. I feel more and more every day that I made a great mistake in not going there when I was untrammelled by family ties and had the opportunity.

M. H. Freeman

Martin R. Delany, *Official Report of the Niger Valley Exploring Party* (New York, 1861)

Martin R. Delany

In August 1858, Delany presided over another Emigration Convention in Chatham, Canada. Its delegates included a number of John Brown's Canadian supporters. Aware by then that Brown's strike for freedom had been postponed, they appointed Martin Delany as Chief Commissioner of a Niger Valley Exploring Party. Accompanied by Robert Campbell, a young schoolteacher from Philadelphia, Delany spent nine months in Africa. In Abeokuta, a walled city in present-day Nigeria, the Alake (king) and his chiefs agreed to permit American blacks to settle there. A formal treaty was negotiated:

This Treaty, made between His Majesty, OKUKENU, Alake; SOMOYE, Ibashorun; SOKENU, OGUBONNA, and ATAMBALA, Chiefs and Balaguns, of Abeokuta; and MARTIN ROBISON DELANY and ROBERT CAMPBELL, Commissioners from the African race of the United States and the Canadas, covenants:

ART. 1. That the King and Chiefs on their part, agree to grant and assign unto the said Commissioners, on behalf of the African race in America, the right and privilege of settling in common with the Egba people, on any part of the territory belonging to Abeokuta, not otherwise settled.

ART. 2. That all matters requiring legal investigation among the settlers be left to themselves, to be disposed of according to their own custom.

ART. 3. That the Commissioners, on their part, also agree that the settlers shall bring with them, as an equivalent for the privileges above accorded, Intelligence, Education, a Knowledge of the Arts and Sciences, Agriculture, and other Mechanical and Industrial Occupations, which they shall put into immediate operation, by improving the lands, and in other useful vocations.

ART. 4. That the laws of the Egba people shall be strictly respected by the settlers; and, in all matters in which both parties are concerned, an equal number of commissioners, mutually agreed upon, shall be appointed, who shall have power to settle such matters.

As a pledge of our faith, and the sincerity of our hearts, we each of us hereunto affix our hand and seal this 27th day of December, 1859.

Martin R. Delany, *Official Report of the Niger Valley Exploring Party* (New York, 1861)

While Delany and Campbell were in Africa, Henry Highland Garnet was also organizing a back-to-Africa movement. Founder of the African Civilization Society, Garnet hoped that black Americans would open up commerce between Africa, the United States and Great Britain, as well as establish "a grand center of Negro nationality." Opponents of emigration were particularly critical of Garnet because the Civilization Society accepted support from members of the Colonization Society. Garnet held meetings in Boston and New York to answer his critics. In one of his speeches he said:

Let me state a few facts for your consideration. On the coast of Africa there are now eight thousand white men engaged in commerce and trade. They are at the mouth of every river, obtaining all the ivory, gold, palm oil and valuable skins. They bring these to England and the United States and they are becoming rich.

There is a gentleman at Staten Island, New York, who manufactures "sperm candles." They are made of bleached palm oil.* This gentleman sends out ships to Africa that come back laden with palm oil. He has accumulated a fortune of millions of dollars and lives in a princely palace in Fifth Avenue.

White men are daily equipping their vessels and filling their pockets and laughing at us poor colored people quarreling among ourselves and destroying the character of every

* Genuine sperm-oil candles were made from whale oil.

man who fails to agree with us. If [we had] a dozen ships keeping up a trade between these countries, that fact would do more for the overthrowing of slavery, in creating a respect for ourselves and breaking down the walls of prejudice, than fifty thousand lectures.

The Weekly Anglo-African, September 17, 1859

On his return to America, Delany joined forces with Garnet and the African Civilization Society. While Delany signed up families for the Niger Valley, Garnet went to England to raise money for the settlement. For a time it seemed as if the dream of Newport's African Union Society was about to be realized.

But interest in Africa waned when the government of Haiti launched a campaign to attract black settlers from the United States. Haiti was nearby, not far across the sea, and the Haitian government was offering to pay moving expenses and sell land cheaply to black emigrants. So many families decided to go to Haiti that John Jones sent a notice to the Chicago newspapers:

MEN OF CHICAGO! Take notice there is one colored man in this city who is not going to Haiti, but expects to remain with you until he slips off this mortal coil; and, indeed he expects to be with some of you in that other world. So gentlemen you see that we will, in all probability, remain together for all time to come. In view of this fact, I ask a part of your patronage in the Clothes Cleaning and Repairing business. You will find me at my old stand, 119 Dearborn Street.

John Jones

Douglass' Monthly, May 1859

Even Frederick Douglass who opposed all emigration said, "If we go anywhere, let us go to Haiti." He accepted an invitation to visit the island republic, but ten days be-

*fore his departure the Confederates fired on Fort Sumter,
and he cancelled his trip. "We shall stay here and watch the
current of events," he wrote. "This is no time to leave the
country."*

*In the decade that ended with the Civil War, fifteen thou-
sand black Americans moved to Canada, five thousand to
Liberia and two thousand to Haiti. The exodus continued,
at a slower rate, during the first years of the war. Convinced
that whites and blacks could never live side by side in harmony, Lincoln proposed a black colony in Central America
and Congress appropriated half a million dollars for those
who wished to go. Most blacks rejected Lincoln's proposal.
A typical comment was headed, "We Will Not Go":*

New Bedford, November 15, 1862

Mr. Editor:

The President knows that we will not go to Africa, as
paradisical as it is portrayed. Neither will we listen to the
siren [song] of beauteous Haiti. So he says, "Never mind
if I have no reason or justice in what I say. (Alas! When
had the Government used reason or justice when the blacks
were concerned?) Here is land in Central America to which
I will send you. There are large coal mines there which you
will be able to realize fabulous sums from, and you will be
within one month's sail of the Capitol, and the paternal
flag shall protect you."

Oh! Abraham Lincoln, Abraham Lincoln! At the cabinet
meeting at which that plan was suggested there was one
more present than was visible to the human eye. That
[plan] could have only emanated from the Prince of Darkness.

E.J.J.

The Pacific Appeal, December 13, 1862

Henry Highland Garnet was one of the few spokesmen to

*back Lincoln's plan. He saw Central America as a homeland
for the slaves of the South:*

Mr. Editor:

In regard to the Central American plan, as proposed by
the President for *the purpose of saving our emancipated
brethren from being returned to slavery*—of that I do most
sincerely approve.

Where are the freed people of the South to seek a refuge?
Neither the North, the West, nor the East will receive them.
Nay—even colored people do not want them here. They
all say, white and black—"these Southern Negroes if they
come here *will reduce the price of labor and take the bread
out of our mouths.*"

Let the government give them a territory and arm and
defend them until they can fully defend themselves, and
thus hundreds of thousands of men will be saved.

Henry Highland Garnet

The Pacific Appeal, October 11, 1862

*Five hundred blacks—including Lewis Douglass, son of
Frederick Douglass—signed up to go to Central America.
But before their chartered ship could depart, Lincoln is-
sued the Emancipation Proclamation. A month later, Lewis
Douglass joined the Army of the United States.*

VI · O, FREEDOM
(1861–65)

Suppose you had kept your freedom without enlisting
in this army. Your children might have grown up free, but
it would have been always flung in their faces—"Your
father never fought for his own freedom." Never can say
that to this African race any more. Never can say that,
because we showed them we could fight by their side.

Corporal Thomas Long, First South Carolina Volunteers

1. A White Man's War

*President Lincoln had declared that his aim was to pre-
serve the Union, not to free the slaves. "This is a white
man's war" Northerners insisted after the fall of Fort Sum-*

ter. Commander-in-Chief George B. McClellan underlined this in a proclamation to Virginians: "Understand one thing clearly. Not only will we abstain from all interferences (with your slaves) but we will, with an iron hand, crush any attempt at insurrection on their part."

Responding to these statements, editorials and letters in the black press advised readers to "wait and see":

The American flag is our flag; for we are Americans. But the usual interpretation of it is not ours, alas! but that of our bitterest enemies. Withered forever be the hand, and paralyzed the arm of the colored American who lifts up either in support of the Federal Flag; until its supporters, seeing the justice of our claims and the greatness of our sufferings, shall inscribe upon it the glorious motto—the new watchword of the John Brown Abolitionists—

EMANCIPATION OR EXTERMINATION!

The Weekly Anglo-African, April 27, 1861

No! No!!! Your answer must be No! No black regiments, no war measure to be adopted or encouraged by us. Our policy must be neutral, ever praying for the success of that party determined to initiate the policy of justice and equal rights.

The Weekly Anglo-African, September 25, 1861

Shall we now fly to arms and sacrifice our lives to bind new chains upon our already festered limbs? No! God forbid.

We are in advance of our fathers. They put confidence in the word of the whites only to feel the dagger of slavery driven still deeper. Our enslaved brothers must be made freedmen. We of the North must have all rights which white men enjoy. Until then we are in no condition to fight under the flag which gives us no protection.

The Weekly Anglo-African, October 19, 1861

Most white abolitionists rallied round the President. William Lloyd Garrison cancelled the annual meeting of the American Anti-Slavery Society and urged all-out support of the Union. Even Gerrit Smith who had run against Lincoln in the 1860 election now called for unity on the part of everyone in the North. Dr. James McCune Smith sent a sharp letter to his old friend:

New York, August 22, 1861

Hon. Gerrit Smith
Dear friend:

I charge you and charge the Garrison party with being unequal to the exigency of the hour. After lives spent in signal devotion to the cause of the slave you fairly abandon that cause in the hour of its trial and triumph. This is strong language. What are the facts? Because the South chose to storm Sumter, the Garrison host abandoned its May meeting in New York and you cried hosanna to the coming hour of Emancipation. You lent the sanction of your great name to the support of an Administration which, with trembling knees, endeavored to pacify the South by returning fugitive slaves!

And today when a field has been opened for you to do most effectual antislavery work you say: "For whilst the other President (Davis) is cheered and strengthened by the entire devotion to his cause of all around him," etc.

Is this true? Is it not virtually ignoring one half of those around Jeff Davis? I mean his slaves.

Let me tell you how I see this situation and what I expect from you. *First.* The whole nation is upon the anxious seat, inquiring, "What shall we do to be saved?" *Second.* The only salvation is *Immediate Emancipation. Third.* As soon as the people are convinced of this great truth, they will ordain and carry out *Immediate Emancipation.*

You can write in your own strong style a pamphlet entitled "Slavery the sole cause, Emancipation the sole remedy for the Rebellion." Let this pamphlet be showered in millions of copies through every household in the North and wherever it can reach in the South. The people thus moved would cause the Administration and Congress to move; and if these last moved too slowly they would topple in the mud and leave room for veteran antislavery men to do the good work.

James McCune Smith

Gerrit Smith Miller Collection, George Arents Research Library at Syracuse University

Despite Union insistence that this was "a white man's war," black men from all over the North offered their services:

Oberlin, Ohio, November 27, 1861

The Hon. S. Cameron, Secretary of War
Sir:

Very many of the colored citizens of Ohio and other states have had a great desire to assist the government in putting down this injurious rebellion.

Since they have heard that the rebels are forming regiments of free blacks and compelling them to fight against the Union, they have urged me to write and beg that you will receive one or more regiments of the colored men of the free states. We are partly drilled and would wish to enter active service immediately. To prove our attachment and our will to defend the government we only ask a trial.

William A. Jones

National Archives

Their offers were rejected. Military companies applying to the governors and legislatures of their states were also rebuffed. Henry Highland Garnet recalled the experience of black New Yorkers:

The colored men of this city had gone to the governor and offered their services as men—not as black men—to fight the battles of their native land. When the offer became public, the white people were horror-stricken, fearing lest white men and black should fight shoulder to shoulder to save the country. And when about to organize, the Superintendent of Police sent a posse of police to tell them that they must not hold any meeting but must disband. Then they said they would wait till they were called for.

The Liberator, January 16, 1863

William H. Parham, a schoolteacher in Cincinnati, told Jacob C. White, Jr., what happened to black patriots there:

Cincinnati, October 12, 1861

Kind friend:
When Sumter fell, the Northern heart was fired with indignation. Some of our colored men, thinking they were a part of this Northern heart, imagined themselves very indignant, and as all the rest of this heart was forming Home Guards concluded they must do likewise. Meetings were held at which ardent speeches were made calling upon all colored Americans to rally under the stars and stripes. Judge the surprise of these patriotic individuals when waited upon by the Chief of Police and informed that all that kind of thing must be stopped, that they had nothing to do with the fight. It was a *white men's fight with which niggers had nothing to do.*

I agree with you that the time for black men to fight has not yet come.

William H. Parham

Jacob C. White Collection, Moorland-Spingarn Collection, Howard University Library

A year later, when Confederate forces were advancing

on Cincinnati, Parham wrote to White again:

Cincinnati, September 7, 1862

Friend White:

Last night it was rumored that the "Rebs" had made their appearance within five miles of this city. When I retired I knew not whether I should wake up a subject to Jeff Davis or Abe Lincoln. However, the rumor proved unfounded.

Never in all my life, my dear friend, have I witnessed anything which approximated the scenes of the eventful past week. Since Tuesday last, preparations for defense have absorbed everything else. All places of business have been closed—butchers, bakers, and apothecaries excepted, likewise all places of amusement. Every able-bodied man was expected to do something toward placing the city in an attitude of defense—some to dig trenches, others to shoulder muskets. Those who failed to volunteer were taken from their homes at the point of the bayonet.

Our troubles with the Irish are not yet at an end. On Friday a party of them attacked a house occupied by a colored family. When one of the inmates appeared at the door, gun in hand, this had no other effect than to increase their violence. One of them rushing up to him, wrestled the weapon from his grasp and commenced beating him with it. The shock occasioned by the blow caused the gun to go off, killing the assailant instantly.

William H. Parham.

Jacob C. White Collection, Moorland-Spingarn Collection, Howard University Library

With the Confederates at the gates of the city, the mayor called on blacks as well as whites to come to its defense. But the blacks were roughly handled by the police, most of whom were Irish. "They were torn from their homes, from their shops, and driven to the mule pen on Plum Street at the point of a bayonet," one conscript said. Another de-

scribed the behavior of the captain in charge of the black recruits:

Coming into the yard, he ordered them all to rise, marched them to another part, then issued the order, "D—n you, squat." Turning to the guard he added, "Shoot the first one who rises." Reaching the other side of the river, the same squad were marched from the sidewalk into the middle of a dusty road and again the order, "D—n you, squat," and the command to shoot the first one who should rise.

Peter H. Clark, *The Black Brigade of Cincinnati*
(Cincinnati, 1864)

Mistreatment of black Home Guard recruits was so blatant that sympathy swung to their side. Permitted to form a Black Brigade, a thousand strong, they played an important role in defending the city. In Cincinnati people stopped talking about "a white man's war."

A shift in public sentiment had been building also in other parts of the North. Some of this was due to the heroism of two black sailors who, singlehandedly, gave the Union its first victories at sea. Both were cooks aboard merchant vessels which were captured by the Confederate privateer, Jeff Davis. *Frederick Douglass recounted William Tillman's story:*

The schooner S. J. *Waring*, when scarcely beyond the waters of New York, was captured by the privateer *Jeff Davis*. The captain and the mate of the *Waring* were sent home and a prize crew were put on board. Three of the original crew, two seamen and William Tillman, the colored steward, were retained. Tillman very soon ascertained, from conversations which he was not intended to hear, that the vessel was to be taken to Charleston and that he was to be sold as a slave.

Tillman declared that they should never succeed in

getting him to Charleston alive. Only one of his fellow prisoners, a German named Stedding, consented to take part in the dangerous task of recapturing the vessel. They were within fifty miles of Charleston. Night and sleep had come down upon them—for even pirates have to sleep. Stedding discovered that now was the time and Tillman began his fearful work—killing the pirate captain, mate and second mate, thus making himself master of the ship with no other weapon than a hatchet.

Neither [Tillman] nor his companions possessed any knowledge of navigation but they managed to reach New York.

Well done for Tillman! The New York *Tribune* says that the nation is indebted to him for the first vindication of its honor on the sea.

Douglass' Monthly, August 1861

Tillman received a hero's welcome in New York as well as $6,000 prize money from the owners of the Waring. *So many people wanted to see him that P. T. Barnum invited him to his American Museum. His bloody hatchet was still on display there when a second rescue took place. The schooner* Enchantress, *sailing from Boston to Cuba, was also overtaken by the* Jeff Davis. *Removing her crew, except for Jacob Garrick, the cook, the Rebels took over. Hailed by a Union man-of-war, they passed themselves off as the original Union crew. Garrick explained how he gave away the show:*

After dinner I took my dishes to the galley and washed them. In going back to the cabin, I saw a vessel coming. She hauled right up for us. I kept looking from one galley door to the other, according as we would go about, to see how near the steamer was getting.

When the steamer got close, I heard a hail, "What schooner is that?" The reply was, "The *Enchantress*." "Where bound to?" "Cuba." As soon as that was said, I jumped overboard.

I sang out, "A captured vessel of the privateer *Jeff Davis*, and they are taking her into Charleston." I sang it out so they could hear me on board the steamer. The steamer's boat picked me up. Then they took the prize crew off the schooner.

William Smith, *The* Jeff Davis *Piracy Cases*,
(Philadelphia, 1861)

But the real shift in public attitudes was brought about by the slaves of the South. It was they who changed the war to preserve the Union into a war of liberation.

2. Many Thousands Gone

There were four million slaves in the South, working on plantations and on Rebel fortifications. Lincoln, trying to appease the slave states that had remained loyal to the Union, was afraid to call on slaves to leave their masters. They did not wait for his invitation. As one slave said, "When my master and somebody else quarrel, I'm on the somebody else's side."

The war was only a few weeks old when a group of slaves paddled across Chesapeake Bay in a stolen canoe to present themselves to General Benjamin Butler, commander of Union forces in Virginia. Instead of returning them to their masters, Butler declared them "contraband of war" (captured enemy property) and put them to work building a bake house for his men. In two months, nine hundred "contraband" teamsters, blacksmiths, cooks, and laundresses were working for him.

The same thing happened whenever Union forces entered slave territory. After a Northern fleet captured the Sea Islands of South Carolina in November 1861, the whites fled. Before long, the eight thousand slaves they left behind were raising food and cotton for the Union. Charlotte Forten who went to the Sea Islands to teach in a newly opened school, reported the reactions of the "contrabands":

I enjoy hearing two of our men—Harry and Cupid—rejoice over the flight of the Secesh at the "gunshoot." They call the taking of Bay Point, which is opposite Hilton Head, the "gun shoot." It was immediately after this that these islands were deserted by the Southerners. Shortly afterward, a few of them had the temerity to return and try to induce the Negroes to go off with them.

Harry says that his master told them that the Yankees

"Contrabands" going to join the Union forces

would certainly shoot every one of them. "Very well, massa," said he. "If I go with you, I be as good as dead. So if I got to dead, I believe I'll stay and wait for the Yankees." He said he knew all the while there was no truth in what his master said.

Nevertheless the master thought that some of the people could be induced to go with him. So he very coolly ordered them to remove all the furniture from the house to an island opposite and then go thither themselves. "So," as Cupid says, "they could get us all together in a heap and just sweep us right off into the boat. And then they tell me that I could just row my wife and children down to a certain point and then I could come back myself if I choose. As if I was going to be such a goat!" The people, instead of obeying their master, secreted themselves so that when he and his friends returned, not a single one of those Negroes could be found to accompany them into slavery.

The Liberator, December 19, 1862

An ex-slave told what happened when Union gunboats steamed up a river in South Carolina:

The people was all a hoeing. They was a hoeing in the rice field when the gunboats come. Then every man drop them hoe and left the rice. The master he stand and call, "Run to the wood for hide. Yankee come, sell you to Cuba! Run for hide!" Every man he run, and my God! run all the other way! Master stand in the wood. He say, "Run to the wood!" and every man run by him, straight to the boat.

Thomas W. Higginson, "Up the Edisto,"
Atlantic Monthly, August 1867

"Contrabands" on the way to work

There were similar reports, some tragic, from Florida, Louisiana, Virginia and Kentucky. A free black in Louisville told of slaves who swam across the Ohio River:

During summer and fall, numbers were found drowned who had braved the perils of the Ohio in order to obtain freedom. One man and his wife I saw and conversed with swam the river with their trunk, wading up to their necks and pushing their trunk before them, holding on to it as a buoy when too deep to wade. They reached the shore and are now safe in the land of the free.

The Pacific Appeal, March 7, 1863

A correspondent for Douglass' Monthly *described the scene at Cairo, Illinois, where the Ohio joined the Mississippi:*

Cairo, September 25, 1862

Friend Douglass:

Cairo now begins to look as though the jubilee sure enough has come. Every morning when I go down to the levee I find it dotted over with new arrivals of contrabands. Old men and young men, old women and young women, and children are here. The town is literally alive with them.

I have heard various accounts of what they thought and did when they heard *"them big guns roar"*—how the men and women in the fields would begin to fall back upon their dignity and disregard the commands of the overseer. The overseers would tell them, "Now when you see the Yankees coming you must break for the woods." They would say, "No, we think the best way would be to run to the Yankees and throw ourselves on their mercies, and they will be less liable to hurt us."

I am constantly asked by both men and women whether they can get work in the North—what the wages are and whether they can make money there, and whether it is very cold in the winter.

H. Oscar

Douglass' Monthly, November 1862

Pressures on Lincoln were mounting. The war was well into its second year. Confederate troops were on the offensive in Virginia, Tennessee and Kentucky. Union men were slow to volunteer, and there was angry opposition to a draft. And yet Lincoln hesitated to tap the tremendous source of fighting power that the slaves offered him. Time and again, Frederick Douglass pointed out, "We are striking with our soft white hand, when we should be striking with the iron hand of the black man, which we keep chained behind us."

At last, Lincoln decided to break the chains. In September 1862 he issued a preliminary proclamation which promised freedom to the slaves of the Rebel states on January 1, 1863.

For a hundred days blacks and their white friends watched, waited, worried. Would the Rebels make peace to save slavery? Would Lincoln change his mind? On the first of January, blacks gathered in churches and halls across the nation to await the news. Henry M. Turner, pastor of Israel Bethel Church in Washington, recalled the momentous day:

Long after sunset Israel Church and its yard were crowded with people. Seeing such a multitude in and around my church, I hurriedly went to the office of the first paper in which the proclamation of freedom could be printed, and squeezed myself through the dense crowd that was waiting. The first sheet run off with the proclamation in it was grabbed for by three of us, but some active young man got possession of it and fled. The next sheet was grabbed for by several and was torn into tatters. The third sheet I succeeded in procuring and off I went.

Down Pennsylvania Avenue I ran as for my life. When

the people saw me coming with the paper in my hand they raised a shouting cheer that was almost deafening. As many as could get around me lifted me to a great platform and I started to read. I had run the best of a mile. I was out of breath and could not read. Mr. Hinton to whom I handed the paper read it with great force and clearness.

While he was reading every kind of demonstration was going on. Men squealed, women fainted, dogs barked, white and colored people shook hands, songs were sung. By this time cannons began to fire at the Navy Yard in the wake of the roar that had been going on behind the White House. Every face had a smile and even the dumb animals seemed to realize that some extraordinary event had taken place.

Great processions of colored and white men marched to

Freed children dancing

and fro in front of the White House and congratulated President Lincoln on his proclamation. The President came to the window and made responsive bows.

The jubilation that attended the proclamation of freedom I am sure has never been surpassed. Rumor said that the very thought of being set at liberty and having no more auction blocks, no more separation of parents and children, was so heart-gladdening that scores of colored people literally fell dead with joy. It was indeed a time of times and a half time. Nothing like it will ever be seen again in this life.

Henry M. Turner, *The Negro in Slavery, War and Peace*
(Philadelphia, 1913)

3. The Colored Volunteer

As the shouts died down, there were second thoughts about the proclamation. It could not be enforced in the Deep South until Union armies were victorious there, and it did not attempt to free slaves in Border States which were loyal to the Union. A Californian pointed this out:

February 25, 1863

Mr. Editor:

Our honest but incompetent President adopts a halfway measure which purports to give freedom to the bulk of the slave population beyond the reach of our arms, while it ignores those whom alone we have the power to redeem. The proclamation should have been made to include every bondsman on the soil of America. Then indeed we could have boldly claimed the services of every loyal man, white or black, in suppressing this hell-born rebellion. The proclamation has been brought forth by timid and heaven-doubting midwives and proved an incompetent and abominable abortion.

J.H.H.

The Pacific Appeal, March 7, 1863

But most people recognized the proclamation as the beginning of the end of slavery. In it Lincoln had said that black men would be "received into the armed service of the United States." The War Department had already authorized two black regiments in the South: the First South Carolina Volunteers, composed of ex-slaves, and the First Regiment Louisiana Native Guards. The Native Guards were free blacks who had been enrolled in the Confederate militia. They had refused to leave New Orleans when North-

ern troops took the city in the spring of 1862. Instead, they offered to fight for the Union.

In L'Union, the French-English newspaper published by New Orleans' black community, there were frequent notices calling for volunteers. The following promised that soldiers would receive bounties of $100 or 160 acres of land after the war as well as pay and support for their families while they were in service. Sergeants and corporals who spoke English in addition to French were wanted:

ATTENTION! NATIVE-GUARDS!
Ralliez-vous sous le Drapeau de l'Union!

On demande des hommes bien constitués pour former une compagnie du 3è régiment des Volontaires de la Louisiane, pour le service des Etats-Unis.

$100 ou 160 acres de Terre à la fin de la guerre.

$38 en avance!

Provisions pour familles aussitôt la compagnie enrégimentée.

Paie: $13 á $22 par mois.

On demande des sergents et des caporaux parlant l'anglais et le français.

Louis N. Fouché, officier recruteur

L'Union, November 5, 1862

One native of New Orleans, H. Ford Douglass, had said that he would be willing to join a foreign army to fight against the United States. He did an about-face after the war began. Seeing a chance to strike a blow against slavery, he somehow managed to enlist in a white regiment. On duty in Louisiana when the first black regiments were authorized, he wrote the following to Owen Lovejoy, an antislavery congressman from Illinois:

Providence, Louisiana, February 3, 1863

Hon. Owen Lovejoy
My dear Sir:

In my desire to serve the great cause of freedom I have

First South Carolinas in battle

enlisted as a soldier. I belong to Company G, 95 Regiment Illinois Volunteers.

My mistake was in not waiting until the government called colored men into the service. Then I could have occupied something like an equal position among my comrades. But as it is now, although I am respected by my own regiment and treated kindly by those who know me, still there are those in other regiments with whom I come in contact who have no regard for my feelings simply because I have the hated blood coursing in my veins.

My position therefore, which might be very pleasant, especially when I have the consciousness of fighting in a cause so holy, is anything but agreeable. Under the circumstances I wish you to interest yourself in my behalf. I would like to get a transfer to South Carolina where there are colored regiments in the course of formation or else a commission to recruit for one to which I could be attached after it was formed.

There could be no legal objection on this point for I am already a U.S. soldier. I have now been six months in the service with the advantages of drill in many of its most important details. I think I could render more efficient service with those that I have been identified in the moral conflicts of the past than I can in my present position. You will agree with me that the Negro ought to have an intelligent idea of what he is fighting for—in this I think I could be useful.

H. Ford Douglass

National Archives

Douglass was transferred to a Louisiana black regiment and was authorized to raise an independent company of scouts. At first as a lieutenant and later as a captain, he saw service throughout the war.

His experience was unusual. Outside of Louisiana, where the Native Guards had always had black officers, no black men except doctors received commissions until 1865. Nor were they allowed to organize their own companies, a privilege granted to many whites. After the Emancipation Proclamation gave the go-ahead for black troops, the War Department and state governors were bombarded with letters like the following:

St. Cloud, Minnesota, April 15, 1863

To the Hon. Edward Stanton
Dear Sir:

[I am] a loyal citizen of Minnesota of African descent living in the Northwestern part of the U.S. where there are but few of my race, not enough to raise a company. Willing to do anything to help put down the Rebellion, I ask to go into Illinois where there are hundreds of my race ready to volunteer in the U.S. service. I ask of you as the head of the

War Department to give me a commission as Captain to raise
a company or regiment of my people.

R. I. Cromwell

National Archives

*Cromwell did not get the assignment. A black man who
wanted to fight had to wait for his state to raise a black
regiment—or go elsewhere. The first regiment of Northern
blacks was organized in Massachusetts. A team of recruiters,
which included Frederick Douglass, Martin R. Delany,
Henry Highland Garnet and William Wells Brown, traveled
through the North signing up volunteers. Among those who
joined were Douglass' two sons and Delany's oldest. Of-
ficered by white abolitionists, the 54th Massachusetts Volunteers marched off to war singing a song that one of their men
had written:*

McClellan went to Richmond with two hundred thousand
    brave;
He said, "keep back the niggers," and the Union he would
    save.
Little Mac he had his way—still the Union is in tears—
Now they call for the help of the colored volunteers.

O, give us a flag, all free without a slave,
We'll fight to defend it, as our Fathers did so brave.
The gallant Comp'ny "A" will make the rebels dance,
And we'll stand by the Union if we only have a chance.

So rally, boys, rally, let us never mind the past;
We had a hard road to travel, but our day is coming fast,
For God is for the right, and we have no need to fear,—
The Union must be saved by the colored volunteer.

William Wells Brown, Negro in the American Rebellion

(Boston, 1867)

*The 54th Massachusetts Volunteers saw their first action
in the summer of 1863 when they stormed Fort Wagner,*

a Confederate stronghold in Charleston's harbor. They planted their flag on the parapet of the fort, then were forced to retreat under withering enemy fire. Their colonel was killed, and more than two hundred men were wounded or taken prisoner. A sergeant of the 54th remembered:

Our column charged the fort, passed the half-filled moat and mounted to the parapet. Many of the men clambered over and some entered by the large embrasure in which one of the big guns was mounted. But the rebel fire grew hotter and a fieldpiece every few seconds seemed to sweep along our rapidly thinning ranks. Men all around me would fall and roll down into the ditch.

Just at the hottest moment of the struggle, a battalion charged up to the moat and commenced to fire upon us. I was one of the men who shouted, "Don't fire on us! We are the Fifty-fourth!" I have heard it was a Maine regiment. This is God's living truth!

Immediately after I heard an order, "Retreat!" Some twelve or fifteen of us slid down the parapet. The line of retreat seemed lit with infernal fire. The hissing bullets and bursting shells seemed angry demons.

I was with Hooker's division in the battle of Fredericksburg, but hot as the fire was there, it did not compare to the terrific fire which blazed along the narrow approach to Wagner.

George W. Williams, *A History of the Negro Troops in the War of the Rebellion* (New York, 1888)

Although the 54th was driven back, their assault on Fort Wagner established the reputation of blacks as fighting men. A sister regiment, the 55th Massachusetts, joined in the siege of Charleston and was the first to enter the city when it fell. A sergeant in the 55th wrote:

I have seen considerable service, both in the infantry and in artillery. It was my privilege to be the first non-commissioned officer that reached the enemy's guns in the fight on James Island on the first of July. I found one of them loaded and fired it. Afterwards loaded it with another charge and fired that also. The two guns were afterwards given in my charge by the Colonel.

Could you have been on the battlefield and seen them under a shower of shot and shell when it seemed as though the day was lost—could you have seen the old 55th rush in, you would have thought that nothing human could have withstood their impetuosity. We know no defeat. The guns we were bent on having and there they are next to my tent door.

The Liberator, October 7, 1864

By the summer of 1863 black soldiers were in demand. A stiff new Conscription Act required the states to draft men of

Black soldiers pose for a recruiting picture

military age if they could not fill their quotas with volunteers. Every black who joined up made it possible for one white to stay out of the army. Connecticut, Rhode Island, Ohio, Michigan sent agents across the country, to Canada and to Union-held territory in the South, to find black volunteers. With the states competing against each other, blacks were offered substantial bounties for enlisting. Martin Delany who had postponed his dream of going to Africa teamed up with John Jones to recruit in the Midwest. One of his handbills:

BLACK NATIONAL DEFENDERS!

The State of Connecticut is authorized to raise Colored Troops; and any number of her quota of 5,000 may be colored men. 29th Regiment Connecticut Volunteers, is now being formed at Camp Buckingham, composed entirely of Colored Men, located at the beatiful City of New Haven, the seat of Yale University.

STATE BOUNTY,
$200.00 CASH!

On being sworn in.

By an old law of the State, 30 dollars a year are allowed to each soldier for clothing, 10 dollars of which is paid down at the time of entering the service, the other 20 dollars being paid in four month payments each, making 210 dollars Bounty—cash, on joining the Regiment—and 20 dollars more during the year.

An important fact connected with this recruiting is, that the contract for raising the troops has been given to a Colored Man; and Connecticut is the first State, since the war commenced, which has been thus liberal and considerate.

This fact alone should be an inducement for **COLORED MEN** to rally to her standard: all the Recruiting Agents in the West being Colored; and this principle should prevail everywhere. Colored Men should recruit Colored Men, as best adapted to it.

The most liberal compensation will be given to Good Agents,

about 50 such being now wanted, and to whom will be paid Cash so soon as service is rendered.

APPLY WITHOUT DELAY TO

DR. M. R. DELANY.

State Contractor, Head-quarters of the West and South-Western States and Territories, 172 Clark Street, Top Story, Chicago, Ill.

JOHN JONES, Assistant.
W. F. STAINES, Evansville, Ind.

National Archives

Many unscrupulous agents pocketed the bounties due black volunteers. To protect his recruits from being swindled, Delany personally escorted them to the army camps. In the following letter to Mary Ann Shadd Cary, who left her home in Canada to help win the war, he explained his terms. Mrs. Cary, probably the only woman to work as a recruiter, was also employed by the state of Indiana.

December 7, 1863

Mrs. Cary
Madame:

I have just returned from the East where I have completed a contract with the State authorities of Connecticut with the sole right of raising black troops in the West and South-west. She wants 5,000 men to make up her quota. The first black regiment to be raised is the 29th Regiment Connecticut Volunteers.

To all "slaves" obtained, a state-bounty of $120. cash will be paid *immediately* on being sworn in, with the same pay per month, clothing and political status as white men. Free colored men get $200. bounty cash.

I will pay you $15 cash for all slave men (or freedmen) on delivery and examination by me here in Chicago, I bearing the expense of transportation.

This presents a good opportunity to do good to the oppressed and justice to those who help them. I am still an agent for Rhode Island and if any prefer heavy artillery, you may take them for that.

M. R. Delany

Mary Ann Shadd Cary Papers, Moorland-Spingarn Collection, Howard University Library

Although she was not an official recruiting agent, Sojourner Truth traveled through the Midwest to urge support for the Union. In Indiana, Copperheads—Northerners who sided with the South—threatened to burn down the hall where she was to speak. "Then I will speak upon the ashes," she said. Her report of the meeting:

The ladies thought I should be dressed in uniform so they put upon me a red, white and blue shawl, a sash and apron to match, a cap on my head with a star in front, and a star on each shoulder. When I was dressed I looked in the glass and was fairly frightened. Said I, "It seems I am going to battle." My friends advised me to take a sword or pistol. I replied, "I carry no weapon. I feel safe even in the midst of my enemies, for the truth is powerful and will prevail."

They put me into a large, beautiful carriage with the captain [of the Home Guard] and other gentlemen, all of whom were armed. The soldiers walked by our side and a long procession followed. As we neared the court-house, I saw that the building was surrounded by a great crowd. But when the Rebels saw such a mighty army coming, they fled. By the time we arrived they were scattered over the fields, looking like a flock of frightened crows. Not one was left but a small boy, who sat upon the fence, crying "Nigger, nigger!"

We now marched into the courthouse, escorted by double files of soldiers with presented arms. The band struck up "The Star-Spangled Banner," in which I joined and sang with all my might, while amid flashing bayonets and waving banners our party made its way to the platform.

Olive Gilbert, *Narrative of Sojourner Truth*
(Battle Creek, Michigan, 1876)

4. Copperhead, Johnny Reb and Uncle Sam

The war was unpopular in many quarters. Businessmen with ties to the South called for peace at any price while workmen were afraid that freed slaves would flock to the North and compete for their jobs. Neither group was eager to fight and die for "a war for the nigger." The sight of a black man in uniform was sometimes enough to touch off a riot. In the spring of 1863, two black Canadians, Dr. Alexander T. Augusta and Dr. Anderson Abbott, were enrolled as Surgeons for the black troops, with the rank of Major. Dr. Abbott described what happened on a train in Baltimore:

While sitting in the car at Baltimore depot a man came

Major Alexander T. Augusta
    (*Moorland-Spingarn Collection, Howard University Library*)

up and pulled off one of [Augusta's] shoulder straps. Augusta defended himself until a squad of soldiers came to his assistance. Augusta was arrested and carried up town to the provost marshal, followed by a hooting mob. After [showing] proofs of his rank as a commissioned officer he was escorted to the depot under guard. When opposite a doorway a man standing on the steps struck Augusta a powerful blow on the nose, knocking him down. Immediately the mob rushed upon him. A squad of military detectives dispersed the mob with their revolvers while Augusta, stunned and bleeding, escaped into an adjoining drug store. It was a wonder that he escaped with his life.

Anderson R. Abbott Papers, Toronto Public Library

When a rumor spread through Detroit that a black man had raped a white girl, mobs shouting, "Kill all the damned niggers!" stormed the black section of the city. Several men were killed, thirty-two houses destroyed and more than two hundred left homeless. When it was all over, the rapist turned out to be white and the girl, a prostitute. The chief target of the mob was a cooper shop belonging to a prosperous black businessman. His daughter, Louisa Bonn, and two of his employees described their experiences:

Louisa Bonn: They commenced breaking in the doors and windows of the cooper shop. Myself and child, mother and Mrs. Dale and her three children kept in the back part of the house. Then the dining room caught fire. I started to go out the front door with my babe in my arms. On going to the door, a man met me with a large boulder in his hand. I then returned in the house, the sheets of flames approaching me and my babe. Finding I could not get out I commenced screaming. Two gentlemen ran to me and told me I should not be hurt. I thought my mother was burned up! No tongue can describe the feelings of my mind on that occasion.

Louis Houston: Finding the house being consumed, I went to the back part of the lot to go through a hole in the fence.

Stones and bats were flying. On reaching the spot I found one of our hands who, a few moments before, worked at my side, knocked in the head with an axe. He appeared lifeless. I went up the alley. Here the mob overtook me. They beat me over the head till I heard some one say, "he is dead!" Near night I came to enough to get home.

Lewis Pearce: I was knocked down by a stone in the yard while the house was burning. I found the flames so intense that I drew a wheelbarrow over me. There I lay till a couple of policemen dragged me out. I then staggered over to Mrs. Jones, being weak from loss of blood. I had not been there but a few moments before they came and said, "Get out of there." I got out into the privy to conceal myself and soon a couple of fellows brought me out on St. Antoine Street, beating me all the way. The mob fell on me and with kicks and clubs beat me till they thought life was extinct. My head was bruised, my knee cap was broke right in two. I am now getting better but never shall overcome the effects of the injuries.

A Thrilling Narrative from the Lips of the Sufferers
of the Late Detriot Riot (Detroit, 1863)

Then for four frightful days in July 1863, a mob roamed the streets of New York, killing, burning, looting. The rioters were protesting the new Conscription Law which permitted rich men to escape the army by paying for a substitute, but drafted the poor. However, most of their anger was directed against blacks. Dozens of men were lynched, the Colored Orphan Asylum was burned to the ground, and thousands of refugees fled the city. Fifteen-year-old Maritcha Lyons was one of the refugees. She later wrote:

On the afternoon of July [13th], a rabble attacked our house, breaking windowpanes, smashing shutters and partially demolishing the front door. Before dusk arrangements had been effected to secure the safety of the children. As the evening drew on, a resolute man and a courageous woman quietly seated themselves in the hall, determined to sell their lives as dearly as may be. Lights having been extinguished, a lonely vigil passed in mingled indignation, uncertainty and dread. Just after midnight a yell announced that a second mob was gathering. As one of the rioters attempted to ascend the front steps, father advanced into the doorway and fired point blank into the crowd. The mob retreated hastily and no further demonstration was made that night. The next day a third and successful attempt at entrance was effected. This sent father over the back fence while mother took refuge on the premises of a neighbor.

In one short hour, the police cleared the premises. What a home! Its interior was dismantled, furniture was missing or broken. From basement to attic evidences of vandalism prevailed. A fire, kindled in one of the upper rooms, was discovered in time to prevent a conflagration.

Under cover of darkness the police conveyed our parents to the Williamsburg ferry. There steamboats were kept in

Colored Orphan Asylum burning during New York riots, 1863
(*New York Public Library Picture Collection*)

readiness to transport fugitives or to outwit rioters by pulling out into midstream. Mother with her children undertook the hazardous journey of getting to New England. After a brief rest in New London, we reached Salem tired, travel-stained, with only the garments we had on.

Lyons-Williamson Papers, Schomburg Collection

Albro Lyons' partner, William P. Powell, who managed a Colored Sailors Home, had a more hair-raising escape:

New Bedford, Massachusetts, July 18, 1863

Friend Garrison:

On the afternoon of the 13th the Colored Sailors Home was invaded by a mob of half-grown boys. From 2 to 8 P.M. myself and family were prisoners. The mob commenced throwing stones at the windows until they succeeded in making an opening. My family, including my invalid daughter, took refuge on the roof of the next house. I remained till the mob broke in and then narrowly escaped the same way. This was about 8½ P.M. We remained on the roof for an hour. It began to rain, as if the very heavens were shedding tears over the dreadful calamity.

How to escape from the roof of a five-story building with four females—and one a cripple—without a ladder was beyond my *not* excited imagination. But God came to my relief in the person of a little deformed, despised Israelite who took my poor helpless daughter under his protection in his house. He also supplied me with a long rope. Though pitchy dark I took soundings with the rope to see if it would touch the next roof, after which I took a clove-hitch around the clothesline which led from one roof to the other over a space of about one hundred feet. I managed to lower my family down to the next roof and from one roof to another, until I landed them in a neighbor's yard. We were secreted in our friend's cellar till 11 P.M. when we were taken by the police and locked up in the station house for safety. In this dismal place we found upward of seventy men, women and children—some with broken limbs—bruised and beaten from head to foot. We stayed in this place for 24 hours, when the police escorted us to the New Haven boat. All my personal property to the amount of $3,000 has been scattered to the four winds. I am now an old man, stripped of everything which I once possessed, but I thank God that He has spared my life which I am ready to yield in the defense of my country.

William P. Powell

The Liberator, July 24, 1863

There were those who did not escape at all. An eyewitness reported:

"Mother! They may kill the body but they cannot touch the soul!" was the language used by poor Abraham Franklin as he was borne from his mother by the barbarous mob on the morning of the 14th. This young man, aged 23, had been an invalid for about two years. When the mob broke in they found him in bed. They bore him into the street and there they beat him to death, hanged him to a lamppost, cut his pantaloons off at the knees, cut bits of flesh out of his legs and afterwards set fire to him. All this was done beneath the eyes of his widowed mother. Patrick Butler and George Glass, both Irishmen, have been arrested for the murder.

The Pacific Appeal, September 5, 1863

Few rioters were brought to trial; none were executed for murder. The riot, however, marked a turning point. To the surprise of the black community, New York's leading merchants came forward with offers of help. They raised almost $50,000 for the riot victims and helped to rebuild the Colored Orphan Asylum. Henry Highland Garnet, who had escaped the mob only because his daughter had wrenched his nameplate from his door with an axe, took charge of

Man hanged by New York rioters
(*New York Public Library Picture Collection*)

the distribution, assisted by other black ministers. Nine months later when New York's first black regiment paraded through the city, thousands lined the streets to cheer them.

Although the Copperhead attacks virtually ceased, black soldiers were singled out for special treatment by the Rebels. The Confederate Congress ruled that black prisoners of war were to be sold as slaves or put to death and their white officers executed. Even after Lincoln threatened to retaliate if the laws of war were violated, Rebels continued to mistreat black soldiers. A soldier testified to this at a U. S. Army hearing:

Samuel Johnson being duly sworn deposes and says:

I am an orderly sergeant of Co. D 2nd U. S. Colored Cavalry. In April last I went to Plymouth, N.C., to take charge of recruits and was there at the time of the capture of Plymouth by the Rebel forces. When I found the city was believed by the Rebels to be a citizen and was employed a suit of citizens' clothing which I put on. When captured I was being surrendered I pulled off my uniform and found

New York's black regiment

in endeavoring to raise sunken vessels of the Union fleet.

All the Negroes found in blue uniform or with any outward marks of a Union soldier upon him was killed. I saw some taken to the woods and hung. Others I saw stripped of all their clothing and then stood upon the banks of the river and shot. Still others were killed by having their brains beaten out by the butt end of muskets. The Regiments most conspicuous in these murderous transactions were the 8th N.C. and I think the 6th N.C.

National Archives

When Confederates led by General Nathan Bedford Forrest captured Fort Pillow in Tennessee, they killed more than three hundred men who had surrendered. Shocked by reports of soldiers buried and burned alive, a Congressional Committee investigated the massacre. Selections from

Massacre at Fort Pillow
(*General Research and Humanities Division, New York
Public Library, Astor, Lenox and Tilden Foundations*)

the testimony of twenty-one black survivors:

Duncan Harding (colored) private, Company A, 6th U.S. heavy artillery sworn and examined.

Question. Were you in Fort Pillow at the time it was captured?

ANSWER. Yes, sir. I was a gunner. I was shot in the arm. They picked me up and marched me up the hill and while they were marching me they shot me again through the thigh.

Question. When you were shot the last time had you any arms?

ANSWER. No, sir.

Question. Were any officers about when you were shot last?

ANSWER: Yes, sir.

Question. Did they say anything against it?

ANSWER. No, sir; only, "Kill the Godamned nigger."

Nathan Hunter (colored) private, Company D, 6th U.S. heavy artillery, sworn and examined.

They shot me for dead and I lay there until next morning when the gunboat came. They thought I was dead and pulled my boots off. I was not shot until we were done fighting.

Question. Did you see any others shot?

ANSWER. Yes, sir. They shot down a whole parcel along with me. Their bodies were lying along the river bank. They kicked some of them into the river after they were shot.

Daniel Tyler (colored) private, Company B, 6th U.S. heavy artillery, sworn and examined.

Question. How did you lose your eye?

ANSWER. They knocked me down with a carbine and then they jabbed it out.

Question. After you had surrendered?

ANSWER. Yes, sir. I was going up the hill. A man knocked me down and then took the end of his carbine and jabbed it in my eye and shot me.

Thomas Adison (colored) private, Company C, 6th U.S. heavy artillery, sworn and examined.

Question. What happened after you were wounded?

ANSWER. I went down the hill after we surrendered. They shot me again in my face, breaking my jaw bone. A fellow turned me over and searched my pockets and took my money. He said, "Godamn his old soul. He is sure dead now." They shot a great many that evening.

Question. The day of the fight?

ANSWER. Yes, sir. I heard them shoot little children not more than that high (holding his hand off about four feet from the floor) that the officers had to wait on them.

Question. Did you see them shoot them?

ANSWER. I did not hold up my head.

Question. How did you know that they shot them then?

ANSWER. I heard them say, "Turn around so that I can shoot you good." Then I heard them fire and I heard the children fall over. One was named Dave, and the other was named Anderson.

Manuel Nichols (colored) private, Company B, 6th U.S. heavy artillery, sworn and examined.

After I surrendered a man shot me under the ear. I fell down. One of their officers came along and hallooed, "Forrest says, no quarter! no quarter!" and the next one hallooed, "Black flag! Black flag!"

Question. How near to you was the man who shot you?

ANSWER. Right close to my head. When I was shot a man turned me over and took my pocketknife and pocketbook. I had some of these brass things that looked like cents. They said, "Here's some money." I said to myself, "You got fooled that time."

Major Williams (colored) private, Company B, 6th U.S. heavy artillery, sworn and examined.

I saw a white man burned who was nailed up against the house. I think it was a lieutenant in the Tennessee cavalry.

Question. How was he nailed?

ANSWER. Through his hands and feet right against the house.

Question. Was his body burned?

ANSWER. Yes, sir. Burned all over—I looked at him good.

Jacob Thompson (colored) sworn and examined.

Question. Were you a soldier at Fort Pillow?

ANSWER. No, sir, but I went up in the fort and fought with the rest.

Question. Did you see anybody shot?

ANSWER. Yes, sir. They just called them out like dogs and shot them down. I reckon they shot about fifty, black and white, right there. They nailed some black sergeants to the logs and set the logs on fire.

Question. Did they kill them before they burned them?

ANSWER. No, sir. They nailed them to the logs; drove the nails right through their hands.

Ransom Anderson (colored) Company B, 6th U.S. heavy artillery, sworn and examined.

Most all the men that were killed on our side were killed

after the fight was over. They put some in the houses and
shut them up and then burned the houses.
Question. Were any of them alive?
ANSWER. Yes, sir. They were wounded and could not walk.
They told them they were going to have the doctor see
them, then shut them up and burned them.
Question. Was the door fastened up?
ANSWER. Yes, sir. It was barred with one of those wide bolts.

House of Representatives Report No. 65,
38th Congress, 1st session

*Recuperating in an army hospital, one of the survivors
said:*

I hope to recover and get away from here very soon. I
want to be in my place again for I have something to avenge
now and I cannot bear to wait.

Harper's Weekly, April 30, 1864

*Across the South, black soldiers went into battle cry-
ing, "Remember Fort Pillow!" Writing to his father, Amos G.
Beman, Charles T. Beman described their resolute mood:*

Point of Rocks, Va., June 20, 1864

Dear Father:

Since I last wrote almost half of the 5th Massachusetts
Cavalry have been in several engagements and about thirty
have been killed and wounded. About 1 A.M. Wednesday
we heard the bugle and sprang to our arms. We started
towards Petersburg and when about four miles on our way,
we came in front of the Rebels' works. We had to pass
through a strip of woods while the shell, grape and canister
came around us cruelly. Our Major and Col. Russell were
wounded and several men fell. To advance seemed almost
impossible but after a terrible charge, amidst pieces of barbarous iron, solid shot and shell we drove the desperate

graybacks from their fortifications and gave three cheers for our victory.

The colored troops here have received a great deal of praise. The sensations I had in the battle were coolness and interest in the boys' fighting. They shouted, "Fort Pillow," and the Rebs were shown no mercy.

Charles Torrey Beman

Beman Papers, Beinecke Library, Yale University

Even in the army, black soldiers had to fight for equal treatment. Although they had been promised the same pay as white enlisted men—$13 a month plus a clothing allowance—they were given only $10, with $3 deducted for clothing. In protest, the men of the 54th and 55th Massachusetts Regiments refused to accept any pay at all. They *went payless for eighteen months until Congress ended the discrimination. A private in the 54th wrote:*

Morris Island, South Carolina, January 15, 1864

Mr. Editor:

When I enlisted in this regiment it was not to secure the paltry wages that was offered but that I might be one of the many that have come out to fight for the elevation of a downtrodden race. Since then I have been where shot and shell fell around me like hailstones. While I write, heavy firing can be heard from Battery Gregg, paying her compliments to the city of Charleston.

When the sun rises then commences our hard fatigue, and continues until the sun goes behind the western hills. We lay ourselves down to rest, not knowing what moment we may be called on to face the enemy. We have fulfilled all our agreements to the Government, but thus far the Government fails to fulfill their part of the contract by paying us. We are in hopes something may be done soon. I cannot say where the 54th may yet go. But wherever we are, whatever may be our fate, we shall always try and be an honor to the race which we represent.

Daniel Walker, Co. H, 54th Regiment

The Pacific Appeal, March 12, 1864

The soldiers also complained because all of their officers were white. In the last year of the war, some men were commissioned as officers in the field, only to have their commissions disapproved by General Charles W. Foster, chief of the Bureau of Colored Troops. James M. Trotter, who wrote the following letter to Francis J. Garrison, was a twenty-two-year-old schoolteacher from Cincinnati. He met Francis, son of William Lloyd Garrison, while the 55th was in training in Massachusetts. Trotter and his fellow sergeants were offi-

cially mustered in as lieutenants in June 1865.

> Camp of 55th Massachusetts Volunteers
> Folly Island, South Carolina, August 2, 1864

Dear Franky:

You have heard that First Sergeants Shorter and Dupree and Sergeant Major Trotter have been commissioned as Second Lieutenants. So far, very good, but General Foster will not muster them into the service as officers, claiming that "There is no law *allowing* it, they being colored men." Do you know of any law that prohibits it? I am performing the duties for which I was commissioned, but this half-and-half arrangement is very unpleasant.

I am sorry to have to tell you also that most all the line officers give us the *cold shoulder.* Indeed, when our papers returned those who have all along claimed to be our best friends seemed to feel the most lively satisfaction at the result. Oh how discouraging! How maddening, almost!

An officer told me that it was "too soon," that time should be granted white officers to *get rid of their prejudices,* so that a white Lieutenant would not refuse to sleep in a tent with a colored one. Of course he supposed that an objection of this kind would be made always by the white Lieut., and that an educated decent colored officer would never object to sleeping with the former whatever might be his character. Yes, Franky, there is really more turning up the nose on account of the commissions in our very midst than elsewhere; and no other reason is given except color. When you write your father please tell Mr. Garrison about the refusal of General Foster to muster as officers colored men, so that it may [be] referred to in *The Liberator.*

James M. Trotter

Francis J. Garrison Papers, Schomburg Collection

5. They Also Served

Two hundred thousand black men served in the Union army; thirty thousand joined the navy. Another quarter of a million men and women worked for the Union as spies, scouts, nurses, cooks, laborers. Among the thousands of slaves who contributed to the war effort, Robert Smalls was the most prominent. A twenty-three-year-old pilot on the Confederate gunboat Planter, *based in Charleston, Smalls and a slave crew sailed the boat past the guns of Fort Sumter and turned it over to the Union fleet. He also brought*

Teamsters working for the Union army

valuable information about the disposition of Confederate forces in and around the city. In 1864, Smalls told a black audience in Philadelphia how he had captured the Planter:

While at the wheel of the *Planter,* it occurred to me that I could not only secure my own freedom but that of numbers of my comrades. Moreover, I thought that the *Planter* might be of some use to "Uncle Abe." I was not long in making my thoughts known to my wife. She desired to know the consequences in case I should be caught. I replied, "I shall be shot." "It is a risk, but you and I and our little ones must be free. I will go," said she, "for where you die I will die."

I reported my plans to the crew (all colored) and secured their secrecy and co-operation. On May 13, 1862, we took on board several large guns at the Atlantic Dock. At evening of that day, the Captain went home, leaving the boat in my care.

At half past 3 o'clock in the morning of the 14th, I left the Atlantic Dock with the *Planter,* took on board my family and several other families, then proceeded down Charleston River slowly. On reaching Fort Sumter I gave the signal which was answered from the fort, thereby giving permission to pass. I then made speed for the blockading fleet. When out of range of Sumter's guns, I hoisted a white flag and at 5 A.M. reached a U.S. blockading vessel, commandered by Captain Nichols, to whom I turned over the *Planter.*

A. M. E. Review, January–March 1955

Smalls remained aboard the Planter, *at first as pilot and later as captain, until 1866. A newspaper story gave the circumstances of his promotion:*

Our readers will remember the brave man who took the steamer *Planter* out of Charleston harbor. He is a very skillful pilot and has since served up and down all that coast.

Robert Smalls

THE STEAMER PLANTER.

In the latter part of November, the *Planter*'s captain, a white man, refused to stick by his vessel where she was under fire. Chief Quartermaster Elwell ordered Mr. Smalls to be made captain, in a letter ending as follows:

"He is an excellent pilot, of undoubted bravery, and is in every respect worthy of the position. The present captain is a coward, though a white man. Dismiss him, therefore, and give the steamer to this brave black Saxon."

Captain Smalls is, we believe, the highest in command of any colored person in the land or sea service of the United

States. He has already gained for himself much honor and success. We wish him more.

The Pacific Appeal, January 30, 1864

Other slaves with an intimate knowledge of the South-ern terrain acted as spies for the Secret Service and scouts for the Army. Garland H. White, formerly the slave of Robert Toombs, a Confederate leader, was a chaplain with a black regiment when he wrote the following:

At the front near Petersburg, Virginia,
July 29, 1864

Hon. William H. Seward, Secretary of State
Dear Sir:

I know it would be of great importance to the government to have me detailed to General Sherman's army in Georgia to act as a guide. I am acquainted with most of the large plantations of the Chattahoochee River. Mr. Toombs' large plantation is on the same river, 36 miles below Columbus. I have traveled all through that portion of Georgia on rail-roads, steamboats and country roads. I am also acquainted with the roads leading to Americus where there is a large prison containing several thousands of our Union soldiers. This place is about 50 miles from Columbus. It would be of great importance to open a campaign in that portion of my old state. I have never heard of Union troops making a raid in these parts. The rivers to Columbus and Macon are both navigable for boats drawing 7 & 8 feet of water during the spring and fall months. All the cotton & other goods were shipped on those streams. With my humble knowledge of the geography of Georgia I am very certain that gunboats can pass through the state with more facility than most per-sons ever imagined.

Garland H. White, Acting Chaplain

National Archives

Raid on the Combahee River, South Carolina

Harriet Tubman was sent to South Carolina to work as a scout. Commanding a corps of ex-slaves, she traveled through the countryside to collect information for army raids and to urge slaves to leave their masters. When she led a fleet of gunboats up the Combahee River, almost eight hundred slaves crowded the riverbank, trying to get aboard. She told a Northern friend:

I never see such a sight. You'd see a woman with a pail on her head, rice a smoking in it just as she'd taken it from the fire, young one hanging on behind, one hand round her forehead to hold on, the other hand digging into the rice-pot, eating with all its might. Hold of her dress two or three more, down her back a bag with a pig in it. One woman brought two pigs, a white one and a black one. We took 'em all on board. Named the white pig Beauregard [a Confederate general] and the black pig Jeff Davis.

Sarah Bradford, *Harriet the Moses of Her People*
(Auburn, N.Y., 1869)

After the Combahee raid, Mrs. Tubman, who was about forty-three at the time, wrote to the North to ask for some appropriate clothing. Bloomer dresses, popularized by the woman's rights movement, were knee-length skirts worn over wide trousers.

I want a bloomer dress, made of some coarse, strong material to wear on expeditions. In our late expedition up the Combahee River I was carrying two pigs for a poor sick woman who had a child to carry. The order "double quick" was given. I started to run, stepped on my dress, it being rather long, and fell and tore it almost off. When I got on board the boat, there was hardly anything left of it but shreds. I made up my mind that I would never wear a long dress on another expedition, but would have a bloomer as soon as I could get it. So please make this known to the ladies.

You have without doubt seen a full account of the expedition I refer to. Don't you think we colored people are entitled to some of the credit for that exploit? We weakened the Rebels by bringing away 756 head of their most valuable livestock, known in your region as "contrabands," and this without the loss of a single life on our part, though we had good reason to believe that a number of Rebels bit the dust. Of those 756 contrabands, nearly all the able-bodied men have joined the colored regiments here.

Boston *Commonwealth,* July 17, 1863

Susie King, a Georgia slave who escaped early in the war, also worked for the army in South Carolina. Enrolled as a laundress in the First Carolina Volunteers, she traveled to the front with her regiment. Many years later she wrote:

I learned to handle a musket very well and could shoot straight and often hit the target. I assisted in cleaning the guns and used to fire them off, to see if the cartridges were dry, before cleaning and reloading. I thought this great fun.

Harriet Tubman

I was also able to take a gun apart and put it together again.

Fort Wagner being only a mile from our camp, I went there two or three times a week and would go up on the ramparts to watch the gunners send their shells into Charleston. Outside of the fort were many skulls lying about. Some thought they were the skulls of our boys; others thought they were the enemies'. They were a gruesome sight, those fleshless heads and grinning jaws, but by this time I had become accustomed to worse things.

We landed on Morris Island between June and July 1864. Orders were received for the boys to prepare to take Fort Gregg. I helped to pack haversacks and cartridge boxes. About four o'clock, July 2, the charge was made. The firing could be plainly heard in camp. I hastened down to the landing when the wounded began to arrive, some with their legs off, arm gone, foot off and wounds of all kinds imaginable.

I asked the doctor at the hospital what I could get for them to eat. They wanted soup, but that I could not get. I had a few cans of condensed milk and some turtle eggs, so

I thought I would try to make some custard. Cooking with turtle eggs was new to me but the result was a delicious custard. The men enjoyed it very much. ,

There are many people who do not know what colored women did during the war. Hundreds of them assisted Union soldiers by hiding them and helping them to escape. Many were punished for taking food to the prison stockades for the prisoners. When I went into Savannah in 1865 I was told of one of these stockades in the city. The colored women would take food there at night and pass it to them through the holes in the fence. The soldiers were starving and the women did all they could towards relieving those men, although they knew the penalty should they be caught.

Susie King Taylor, *Reminiscences of My Life in Camp*
(Boston, 1902)

Women working in an army camp

Black women from all over the North went to Washington to nurse the soldiers and to act as counselors and teachers to the twenty thousand freedmen who were living in shacks and barracks in and around the capital. John H. Rapier, Jr., gave his uncle an enthusiastic report on wartime Washington:

Helping a Union soldier

James P. Thomas, Esquire

Dear Uncle:

There are many ladies here engaged in teaching and general supervision of the freedmen. They are the most earnest laborers I have ever seen in any cause. Wind, rain and storm never stop them. Night and day these angels of mercy [are] in the miserable hovels of these poor people, doing the most menial duties.

Foremost and bravest of these is a Miss Harriet Carter of Massachusetts. Do not imagine Miss Carter to be an old and homely one who has sighed for someone to love her and has taken up this occupation, perhaps as a penance for saying "no" when she ought to have said "yes." By no means —Miss Carter is twenty-four, with pretty eyes and a wilderness of the softest brown hair you ever felt. As full of learning as an Episcopal minister, and would make even Henry Green laugh at her humor and wit. In my daily rounds I always encounter her and have a half hour's pleasant chat before I resume the duties of the day.

On the 14th the most eventful event of my life occurred. I drew $100 for medical services rendered the U. S. Government. My draft was in favor of "Acting Assistant Surgeon, Rank 1st Lieutenant, U.S.A." I read the address several times. I liked it, though I confess it read strange to me. In the spring I want my drafts payable to Major John H. Rapier, Surgeon, U.S.A.

Colored men in the U.S. uniform are much respected here. In visiting the various departments you receive the military salute from the guard as promptly as if your blood was a Howard or Plantagenet instead of Pompey or Cuffee's. I had decided not to wear the uniform but have altered my mind and I shall appear hereafter in full dress—gold lace, pointed hat, straps and all.

Mr. Fred Douglass spoke here last night and today the President sent for him. Did you ever hear such nonsense? The President of the U.S. sending for a "nigger" to confer with him on the state of the country! I am invited to take supper with Mr. Douglass tonight. He visited the Hospital today.

John, Jr.

Rapier Papers, Moorland-Spingarn Collection,
Howard University Library

6.   Victory—and Then?

Barriers were crashing down everywhere. Frederick Douglass was not the only black man to visit the White House. Dr. Augusta and Dr. Abbott had broken precedent a year earlier by attending a Presidential reception. Dr. Abbott wrote:

We appeared at the White House in full uniform. We were met by Mr. B. B. French, a Commissioner of the Treasury Department, who conducted us to the President. Mr. French introduced Dr. Augusta first. Robert Lincoln who had been standing beside his mother came up to the President and asked a question, which I took to be, "Are you going to allow this innovation?" The President replied promptly, "Why not?"

Then I was introduced and the President shook hands with me also. We passed on to Mrs. Lincoln and [I] was introduced [to] that lady. We then entered the East Room. The moment we entered we became the cynosure of all eyes. I never experienced such a sensation before. We could not have created more surprise if we had been dropped down through a skylight. I suppose it was because it was [the] first time in the history of the U.S. when a colored man had appeared at one of these levees. What made us more conspicuous of course was our uniforms. Colored men in the uniforms of U.S. military officers of high rank had never been seen before.

I should have liked to crawl into a hole. But I bit my lip, took Augusta's arm, and sauntered around the room pretending to view the very fine pictures which adorned the walls. Wherever we went a space was cleared for us. Some stared merely from curiosity—others with an expression of friendly interest, while others scowled in a way that left no [doubt] as to what views they held on the Negro question. We faced stares and fascinated eyes for about half of an hour and then secured our wraps. So ended our first visit to the White House.

Anderson R. Abbott Papers, Toronto Public Library

In February 1865, the Reverend Henry Highland Garnet preached a sermon in the Hall of the House of Representatives; John S. Rock was admitted to argue cases before the Supreme Court; and Martin R. Delany was commissioned as a major in the U. S. Army, the first black line officer of high rank.

On April 3, black troops singing "John Brown's Body" marched into Richmond, capital of the Confederacy. T. Morris Chester, the only black reporter to work for a white newspaper, the Philadelphia Press, sat in the hall of the Confederate Congress to write the following dispatch:

The great event after the capture of the city was the arrival of President Lincoln. With a file of sailors for a guard of honor, he walked up to Jeff Davis' house, the headquarters of General Weitzel. The news sped as if upon the wings of lightning that "Old Abe" had come. By the time he reached General Weitzel's headquarters thousands of persons had followed him. When he ascended the steps the people shouted louder and louder until it seemed as if the echoes would reach those patriot spirits who had died without witnessing the sight.

When a carriage was brought in front, Mr. Lincoln, with his youngest son, Admiral Porter, General Kautz and General Devans entered. There is no describing the scene along the route. The colored population was wild with enthusiasm. Old men thanked God in a very boisterous manner and old women shouted as high as they had ever done at a religious revival.

Nothing can exceed the politeness which the whites every-

Greeting President Lincoln in Richmond

where manifest to the Negroes. Not even the familiarity peculiar to Americans is indulged in—calling blacks by their first names. Even masters are addressing their slaves as "Mr. Johnson," "Mrs. Brown." A cordial shake of the hand and a gentle inclination of the body approaching to respectful consideration, are evident in the greetings which now take place between the oppressed and the oppressor.

Everyone declares that Richmond never before presented such a spectacle of jubilee. Those who participated in this informal reception of the President were mainly Negroes. There were many whites in the crowd, but they were lost in the great concourse of American citizens of African descent.

I visited several of the slave jails where men, women and children were confined for the examination of purchasers. The owners, as soon as they were aware that we were coming, opened wide the doors and told the confined inmates they were free. The poor souls could not realize it until they saw the Union army. Even then they thought it must be a dream, but when they saw Abraham Lincoln they were satisfied that their freedom was perpetual. One enthusiastic old Negro woman exclaimed, "I know that I am free, for I have seen Father Abraham."

Philadelphia *Press*, April 11, 1865

Two days before Chester's article appeared, General Robert E. Lee surrendered to General Grant. Even Lincoln's assassination the following week could not silence the jubilee. All over the South, doors of slave jails opened and soldiers carried the news of freedom to remote plantations. A soldier described his new peacekeeping assignment:

Camp Hancock, South Carolina, July 7, 1865

Mr. Editor:

Our duty is to let the colored people know that they are free citizens of the United States, and to protect them as such. Also to prevent their former owners from driving them off the plantations and cheating them out of their share of the crop. These former slaveholders grieve and fret a great deal about having to pay the freedmen for their labor, but they have to do it.

We have had some grand meetings. The people came from miles around and listened to freedom songs and speeches, such as people [here] never heard before. We have organized a debating society and devote our leisure to debating such questions as are most beneficial to us as a people. We are all anxious to get home now the war is over but faithful to our Uncle Sam we will wait until our turn comes.

Charles Gilbert, 26th Regt., U. S. Colored Troops

The Anglo-African, August 12, 1865

The war was over, but there was much unfinished business to be settled. What should be done with the four million

*slaves who were now free? The freedmen had an immediate
answer. They wanted to find their families—the mothers,
fathers, sons, daughters who had been sold away so many
years before. All during the summer of 1865, and for many
years thereafter, black newspapers carried columns headed
INFORMATION WANTED:*

Andrew Dennis and Richard Dennis, generally called
Dick. When last heard from some six years ago they resided
in Georgia. It is supposed they joined the Union Army.
Their mother, brother George and sister Cecelia are residing
in San Francisco and wish information respecting them.

Mrs. Sarah Lee, a colored lady living at Eldora, Iowa,
wants to know the whereabouts of her sons Gideon or
Sandy, also a daughter, Martha. The family formerly lived
at Tuscumbia, Alabama.

Mrs. Thos. L. Johnson who was sold away from Georgetown, D.C., when quite a child and who, at the breaking out
of the war, was taken to Richmond, is very desirous of finding her father, Joseph Thompson, who for many years was
a gardener in and around Washington.

Henry, Edward and Jinney Haney who when last heard
from were in Fort Smith, Arkansas. They can hear from
their mother and sisters by directing a letter to Mrs. A.
Haney, Frankfort, Kentucky.

The Anglo-African, August 19, 1865

*Some blacks who had been living in the North went
back to their homes in the South. Henry Highland Garnet,
a boy of nine when his family escaped from slavery, visited
his birthplace in New Market, Maryland. In a letter to* The
Anglo-African, *he told of his emotions as he stood beside the
grave of his former master and then wandered through his
old neighborhood:*

To us it was a moment of gratitude to God, with a little
triumph mingled in. The old oppressors are all dead, but we

live, and have lifted our free hands above their tombs.

It is beyond our power to describe our feelings. Through tears we gazed upon the loved scene. We remembered the stream called the Branch, because we fell into it once and were nearly drowned. The Spencer plantation is cut up into ten large farms. Everything had changed greatly. The old trees were felled, the old mansion was gone. Everybody whom we once knew was dead. "Our fathers—where are they?" We diligently inquired, and found but two persons, a colored gentleman and lady, who knew us in our childhood. Mr. Doman, son of our father's friend, Uncle Joseph Doman, gave us a basket of fruit, and taking a branch of cedar and other memorials we left New Market, perhaps forever.

Reprinted in Freedmen's Journal, October 1865

But the summer of jubilee soon came to an end. The ex-slaves wanted land, work, the vote. It was as simple as that—and as difficult. On the Sea Islands of South Carolina, freedmen had bought farms abandoned by the Rebels in the early years of the war. Now the former owners were returning to claim their land—and President Andrew Johnson supported them. In October, Oliver O. Howard, head of the Freedmen's Bureau, was sent to tell the freedmen that they must give up their land and go to work for their former masters. The people on Edisto Island sent a petition to the President. Although crudely written, its meaning was clear:

We, the freedmen of South Carolina, wish to address you concerning the sad feelings that is now resting upon our minds. We have for the last four years been studying with the best of our ability what step we should take to become a people.

Major General Howard has called a meeting on Edisto Island. After his address, a great many of the people got aroused. In reference to what he said [one thing] did appear to be very oppressing—that is, we freedmen should work for wages for our former owners. President Johnson, men that have stood upon the field of battle & have shot their masters & sons now going to ask either one for bread or shelter! Such a thing the United States should not expect a man [to do].

The king of South Carolina [Colonel Whaley, a former slaveowner] ask that he might address the audience of freedmen. We said to him, "Here is plenty widow and fatherless that have serve you as a slave now losing a home. Give each one a acre and a half to a family. You have the labors and profit of their youth." The question was asked him by General Howard, "What would [you] sell your land for?" He answer, "I would not take $100 a acre." That is his feeling, so we lose faith in this Southern gentleman. [We beg] the wise President [to give us] a chance to recover out of this trouble.

Mary Ames, *From a New England Woman's Diary in Dixie*
(Springfield, Mass., 1906)

Across the bay in Charleston, other blacks gathered for South Carolina's first Colored People's Convention. The legislature had just passed a series of restrictive Black Laws and the convention delegates asked for their repeal:

To the Honorable Senate and House of Representatives of the State of South Carolina:

We, the colored people of the State of South Carolina do hereby appeal to you for *justice*. The last four years of war have made great changes in our condition. Our State has been called upon to remodel her Constitution from its very foundation and first principles.

We ask that those laws that have been enacted that apply to us on account of our color, be repealed. We do not presume to dictate to you, gentlemen, but we appeal to your instincts of justice and generosity. Is it possible that the only reason for enacting stringent and oppressive laws for us is because our color is of a darker hue?

We are now free. We are now *all free.* But we are still, gentlemen, to a great extent in your power; and we need not assure you with what deep concern we are watching *all* your deliberations.

We would ask your Honorable body for the right of suffrage and the right of testifying in courts of law. These two things we deem necessary to our welfare and elevation.

We do sincerely hope that you will grant your petitioners their desires. We are natives of this State, and we feel assured that nothing is needed to render our future relations mutually beneficial but the bestowment of the rights we ask.

> "Proceedings of the Colored People's Convention of the
> State of South Carolina" (Charleston, 1865)

Their petition was rejected. In other states of the old Confederacy, similar Black Laws were being passed, similar pleas for justice ignored. By the time Henry Highland Garnet returned home after an extended trip through the South, his feeling of triumph had given way to uneasiness:

October 23, 1865

Gerrit Smith, Esq.
My Esteemed Brother:

I am now on my homeward journey from the South after an absence of four months. I have traveled on a tour of observation among my freed brethren from the eastern shores of Maryland to the banks of the Mississippi. I have been to my native plantation in New Market, Kent County, Maryland, from which place my parents fled twenty-nine years ago. I there freely spoke my sentiments by special invitation of ex-slaveholders and was most kindly received. Strange to say, they actually seemed to be quite proud that even a black man, a native of Kent, received some consideration from his fellow men.

I fully intended to spend Saturday and the Sabbath with you. I checked my trunk for Utica where I am to speak to-night and took my carpet bag in hand, intending to get off at Canastota. But, behold, when the train came to the latter station it flew by so swiftly that I could scarcely see the houses.

This I much regretted, for I desired to see you, and tell you about the inner workings of the plan of Reconstruction, the effects of which I fear may be disastrous to the cause of freedom.

Henry Highland Garnet

Gerrit Smith Miller Collection, George Arents Research Library
at Syracuse University

The war was over. Now the fight for a just and lasting peace had begun.

BIOGRAPHICAL DIRECTORY

Only fifteen of the fifty-odd men and women described below have ever been the subjects of extensive biographies or autobiographies. The minimal information about the others was collated from more than two dozen sources, the only ones available, one often contradicting another. It is to be hoped that primary sources for complete, well-authenticated portraits of these significant individuals will be found as Black Studies becomes more firmly established and more fully elaborated.

Anderson R. Abbott (1837–1913) The son of free blacks who had been driven from the South, Abbott was born in Toronto, Canada. Educated there and at Oberlin College, he received a medical degree from Toronto University in 1861. Two years later he was appointed a surgeon in the Union army. After Lincoln's assassination, Mrs. Lincoln gave him the shawl that the President had worn when on his way to his first inauguration. Returning to Canada in 1866, Abbott practiced medicine and was active in civic affairs.

Ira Aldridge (1807–67) A graduate of New York's African Free School, Aldridge went to England in 1824. Performing in the leading theaters of England, France, Germany and Russia, he became one of the great Shakespearean actors of his time.

Richard Allen (1760–1831) Born a slave, Allen bought his freedom when he was seventeen. Ten years later he led a group of black worshippers out of a church in Philadelphia as a protest against their segregation there. Bethel Church, which he founded in 1794, became the nucleus for the African Methodist Episcopal Church with Allen as the first bishop of the new denomination. A leader in civic as well as religious affairs, Allen helped to organize the defense of Philadelphia in the War of 1812 and presided over the first national Colored Convention.

William Allen A graduate of Oneida Institute, Allen studied law in Boston before becoming coeditor of *The National Watchman*, a newspaper published in Troy, New York, in 1842. The first black college professor in the United States, he taught Greek and German at Central College in McGrawville, New York, until 1853. After his marriage to a white student, he and his wife were forced to leave the country. In England, where he continued to teach, he wrote *The American Prejudice Against Color*, an account of the mob attack that drove them from their homeland.

Alexander T. Augusta (1825–90) Born free in Norfolk, Virginia, Augusta obtained his early education by stealth. Leaving the South as a young man, he spent three years in California, then settled in Canada. After graduating from Trinity Medical College in Toronto, he practiced medicine in Canada and the West Indies until the Civil War. In 1863 he received an appointment as surgeon in the Union army, with the rank of major. He was later promoted to lieutenant colonel, the first of his race to hold this rank. After the war he remained in Washington as a doctor and a member of Howard University's medical school faculty.

Benjamin Banneker (1731–1806) Born free in Maryland, Banneker was befriended by white neighbors who loaned him books and scientific instruments. A self-taught mathematician and astronomer, he published a series of almanacs for which he did all of the calculations. He also worked with engineers and surveyors to lay out the new city of Washington, D.C. Although he lived before the days of the antislavery movement, Banneker sent Thomas Jefferson a copy of his first almanac to show him that blacks were not inferior to whites, and to ask his help in combating the "absurd and false ideas which so generally prevail with respect to us."

Philip A. Bell (c. 1808–89) A pioneer journalist, Bell was coeditor of *The Colored American* from 1837–39. Moving to California in the 1850s, he edited *The Pacific Appeal* during the Civil War. In 1865 he founded *The Elevator,* a weekly whose motto was "Equality Before the Law." The paper was still being published at the time of Bell's death.

Amos G. Beman (1803–74) Born in Connecticut, Beman was tutored at Wesleyan University until students forced him to leave the campus. He taught school, then became a minister and Underground Railroad stationmaster in New Haven. A contributor to the abolitionist press, he was one of the first to lecture on the history of Africa. After the Civil War he went South to teach the freedmen.

William Wells Brown (c. 1814–84) Son of a white father and a slave mother, Brown escaped to the North in 1834. Working as a lecturer for antislavery societies in the United States and Great Britain, Brown became America's first black man of letters. He wrote more than a dozen books: novels, plays, autobiographies, histories and accounts of his travels. A self-taught doctor, he also practiced medicine after the Civil War.

Mary Ann Shadd Cary (1823–93) Abraham D. Shadd, Mary Ann's father, was a pioneer black abolitionist. In 1833 he moved his family from Delaware to Pennsylvania so that his children could obtain an education. A schoolteacher, Miss Shadd settled in Canada after the passage of the Fugitive Slave Act of 1850. There she became "editress" of the *Provincial Freeman*—the first black woman editor—and a leader of the black community in Chatham. She married Thomas F. Cary in 1856. A supporter of John Brown, she helped Osborne P. Anderson write his *Voice from Harper's Ferry*. Returning to the United States during the Civil War, she was an official recruiting officer for black regiments. In Washington, D.C., after the war, she taught school, wrote for black newspapers and attended Howard University's law school. Receiving a law degree in 1884, she was an attorney in Washington for the remainder of her life.

Samuel Cornish (c. 1795–c. 1859) Born free in Baltimore and educated in Philadelphia and New York, Cornish was cofounder of *Freedom's Journal*, the first black newspaper. He later edited *Rights of All* and *The Colored American*. A Presbyterian minister, he was a member of the first board of managers of the American Anti-Slavery Society, but broke with the Garrisonians in 1840.

Alexander Crummell (1819–98) Grandson of an African prince, Crummell was born free in New York where he attended the African Free School. One of the group of black students driven away from Canaan Academy in New Hampshire, he was graduated from Oneida Institute. He was refused admission to New York's General Theological Seminary because he was black, but completed his studies in Cambridge, England, and then went to Liberia as minister and teacher. After twenty years in Africa, Crummell returned to the United States. Noted as a scholar, he founded the American Negro Academy.

Paul Cuffe (1759–1817) The son of an African slave and an Indian woman, Cuffe built up a fleet of merchant ships that sailed as far as Sweden, Russia and the West Indies. After a trip to Africa in 1811, he organized African Institutions in the black communities of the North to win support for a back-to-Africa movement. He brought thirty-eight black emigrants to Sierra Leone in 1815, but plans for a second trip were interrupted by his death two years later.

William Howard Day (1825–1900) A New Yorker, Day was graduated from Oberlin College in 1847 and then settled in Cleveland. There he was publisher of *The Aliened American,* one of the first black newspapers in the Midwest and a leader in the fight against Ohio's black laws. In 1857, he moved to Canada where he taught, became active in the emigration movement and wrote for the *Provincial Freeman.* An associate of John Brown's, he was in England raising money for Canadian schools when Brown went to Harper's Ferry. After the Civil War, Day was a minister and teacher in the South. Settling in Pennsylvania in the 1870s, he became general secretary of the AMEZ Church and the editor of a weekly paper, *Our National Progress.*

Martin R. Delany (1812–85) Born free in Virginia, the grandson of an African chief, Delany and his family moved to Pennsylvania so that he could attend school. Active in the antislavery movement, editor of *The Mystery* (1843–47) and coeditor of *The North Star* (1847–49), Delany also attended Harvard Medical School until his fellow students petitioned for his dismissal. In the 1850s, he broke with men like Frederick Douglass to lead a back-to-Africa movement. Traveling to the Niger Valley, he signed a treaty with the rulers of Abeokuta, in present-day Nigeria, for a settlement of black Americans there. His plans interrupted by the Civil War, he became a recruiter for the black regiments and, in 1865, received a commission as a major. At war's end, he remained in South Carolina where he was an official in the Freedmen's Bureau and, later, an unsuccessful candidate for Lieutenant Governor of the state.

Frederick Douglass (1817–95) Born a slave and completely self-taught, Douglass escaped to the North in 1838 and made his first public speech three years later. After six years as a lecturer for antislavery societies, he broke with the Garrisonians to edit his own paper, *The North Star* (later *Frederick Douglass' Paper* and *Douglass' Monthly*). As editor, orator, politician, organizer, he led the black protest movement for almost fifty years. After the Civil War, he was an editor of *New National Era,* Recorder of Deeds for the District of Columbia and U. S. Minister to Haiti.

Sarah M. Douglass (1806–82) Member of a distinguished Philadelphia family, Sarah Douglass was a founder of the Philadelphia Female Anti-Slavery Society and the National Anti-Slavery Convention of American Women. A teacher of black children for more than a half century, she also lectured to adult audiences on physiology when this was considered a taboo subject for women. Although she was born a Quaker, she stopped attending meetings because a special bench was set aside for black people.

George T. Downing (1819–1903) Son of a well-known New York restaurateur, Downing attended the African Free School and Hamilton College. In 1850 he moved to Rhode Island where he owned a catering business in Providence and several summer hotels in Newport. From 1865–77 he ran the House of Representatives restaurant in Washington. A successful businessman, he was active in the civil rights struggle throughout his life.

James Forten (1766–1842) Born free in Philadelphia, James Forten served as a powder boy aboard a privateer during the Revolution. Apprenticed to a sailmaker after the war, he invented a device for handling sails which earned him a fortune. He headed Philadelphia's African Institution until Paul Cuffe's death, but later led the opposition to the American Colonization Society. Writing, speaking and petitioning against slavery and disfranchisement, Forten influenced such white abolitionists as William Lloyd Garrison and Lucretia Mott, as well as his own people. He was a founder of the Colored Convention movement and president of the 'American Moral Reform Society and numerous other self-improvement societies.

Forten family. James Forten's five children were all active in the antislavery movement in Pennsylvania. **Margaretta** and **Sarah Forten** were members of the Philadelphia Female Anti-Slavery Society and contributors to *The Liberator*. Their sister **Harriet,** the wife of Robert Purvis, helped run an important station on the Underground Railroad. **James, Jr.,** and **Robert B. Forten** were frequent speakers at antislavery meetings. Robert's daughter **Charlotte** (1837–1914) was educated in the integrated schools of Salem, Massachusetts, taught there in the 1850s, and during the Civil War went to South Carolina to teach the newly freed slaves.

The journal that she kept during those years gives a rare firsthand account of the lives and attitudes of well-to-do black people of her time. A poet and essayist, Miss Forten married the Reverend Francis J. Grimke in 1878 and spent the last decades of her life in Washington, D.C.

Newport Gardner (c. 1746–1826) Born in Africa where his name was Ocramar Marycoo, Gardner was brought to Newport, Rhode Island, in 1760, as a slave to Captain Caleb Gardner. While still a slave, he ran a singing school which was attended by members of Newport's leading families. After purchasing his freedom in 1791, he became president of Newport's African Union Society, the first teacher in the school started by the African Benevolent Society, and a founder of the Colored Union Church. Composer of songs and hymns, he kept up his knowledge of his native language, hoping always to return home some day. In 1826 he led a party of emigrants to Liberia where he died six months later.

Henry Highland Garnet (1815–82) The grandson of an African chief, Garnet was born a slave in Maryland but escaped to the North with his family in 1824. After studying at New York's African Free School and at Canaan Academy in New Hampshire (until local farmers destroyed the school), he completed his education at Oneida Institute. A minister, editor and antislavery lecturer, he fought discrimination and disfranchisement. More militant than many of his contemporaries, he rejected the idea of non-violence and urged the slaves to revolt. By the 1850s he was a leader in the African emigration movement. Minister of a church in Washington during the Civil War, he was the first black man to speak in the House of Representatives. After the war he was president of Avery College in Pittsburgh and U. S. Minister to Liberia.

Mifflin Gibbs (1823–1915) Born in Philadelphia, Gibbs went to San Francisco during the gold-rush years. A leader in the fight against California's black laws, he moved to British Columbia when gold was discovered there. Although he was successful in business and a member of the Common Council of Victoria, Gibbs returned to the U.S. at the end of the war. After graduating from Oberlin, he was admitted to the bar in Arkansas. Active in Reconstruction politics, he was a judge in Little Rock and, later, U. S. Consul to Madagascar. His brother, Jonathan Gibbs, was secretary of state in Florida during Reconstruction.

Thomas Hamilton (?–1865) A member of a prominent family of black New Yorkers, Thomas Hamilton was the editor of *The People's Press,* a short-lived newspaper issued in 1843, and publisher of *The Weekly Anglo-African* and *The Anglo-African Magazine.* The latter, the first black literary magazine, included philosophical and scientific essays of high quality, poems and fiction. Hamilton also published books by such black writers as William Wells Brown and Martin R. Delany. His brother, **Robert Hamilton,** a music teacher and composer, took over the editorship of *The Weekly Anglo-African* in 1861.

Frances Ellen Watkins Harper (1825–1911) Born free in Maryland, Frances Ellen Watkins, later Mrs. Harper, was a teacher, antislavery lecturer and writer. The author of ten volumes of poetry and a novel, *Iola Leroy,* she lectured and taught in the South after the Civil War. Active in the womens' rights movement, she was a founder of the National Association of Colored Women and one of several black women who fought against lynching.

Thomas Jennings (1791–1859) Although unknown today, Jennings was a leader of New York's black community in the early nineteenth century. A successful tailor, he was a founder of the New York African Society for Mutual Relief and later its president, a member of the first Colored Conventions and a defender of the city of New York during the War of 1812. An early supporter of *The Liberator* and the American Anti-Slavery Society, he later organized a Legal Rights Association to fight discrimination in public transportation. The Association's first case was his daughter Elizabeth's suit against the Third Avenue Railroad Company. **Elizabeth Jennings** taught in New York's public schools; her brothers and sister were, respectively, a dentist, businessman and dressmaker.

John Jones (c. 1816–79) Born free in North Carolina, Jones moved to Chicago in 1845. Self-educated, he became a prosperous tailor and the owner of valuable property in downtown Chicago.

A stationmaster on the Underground Railroad and a friend of John Brown's, he led the fight against Illinois' black laws. After the Civil War he was a member of the Cook County Board of Commissioners, the first black to win elective office in Illinois.

Charles Langston (1817–92) and **John Mercer Langston** (1829–97) The sons of a white planter and his slave mistress, the Langstons were freed on their father's death and sent to Ohio. Both were Oberlin graduates and active in the antislavery movement. A dentist and gentleman farmer, Charles Langston married the widow of Sheridan Leary, one of John Brown's men. Their daughter, Caroline, was Langston Hughes' mother.

John M. Langston was admitted to the Ohio bar in 1854. A recruiter for black troops during the Civil War, he was an official in the Freedmen's Bureau afterward. Dean of Howard University and U. S. Minister to Haiti, he was elected a congressman from his native state, Virginia, in 1888.

Jeremiah W. Loguen (1813–72) A runaway slave, J. W. Loguen settled in Syracuse, New York, where he operated an important Underground Railroad station and was a friend of John Brown's. A minister, he later became bishop of the AMEZ Church. His daughter, Amelia, married Frederick Douglass' son, Lewis.

Maritcha Remond Lyons (1848–1929) The Lyons' were New Yorkers of African, Indian and English descent. **Albro Lyons** (1814–96), Maritcha's father, an active antislavery worker, owned a sailors' boarding house and outfitting store until the 1863 riot destroyed his business and drove him from the city. Relocating in Rhode Island, he became a manufacturer of ice cream. His wife, Mary Lyons, niece of James Hewlett, the actor, helped him to run an Underground Railroad station during their New York years. Returning to the city after the Civil War, Maritcha Lyons became assistant principal of a public school in Brooklyn. Her unpublished autobiography, *Memoirs of Yesterdays—All of Which I Saw and Part of Which I Was* is a rich source of information about New York's black community in the nineteenth century.

William Cooper Nell (1817–74) Born in Boston, Nell worked on *The Liberator* and *The North Star*. A self-taught historian, he collected the stories of the blacks who fought in the Revolution and War of 1812. His *Colored Patriots of the American Revolution,* published in 1855, is still a useful source of information on this period. A loyal supporter of Garrison, Nell led the fight against segregation in Boston's schools. After the Civil War, he was one of the first blacks to be appointed as a clerk in the post office.

James William Charles Pennington (1809–70) Born in Maryland, Pennington escaped from slavery when he was twenty-one. Working during the day, he went to school at night. So learned did he become that in 1849 the University of Heidelberg, Germany, gave him an honorary degree of Doctor of Divinity. A minister in New York where he was active in the antislavery struggle, he wrote *Textbook of the Origin and History of the Colored People,* the first black history book, and *The Fugitive Blacksmith,* an account of his life as a slave.

Robert Purvis (1810–98) Purvis was the son of a white South Carolina merchant and a Moorish-Jewish woman whose mother had been a slave. Independently wealthy and so light-skinned that he could have passed for white, he devoted his life and fortune to the fight against slavery and disfranchisement. "President" of the Pennsylvania branch of the Underground Railroad, and a founder of the American Anti-Slavery Society, he was a supporter of William Lloyd Garrison and an opponent of black separatism.

Rapier family. John Rapier, Sr., a free black, was a barber and plantation owner in Alabama. He sent his sons to Canada and Scotland for their schooling. **John Rapier, Jr.,** became one of the eight black doctors appointed as Army surgeons during the Civil War. **James Rapier** (1839–83) was active in politics during Reconstruction and served a term as congressman from Alabama.

Charles Bennett Ray (1807–86) Born in Massachusetts, Ray attended Wesleyan University until fellow students drove him away. Pastor of the Bethesda Congregational Church in New York, he was also an editor of *The Colored American* and a member of the Committee of Vigilance which helped slaves make their way to Canada.

Charles Lenox Remond (1810–73) Son of a prosperous business-man in Salem, Massachusetts, Remond was the best-known black abolitionist until the rise of Frederick Douglass. A delegate to the World Anti-Slavery Convention in London in 1840, he refused to take his seat because women delegates were excluded. Return-ing home after two years on the antislavery circuit in Great Britain, he addressed Massachusetts legislators, convincing them to end segregation on the railroads of the state. The Remonds' home in Salem was a headquarters for antislavery lecturers and a haven for people like Charlotte Forten and Maritcha Lyons when they were fleeing prejudice in other parts of the North.

John S. Rock (1825–66) Born in New Jersey, Rock was succes-sively a teacher, dentist, doctor and lawyer. In Massachusetts, where he lived after 1853, he became a justice of peace for the city of Boston and a popular speaker at antislavery meetings. In 1865, he was admitted to practice before the U. S. Supreme Court, the first black lawyer to be so honored.

David Ruggles (1810–49) Born free in Connecticut, Ruggles went to New York when he was seventeen. Proprietor of a grocery store, he gave up his business in 1833 to write and speak against slavery. As secretary of the New York Committee of Vigilance, Ruggles led the fight against kidnapping of free blacks. Because of his frank criticism of the police who collaborated with the slave hunters, he was jailed several times. His months in prison destroyed his health. Blind and penniless, he had to give up the Vigilance Committee and his magazine, *Mirror of Liberty*. In 1842, he moved to Northhampton, Massachusetts. There he op-erated a successful water-cure establishment until his death at the age of thirty-nine.

Prince Saunders (1755–1839) Born free in Vermont, Prince Saunders taught school in Boston's African Meetinghouse from 1809-12. A founder of Boston's African Institution and a corre-spondent of Paul Cuffe's, he later emigrated to Haiti. As an of-ficial of the Haitian government, he urged American blacks to settle there.

Robert Smalls (1839–1915) In 1862 Robert Smalls, the slave pilot of the *Planter*, a Confederate gunboat, took over the boat and, with the assistance of the slave crew, turned it over to the Union navy. He spent the balance of the war aboard the *Planter*, as pilot and, later, captain. During Reconstruction and afterward he served three terms in the House of Representatives as a congressman from South Carolina.

James McCune Smith (1813–65) The son of ex-slaves, Smith was educated at New York's African Free School and at the University of Glasgow in Scotland. The first university-trained black doctor in the United States, he used his knowledge to challenge the idea of black inferiority, engaging in debates with such spokesmen for the slaveholders as John C. Calhoun. In addition to practicing medicine and heading the fight for the franchise in New York State, Smith was an editor of *The Colored American* and a regular contributor to *Frederick Douglass' Paper, The Weekly Anglo-African* and *The Anglo-African Magazine*.

William Still (1821–1902) Born in New Jersey, the son of runaway slaves, Still moved to Philadelphia in the 1840s. As chairman of the Philadelphia Vigilance Committee, he forwarded fugitives to Canada and helped them keep in touch with their families in the South. His records and correspondence, published in 1872, include interviews with thousands of runaways who passed through Philadelphia. From 1859–67 Still led a fight against discrimination on the city's streetcars. After the Civil War he became a successful businessman and was active in Pennsylvania politics.

Sojourner Truth (c. 1797–1883) The slave of New York State farmers of Dutch descent, Sojourner Truth won her freedom in 1827 when slavery was abolished in the state. Originally named Isabella, she took the name Sojourner Truth in 1843, after a religious conversion. Walking from town to town, she began to preach at camp meetings. Although she never learned to read or write, she became one of the most powerful speakers in the antislavery and womens' rights movements. During the Civil War she used her voice and presence to rally support for the Union. Active in freedmen's aid societies, she worked to obtain land in the West for black settlers when the war was over.

Harriet Tubman (c. 1820–1913) Born in slavery in Maryland,

Harriet Tubman escaped to the North in 1849. She made dozens of trips to the South to lead more than three hundred slaves to freedom. During the Civil War she served as a spy and scout behind enemy lines in South Carolina. In the last years of her life, she took part in womens' rights meetings and helped to organize the National Federation of Afro-American Women.

Phillis Wheatley (c. 1753–84) Brought from Africa as a slave when she was about seven, Phillis was purchased by John Wheatley in Boston. Mrs. Wheatley befriended the little girl, educated her and later gave her freedom. Miss Wheatley's first book, *Poems on Various Subjects, Religious and Moral,* was published in England in 1773. Although she had influential patrons abroad and in the United States, she ended her short life as a servant in a lodging house.

William Whipper (1805–85) One of the nation's first black capitalists, Whipper owned extensive coal and lumberyards in Columbia, Pennsylvania. A staunch believer in "self-improvement" as the way to win equal rights, he organized the Colored Reading Society for Mental Improvement in 1828 and was a founder of the American Moral Reform Society eight years later. Editor of *The National Reformer,* the first black monthly magazine, Whipper also ran an Underground Railroad station in Columbia.

Jacob C. White, Sr. (?–1872) A Philadelphia barber, White was active in the antislavery and moral reform movements of the 1830s and 1840s. Secretary and agent of the Philadelphia Vigilant Committee, he was a leader of the Underground Railroad in Pennsylvania during those years. His son, **Jacob C. White, Jr.** (1837–1902) was graduated from Philadelphia's Institute for Colored Youth and taught there until 1864. He then became principal of the Robert Vaux Public School, a position he held until his death. As founder of the Banneker Institute, a literary society, he headed a group of young black intellectuals in Philadelphia. During the Civil War he was secretary of the Pennsylvania State Equal Rights League.

Peter Williams (1786–1840) Son of a slave who bought his freedom, Peter Williams was a leader of New York's black community in the first decades of the nineteenth century. A friend and supporter of Paul Cuffe's, he became pastor of St. Philip's Episcopal Church in 1820. He was an officer of the American Anti-Slavery Society when it was first organized, but the bishop of his diocese demanded that he resign in order to avoid controversy.

William J. Wilson Although overlooked by literary historians, William J. Wilson was one of the ablest writers of the black abolitionist movement. A boot and shoemaker by trade, he wrote a regular column for *Frederick Douglass' Paper* under the pen name, Ethiop. When Thomas Hamilton started *The Weekly Anglo-African* and *The Anglo-African Magazine,* Wilson wrote editorials for the weekly and contributed poems and satirical essays to the monthly. His essay, "What Shall We Do With the White People," excerpted in Part IV, is worthy of publication in an anthology of black writing.

Theodore S. Wright (1797–1847) After his graduation from Princeton Theological Seminary in 1828, Wright became pastor of the First Presbyterian Church in New York and an active anti-slavery lecturer. He was a member of the first executive committee of the American Anti-Slavery Society but later broke with the Garrisonians to join the "political abolitionists." He became a spokesman for the Liberty Party in the 1844 election campaign.

Dorothy Sterling spent two full years working on this book. It is her hope that other researchers and historians will follow her lead, since much important material remains to be uncovered. This is the first of a projected three-volume documentary history, that will carry the story of black people in America up to the present.

Mrs. Sterling, a native New Yorker, lives in Wellfleet, Massachusetts. She was educated at Wellesley and Barnard Colleges and worked at Time, Inc., before leaving to devote herself to her family and writing.

For over twenty years Mrs. Sterling has pursued her research into black history and life. During that time she has written such books as *Freedom Train:* The Story of Harriet Tubman, *Captain of the Planter:* The Story of Robert Smalls, *Forever Free, Tear Down the Walls!* A History of the American Civil Rights Movement, *The Making of an Afro-American:* Martin Robison Delany 1812–85, *Lift Every Voice* (with Benjamin Quarles), and *Mary Jane.* She also serves as editorial consultant for Perspective Books, a series of biographies of notable black figures.

INDEX